DOLLAR POLITICS

VOLUME II

October 1974

CONGRESSIONAL QUARTERLY
1414 22nd STREET, N.W., WASHINGTON, D.C. 20037

Congressional Quarterly, Inc.

Congressional Quarterly Inc., an editorial research service and publishing company, serves clients in the fields of news, education, business and government. It combines specific coverage of Congress, government and politics by Congressional Quarterly with the more general subject range of an affiliated service, Editorial Research Reports.

Congressional Quarterly was founded in 1945 by Henrietta and Nelson Poynter. Its basic periodical publication was and still is the CQ *Weekly Report*, which is mailed to clients every Saturday. The *Weekly Report* is cross-referenced quarterly in a cumulative index.

The CQ *Almanac*, a compendium of legislation for one session of Congress, is published every spring. *Congress and the Nation* is published every four years as a record of government for one presidential term.

Congressional Quarterly also publishes paperback books on public affairs. These include the twice-yearly *Guide to Current American Government* and such recent titles as *The Washington Lobby, 2nd Edition* and *President Ford: The Man and his Record.*

CQ Direct Research is a consulting service which performs contract research and maintains a reference library and query desk for the convenience of clients.

Editorial Research Reports covers subjects beyond the specialized scope of Congressional Quarterly. It publishes reference material on foreign affairs, business, education, cultural affairs, national security, science and other topics of news interest. Service to clients includes a 300-word report five times a week and a 6,000-word report four times a month. Editorial Research Reports also publishes paperback books in its fields of coverage. Founded in 1923, the service was merged with Congressional Quarterly in 1956.

Book Service Editor: Robert A. Diamond.
Major Contributor: Bruce Freed.
Other Contributors: Yorick Blumenfeld, Prudence Crewdson, Mercer Cross, Alan Ehrenhalt, Edna Frazier, Robert E. Healy, Margaret Hurst Lowe, Robin Mezoly, John L. Moore, Warden Moxley, Spencer Rich, Richard C. Schroeder, Joanna R. Shelton, Elizabeth Wehr.
Editorial Assistant: Robert E. Healy.
Cover Design: Art Director Howard Chapman.
Production Supervisor: Donald R. Buck.
Assistant Production Supervisor: Richard Butler.

Library of Congress Catalog No. 77-184425
International Standard Book No. 0-87187-061-4

Copyright 1974 by Congressional Quarterly Inc.
1414 22nd Street N.W., Washington, D.C. 20037

TABLE OF CONTENTS

"Watergate is not primarily a story of political espionage, or even of White House intrigue. It is a particularly malodorous chapter in the annals of campaign financing. The money paid to the Watergate conspirators before the break-in—and the money passed to them later—was money from campaign gifts."

—John Gardner, chairman of
Common Cause, April 1973

"...legislation is, at best, a blunt weapon to combat immorality....[The committee was] mindful that revelations of past scandals have often failed to produce meaningful reform. Too frequently, there is a tendency to overreact in the wake of a particular scandal and burden the penal code with ill-considered laws directed to the specific—perhaps aberrational—conduct exposed."

—Senate Watergate Committee
report, July 1974

Introduction

One legacy of Richard Nixon's presidency is the use of a single word—"Watergate"—to cover a broad range of campaign finance abuses. Indeed, the "smoking gun" that precipitated the President's resignation was the disclosure that he had concealed for almost two years his knowledge that the June 1972 break-in had been financed by private contributions to his re-election campaign.

Included in the unprecedented catalog of misdeeds were specific violations of campaign spending laws, violations of other criminal laws facilitated by the availability of virtually unlimited campaign contributions and still other instances where campaign funds were used in a manner that strongly suggested influence peddling or—at the very least—gave the appearance of gross improprieties in the conduct of public office.

Public Finance and Contribution Limits

Watergate is no exception to the typical reaction to scandal that "there ought to be a law." In response to the rising tide of public outrage at the excesses of Watergate, Congress in 1974 moved on campaign finance legislation. Against a background of the unraveling Watergate disclosures and the gathering momentum of the impeachment proceedings, the Senate April 11 and the House Aug. 8—two hours before Nixon announced his resignation—passed major bills regulating campaign finance. Both bills included provisions for public financing of campaigns, limits on private contributions, overall spending ceilings, a tightening of the disclosure requirements of legislation enacted in 1972 and enforcement provisions. The major differences in the two bills were in the public finance provisions and enforcement. As this book went to press, House-Senate conferees reached agreement Oct. 1 on a compromise bill. *(Details, p. 29, 33)*

Public financing of political campaigns combined with strict ceilings on private contributions would represent a radical change in the financing of American politics. Under the existing system of private financing, an estimated 90 per cent of political funds came from one per cent of the population. Public finance proponents contended that this system gave undue influence to wealthy contributors and to pressure groups with a direct stake in specific legislation. *(1974 group spending, p. 55)*

Opponents of public finance and contribution limits countered that these provisions would infringe upon constitutional rights under the First Amendment. The Watergate committee concluded that public financing violated the First Amendment and led to "inherent dangers" by creating a federal bureaucracy that would fund "and excessively regulate political campaigns."

Spending Limits and Disclosure

Legislation enacted in 1972 placed spending limits on communications media campaigning and broadcast spending; it was assumed that the radio-television spending curb would control the most rapidly escalating cost of political campaigns (TV spending had jumped sixfold in the 1960s). *(1972 Law, p. 2)*

The 1972 presidential election demonstrated that TV spending limits had little effect on overall spending. Although both major party candidates spent well below the legal limit for broadcast spending, overall spending rose drastically. An estimated $44-million was spent in the presidential campaigns of 1968; the 1972 Nixon-McGovern race cost well over $100-million. *(Broadcast spending, p. 60; 1972 presidential campaign spending, p. 64)*

Opponents of spending limits raised two principal arguments. First, they viewed limits as violations of constitutional rights of freedom of expression under the First Amendment. Second, they considered spending limits, particularly when applied to congressional races, as favoring incumbents. Challengers, it was argued, had to spend more simply to gain the voter recognition that an incumbent could maintain merely by taking advantage of the perquisites of office—franked (free) mailing privileges, office staffs paid by the federal government and easier access to the news media.

Disclosure, viewed by many as the most useful feature of the 1972 law since it enabled scholars and journalists to obtain a better picture of patterns of spending and investigators to uncover formerly concealed contributions, nevertheless had its critics—again on constitutional grounds. The American Civil Liberties Union maintained that the disclosure requirements of the 1972 law, tightened in the 1974 bills, inhibited contributions to unpopular political causes.

Enforcement

Until the Watergate scandal erupted and the office of the special prosecutor was created to investigate and prosecute Watergate-related offenses, the entire history of campaign finance laws was one of non-enforcement. No candidate for Congress was ever prosecuted under the 1925 Corrupt Practices Act, although it was widely known that most candidates exceeded the spending limits of the act.

Many observers believed that without strict enforcement any campaign finance legislation would be useless. In a major enforcement breakthrough, the Oct. 1 House-Senate compromise would create a potentially powerful independent election commission with power not only to issue regulations to carry out the new law but to seek civil injunctions in court against violations by candidates and contributors. Criminal prosecutions would rest with the Justice Department. *(Agreement, p. 33)*

Dollar Politics, Vol. II, begins with an examination of the 1972 law and its implementation, then turns to Watergate and the pressures that led to the legislative activity in 1974. The evolving campaign finance legislation in the states, the income tax check-off fund and 1974 fundraising activities are discussed in subsequent chapters. The chapter on campaign finance in Europe illustrates how public finance works in the several democracies that have adopted it. The remainder of the book contains extensive statistical studies of the financing of the 1972 congressional and presidential elections, the text of the 1972 law, a complete list of Watergate indictments and a bibliography. Congressional Quarterly's first book on campaign finance, *Dollar Politics*, is described on page 98.

Robert A. Diamond
Book Service Editor
October 1974

MEDIA SPENDING LIMITS, DISCLOSURE MARK '72 ACT

Spurred by rising campaign-financing costs and by fears that well-heeled challengers could use television to "blitz" incumbents, Congress in 1972 cleared the first comprehensive political campaign financing law since the toothless and unenforced Corrupt Practices Act of 1925.

Called the Federal Elections Campaign Act of 1971, the measure was actually signed into law Feb. 7, 1972 (S 382—PL 92-225), and went into effect on April 7, 1972. It combined two sharply different approaches to reform.

One section clamped limits on how much a federal candidate could spend on all forms of communications media. The second part provided, for the first time, for relatively complete and timely public reports by candidates on who was financing their campaigns and how much they were spending on the theory that meaningful disclosure would reduce the likelihood of corruption and unfair advantage. *(Provisions of act, p. 91)*

The media spending limits were separately applicable to the primary campaign and to the general election.

For a House candidate, the limit was set at $50,000 or 10 cents for each voting-age person in the congressional district, whichever was greater. For a Senate candidate, the limit was $50,000 or 10 cents for each voting-age person in the state.

The ceiling, which was to rise automatically with the cost of living, applied to spending for newspaper, radio, TV, magazine, billboard and television advertising.

The heart of this section was a separate requirement that out of the over all total for media, no more than 60 per cent could go for radio and television advertising.

In practice, this meant in the 1972 elections that a candidate for the House could spend no more than $52,150 for *all* media outlays in his primary campaign and no more than $52,150 in his general election campaign. (The cost of living factor had raised these figures from the initial $50,000.) In each case, only $31,290 of the overall media total could go for radio and television.

Because of population differences between states, the figures for Senate races ranged from an overall media limit of $52,150 in thinly populated states like Alaska and Montana (of which only $31,290 could be for radio and TV) to as much as $1.4 million in California (of which about $850,000 could be for radio and TV).

Presidential limits were also computed on the basis of 10 cents per eligible voter. For each presidential candidate, the overall media limit was $14.3 million of which no more than $8.5 million could be used for radio and TV.

Motive for Media Provisions

What lay behind these media provisions—considered the most important at that time—was not so much a passion for campaign reform, but a fear, almost a panic, in the halls of Congress about the rising cost of campaigning and the increasing influence and cost of television.

In the presidential election year 1956, overall campaign spending in all political campaigns in the U.S. was estimated at $155 million, according to the Citizens Research

Foundation of Princeton, N.J. Of this, only $9.8 million was used for radio and TV broadcasts.

Over the next decade, however, broadcasting emerged as the dominant political medium. While overall campaign spending was doubling by 1968 to $300 million, broadcasting outlays increased nearly six-fold to $58.9 million.

Congressional incumbents feared that without some curb on the costs of media, they would simply be unable to finance their campaigns in the future and would become increasingly dependent on wealthy contributors and powerful lobbying groups for the money to seek re-election. A popular slogan of those supporting the bill, voiced frequently by such senators as John O. Pastore (D R.I.), was that without some limitations on TV outlays, only a wealthy man or a corrupt man might eventually be able to run for office.

Two other factors entered into the media and TV limits. Many Democrats saw the limit on TV outlays as a way of overcoming what they viewed as lopsided advantage enjoyed by the Republicans—particularly in the 1972 presidential race—in the ability to raise money. Without any limit, the GOP with its funding advantage, the argument ran, would increasingly be able to blanket the airwaves and make it impossible for Democratic candidates to be heard. In addition, at the time of passage of the 1971 legislation, a grave fear had arisen that rich challengers could use TV "blitzes" to overpower incumbents.

Although in retrospect this fear may seem exaggerated, incumbent Republicans and Democrats shared it at the time and it was violently fanned by two primary races in 1970. In New York, Rep. Richard L. Ottinger (D N.Y.), barely known statewide at the start of the Democratic primary campaign for the U.S. Senate, spent nearly $1-million for TV advertising and ran off with the nomination from several better-known opponents, although he eventually lost the general election.

In Ohio, parking-lot magnate Howard M. Metzenbaum, known to only 10 per cent of the population compared with a 95 per cent recognition figure for astronaut John Glenn, spent about $500,000 on a television campaign and bested Glenn for the Democratic Senate nomination, although he too lost the general election.

For all these reasons, TV, seen as the political supermedium of the future, was seen ripe for some spending limitations, lest the voters turn into a pack of political robots manipulated by media men and advertising agencies.

Disclosure Requirement

The second major thrust of the 1972 law was the institution for the first time of meaningful requirements for candidates to report political spending.

The Corrupt Practices Act of 1925 did contain limits on how much candidates could could spend ($25,000 for a Senate race; $5,000 House), and requirements that contributions over $100 each and expenditures be reported by federal candidates and committees. But all these limits and reporting requirements did not apply to primaries, only general elections. Moreover, they applied only to the candidate personally and not his campaign unit, and they did not apply to political committees operating only within a single state. This meant that reporting was required only for the national committees and other interstate groups, but not for dozens of separate state finance committees set up by presidential candidates nor for a Senate or House member's campaign committee when it operated within a single state. And it meant that the spending limits were essentially meaningless and unenforceable.

The predominant theory at the time of passage of the 1972 law was that merely by writing a good, tight campaign finance disclosure law, Congress could reduce excessive contributions from any one source to any one candidate, who would fear to be seen as dominated by a single "big giver," and give the public the means to identify the political activities of special interest groups and take necessary corrective action at the polls.

Attempts to rewrite the 1925 Act along these lines had been made regularly during the late 1950s and 1960s with little success, although several bills were reported or passed in the Senate. Then, under pressure from the National Committee for an Effective Congress, the new lobby Common Cause, groups associated with Ralph Nader and with support from Senate leaders Hugh Scott (R Pa.) and Mike Mansfield (D Mont.), Congress in 1971 used the general fear of burgeoning TV spending to unite the campaign reporting provisions and the media spending limits in an omnibus bill.

Favorable Political Climate

A purely political factor in passage of the 1972 law was a commitment in 1970 by Scott to work for a broad campaign reform bill. In 1970, a bill containing sharper TV-spending limits than the 1972 measure, but no broad disclosure provisions, was vetoed by President Nixon as unduly restrictive and narrow in its general effect on corrupt campaign practices. Scott, as Senate Republican leader, worked hard to move the Senate to sustain the veto and pledged to senators that if they would vote to sustain, he would help sponsor a broader reform measure that would be acceptable to Nixon as well as Congress in the next session.

Having made this commitment, Scott was bound to support a broad measure in 1971 and, with Mansfield one of the major Democratic sponsors in the Senate, this provided a bipartisan leadership push for passage of a bill in 1971.

What the 1972 act provided, in the disclosure area, was the requirement that any candidate or political committee in a federal campaign file quarterly spending and receipts reports March 10, June 10, Sept. 10 and Jan. 31 each year. Contributors or recipients of $100 or more had to be identified by name, place of business and address.

During election years, added reports were required to be filed 15 days before and 5 days before an election, and any contribution of $5,000 or more had to be reported within 48 hours of receipt.

Closing up numerous loopholes in previous law, the 1972 statute applied the reporting requirements to primaries, conventions and runoffs as well as the general election and to any political committee, even if it operated in only one state, provided it spent or received $1,000 or more a year. This meant, in effect, that the loophole of avoiding reports by having separate campaign fund groups in each state was closed for presidential candidates, and it meant that members of Congress with campaign fund groups operating only in their home states would henceforth have to report.

The reports were to be filed with the House Clerk for House candidates, Secretary of the Senate for Senate candidates, and General Accounting Office (GAO) for presidential candidates. These would be made available for public inspection within 48 hours of being received and periodically published; and reports also were required to be filed with the Secretary of State of each state and made available for public inspection by the end of the day on which received.

On the theory that disclosure alone would be adequate to stop corruption, all the previous ineffective spending and contribution limits were repealed, except provisions barring contributions directly from corporate funds and directly from union funds raised from dues money. (However, *voluntary* funds raised from union members and administered by a union unit were permitted.)

Impact of Law

The first primary and general elections to which the new law applied were the presidential and congressional elections of 1972.

On the basis of 1972 alone, it was impossible to assess precisely how the new statute would work out, but some tentative conclusions on spending limits and disclosure were possible.

Administration of 1972 Law

Neither the TV spending limits nor the campaign financing disclosure limits proved impossible to administer, as some had forecast when they were passed. Although there were thousands of violations of the disclosure law, most proved minor and the three officials (the Clerk of the House, the Secretary of the Senate, and the GAO) charged with collecting and verifying the reports appeared to have the general technical problems in hand. Total administrative costs were running about $2-million a year for the House, Senate and GAO operations combined.

Drop in Broadcast Spending

During the 1972 campaign, Senate and presidential outlays for radio and TV campaign advertising dropped very sharply as compared with 1968 and 1970, but it was not clear whether this was a result of the TV spending limits. In the presidential race, part of the drop was due to the fact that an incumbent president was running (by contrast with 1968) with a landslide in the making and with loads of free air time available to him when he chose to address the nation in "non-political" speeches under his presidential hat, instead of seeking paid time as merely a candidate. He was in a position to spend far less and he did.

The drop in Senate spending was less easily explainable, but many senators said one factor was the realization that electronic media, while enormously effective, were not as much of a quantum leap in campaigning techniques as had previously been believed. The notion that TV could "do it all," which was virtually an article of faith in the late 1960s and in 1970, had begun to fade, and more resources were put out into other forms of advertising and into traditional organizational and legwork efforts. Broadcast spending totals also were reduced by the requirement in the 1972 law that TV stations charge politicians the lowest unit rate for any time slot.

A complicating factor on the use of TV, which many senators learned in 1972, was that TV station coverage was not well-designed for campaign purposes in many areas. In some large states, for example, Kentucky, it was impossible to cover the whole state with stations broadcasting only within that state. To cover border areas, it was necessary to buy time on stations located in other states, only a portion of whose viewers were in Kentucky. This meant that to send a message to one corner of a state, a candidate had to pay for coverage outside the state as well, a wasteful and costly practice.

The same thing was true in some of the large central metropolitan areas located between two or three states. For northern New Jersey, a candidate had to pay rates for New York too, since many of the stations in that area broadcast simultaneously to New York City, Connecticut and northern New Jersey.

Some Senators found it cheaper under these conditions to use other ways of reaching the voters. The great TV boom, if not ended, was at least slowed.

Federal Communications Commission reports showed that while a handful of senators went slightly over their campaign limits, the TV limits as a whole were observed.

Because of the TV "targeting" problems described above, many in Congress began to argue that a flat spending limit for TV was too inflexible. They said an overall spending limit for all campaign costs—similar to that repealed in 1971, but with real scope and enforcement teeth—would be better. Such a proposal, they argued, would still limit any massive use of TV because a candidate would not be able to exceed his total campaign spending limit. But it would allow greater flexibility as to which portion of overall costs went to TV and which to other items. In 1973 and 1974, proposals to repeal the media limits of the 1972 law and substitute an overall spending limit for all items passed the Senate.

Disclosure Provisions

The campaign disclosure provisions of the 1972 law proved extremely useful, enabling scholars and the relevant committees of Congress to get a clear picture for the first time of patterns of spending. Enormous contributions by the milk industry, formerly concealed large contributions by individuals, and even information playing a key role in the Watergate scandal, relating to "laundered money" and corporate contributions, emerged from the reports.

Although there were thousands of late and faulty reports, the disclosure law on the whole probably met with fair compliance.

Sen. Lloyd Bentsen (D Texas), chairman of the Senate Democratic Campaign Committee, Rep. Wayne L. Hays (D Ohio), Sen. Bob Dole (R Kans.) and Sen. Alan Cranston (D Calif.) as well as Ken Davis, administrative assistant to Republican leader Scott, all said the disclosure provisions were having an important impact in reducing excessive and concealed contributions. Senators and representatives by mid-1974 were extremely reluctant in the Watergate climate to be seen accepting a giant contribution from some big businessman or special interest group. (Sen. Charles McC. Mathias of Maryland said he wouldn't accept contributions over $100 from any one source in his 1974 race.) Donors appeared anxious to avoid any appearance they were seeking to buy an excessive amount of good will or influence.

Problems: Dummy Committees and Enforcement

Nevertheless, there remained a great many problems with the disclosure law. The reports, especially those made in the last few days before the election, were extremely dif-

ficult for a reporter or a rival political camp to collate and make sense of. There was little way to rapidly track down multiple contributions by a wealthy individual made to one candidate through a system of dummy organizations with cryptic names. It was extremely difficult to track down an industrywide campaign, made through a series of fronts, to a candidate or a group of candidates.

More important, the crucial question in effectiveness of the law was enforcement. The Justice Department was given sole power to prosecute violations, despite its record of 45 years of somnolence in enforcing previous regulations. (It was traditionally understood that Department of Justice bureaucrats feared to undertake vigorous enforcement lest they endanger the party in power and be fired.)

The question was whether the department would make a powerful, massive effort not only to round up serious violators but to require that reports be on time and complete. Without such a signal from the department the practice of filing slovenly, incomplete reports, or even misleading reports, and filing them late, would clearly vitiate much of the effect of the law and render it null in practice.

Although thousands of violations, some serious, most technical (late or incomplete) were referred to the Justice Department in 1972 and 1973 by the House and Senate and GAO, there were only a handful of prosecutions.

Senators Scott and Edward M. Kennedy (D Mass.), the Senate Rules Committee, Common Cause and numerous others contended that what was needed was an independent enforcement mechanism, isolated from the politics and timidity of the Justice Department. The Senate in 1973 and 1974 passed legislation taking administration of the law out of the hands of House and Senate and GAO officials, and prosecution responsibility out of the hands of the Justice Department, and placing these powers in an independent enforcement commission.

Common Cause and Reporting

To remedy the problem of getting reports to the public and to reporters quickly with the information organized in a meaningful way, Common Cause, the public interest pressure group, at a cost of more than $250,000 and thousands of hours from volunteer workers, organized teams of people in 1972 to go to reporting places and collect and collate information on reports which it then distributed to the press in time for use before election day.

Common Cause legislative director Fred Wertheimer said the aim was to make the law work and to give it a good start. But it was clear that depending on private organizations alone probably would be inadequate and that unless some permanent way were found to speed up collation and distribution of the materials to the public and press, particularly in the late days of a campaign, perhaps at government expense, the practice of disclosure would be severely handicapped and far less useful.

Common Cause vowed to continue monitoring in 1974 and the Citizens Research Foundation of Princeton, N.J., in June 1974 set up a special campaign reporting center in Washington to systematically gather the campaign data from the House and Senate reporting offices and from the GAO as it was filed and channel it to news media with a fee for the service.

Watergate and Public Financing

Beyond all this, the larger question remained: was disclosure, even if done efficiently and rapidly with meaningful organization of information, quick access by

1972 TV Spending Totals

Presidential Race. In the 1972 campaign, the legal limit on radio and TV spending by any one presidential candidate was $8.5 million for the primaries and $8.5 million for the general election. Federal Communications Commission reports showed all candidates spent well under these limits. Total spending on radio and TV combined, for both the primaries and the election, was $14.3 million. Of this, about two-thirds was spent by Democrats. President Nixon, with virtually no contests in primaries, plenty of free air-time for "non-political" speeches in his role as President, and a landslide election victory in the making, needed to spend relatively little.

The $14.3 million figure compared with $28.5 million—three-fifths of it from Republicans—in total spending in 1968. Most of the drop from 1968 to 1972 was accounted for by a nearly $9 million reduction in Nixon outlays. In 1968 as a non-incumbent candidate with a tough presidential election race, he had spent far more than in 1972. Democrats, by comparison, dropped only slightly from 1968 to 1972.

De Van L. Shumway, press man for the Nixon campaign, said TV is basically "an exposure" medium, and since the President now was enormously well known, money that might otherwise have gone to TV was spent on other things like political organizing at the grass roots and "an extensive people to people program."

Senate Races. The FCC report showed that Senate candidates in 1972 spent $6.4 million, of which $3.3 million was laid out by Democrats. The $6.4 million total was a big drop from $16 million in 1970 and $10.4 million in 1968. Buehl Berentson, director of the Senate GOP Campaign Committee, said the 1971 campaign law limitations had a psychological impact in holding down TV and radio spending and led candidates to put more money into other things. Others said the illusion that TV could solve all problems for a campaigner had faded, and still others pointed to the "targeting" problems as the reason for the spending drop. Several Senate candidates apparently overspent the TV-radio limits: both candidates in Kentucky, John Chafee (R) in Rhode Island and Sen. James Abourezk (D) and Chuck Lien (R) in South Dakota. *(Senate totals p. 62)*

House Races. Broadcast spending in 1972 was $7.4 million, compared with $6.1 million in 1970. Of the $7.4 million 1972 total, $4.3 million was Democratic. Nine House candidates apparently exceeded the limits but there were no prosecutions.

Other. Other races at the state and local level were not regulated, but the FCC computed TV-radio outlays for them as well. Candidates for governor and lieutenant governor spent $9.7 million in 1972, compared with $16.4 million in 1970 (when there were more big-state races) and $6.2 million in 1968. Candidates for other state and local offices totalled $21.7 million.

National Totals. Combining all totals—president, House, Senate, governor and local races—overall radio-TV spending by candidates in 1972 was $59.6 million, compared with $59.2 million in 1970 and $58.9 million in 1968.

reporters, and good enforcement against violations, enough to clean up abuses, corruption and the excessive impact of wealth on the political process?

In the light of the Watergate revelations, many believed that it was not—that only specific airtight limits on campaign outlays and on the size of contributions by any individual could curb influence-peddling and corruption. Common Cause and others even went so far as to press for the end of private financing of elections and substitution of government financing for election campaigns, with stiff penalties for violations. Such legislation passed the Senate early in 1974. Thus, even before the 1972 law's impact could be fully measured, efforts were underway in both chambers of Congress to clamp a tight control on total campaign outlays, with real enforcement teeth, and to install a system of public financing.

Disclosure Provisions Mechanics

Early Disputes

The 1972 law had an early stormy history, with Common Cause, the National Committee for an Effective Congress and Ralph Nader's Public Citizen fearful that the Secretary of the Senate and the Clerk of the House, as well as powerful figures like House Administration Committee Chairman Wayne L. Hays (D Ohio), would seek to administer disclosure provisions so they would tell the public the very least about House and Senate members, instead of the most, lest members be injured and become angry.

Common Cause sued Hays when the cost of obtaining a duplicated page of a report filed by anyone was fixed at $1 on House reports. This was eventually reduced to 10 cents, the same per-page fee as charged by the Senate and the comptroller general for journalists and members of the public who wished to have a report duplicated. Common Cause also brought suit to force issuance of regulations controlling verbal earmarking of funds. The organization argued that when a contributor gives a large sum to the House or Senate congressional campaign committee with the verbal understanding that it be passed through to a specific House or Senate candidate, this pass-through arrangement should be required to be made known in the report. Such regulations eventually were issued.

Many of the reform organizations also complained that reporting of violations of the disclosure law to the Justice Department was lagging, and took to the habit of filing their own complaints to encourage the House Clerk to begin doing so. Common Cause's Wertheimer said his organization filed 400 complaints in April and May 1972, motivated by fears that if candidates got the impression the House and Senate did not intend to enforce the reporting requirements stringently, the candidates simply would not comply carefully and the whole effect of the law would be vitiated.

There were disputes, also, particularly between Hays and Clerk of the House W. Pat Jennings, about the level of support needed to run the campaign reporting unit within Jenning's office.

Costs and Volume of Reports

Eventually, these matters were straightened out. There still remained the task of processing and organizing a tremendous volume of reports, of referring violations and of organizing the reports into periodic reference volumes listing in one place all contributions required by the law.

By mid-1974 the House clerk's office adopted a basic microfilm system for recording and making reports available to the public. Copies of any page were available for 10 cents a page.

Paul Wohl, general counsel to the House clerk, said April 29, 1974, that about 28 persons were then working on the campaign reports, using 3M and Kodak equipment (largely rented equipment). Wohl said reports received are usually processed into the microfilm system overnight and "generally speaking we've met the 48-hour requirement" on having the reports available to the public. Wohl gave these figures for the costs of administering the reporting requirements: calendar 1972 (beginning on April 7, the date the new law went into effect), $263,233; 1973: $260,731. He estimated the cost for 1974 would be considerably more because 1974 was an election year and reports would be due for the entire year whereas in 1972 they only started April 7.

Collating Problems

Under the microfilm system used by the House Clerk and Secretary of the Senate as well, any reporter or other member of the public wishing to look up an individual's campaign reports—challengers as well as incumbents must file them—must go to the clerk's office and ask for the roll of microfilm recording the reports filed by that candidate and organizations listed as campaign organizations for him. That roll, viewed in a large "scanner" which enlarges the microfilm into page size or larger, contains the candidate's name and under it the list of all organizations filing in his name.

Thus, under "Joe Smith, candidate for 6th District of Congress" there might be listed "Committee for Joe Smith's Reelection," "Friends of Joe Smith," "Edna Smith," and others who gave to the candidate, with the amount for each. To determine where the organization called "Friends of Joe Smith" got its money, the viewer must obtain a second roll containing information on who contributed to "Friends of Joe Smith."

Most candidates have only a few such organizations listed, but it is conceivable that one or two backers of Smith, anxious to channel plenty of money to him without necessarily being identified easily, could set dozens of little committees with odd names, each with only one or two contributors, and make their contributions to these committees which in turn would turn the money over to Smith.

A reporter or citizen, seeking to get a full picture of Smith's contributors, would first have to look up under the general report for Smith the names of all such organizations. Then he would have to obtain the rolls of microfilm containing the separate details on each such organization and copy down the contributors to each such organization. Only then could he determine whether a handful of persons were channeling large amounts through numerous dummy organizations to one candidate.

With only a handful of scanners to use and with only a few days to work before the final series of reports are filed, 15 days before and then 5 days before election (or primary), persons seeking a comprehensive combined picture of financing face an enormously difficult task.

The GAO, which uses a somewhat different system based on computerized information, has less difficulty in producing information quickly on who is behind multiple filings to any one candidate. It can produce this information rapidly with a computerized readout, according to Larry McCoy, chief of the reports processing and control section in the GAO's Office of Federal Elections.

But neither the congressional administrators nor the GAO were able to produce quick analyses of special efforts by one industry or group of industries to channel funds through various committees to a selected group of candidates.

Thus, if bankers, for example, privately agree that a big effort should be made to support a selected list of 100 candidates for the House and 20 for the Senate, they could set up dozens of different voluntary contributions committees with names not easily identified with the banking industry. It would be extremely difficult for the House Clerk, Secretary of the Senate or GAO to be able to discover quickly what the total picture of banking industry efforts looks like—especially if the industry effort is launched in the last weeks of a campaign.

Lists of contributing organizations seeming to represent the same industry are kept, but putting it all together is clumsy and haphazard.

Treatment of Violations

Wohl said that the House Clerk's office had determined to turn over all apparent violations to the Justice Department, even if minor. Most violations involve late or incomplete reports, or failure to file; some are more serious.

In 1972, the House Clerk's office referred 2,702 violations by candidates and 2,198 by political committees (total 4,900) to the Justice Department.

In 1973, not an election year, the figures were 418 violations by candidates and 779 by political committees (total 1,197).

The House Clerk established a policy that no details of the apparent violations—not the names of those involved or the nature of the violation—would be made public. Common Cause and others said this was simply a way of protecting members and avoiding political damage to them, while weakening the impact of the law

On April 10, 1974, the House Clerk's Office published a comprehensive listing of campaign contributions for 1972 (H Doc 93-284). Some of the problems in obtaining information under the law were made evident in the book. Under each candidate's name were listed the names and amounts obtained by him from campaign committees devoted solely to his re-election. However, organizations which contributed to more than one candidate are listed in a separate section with only their total contributions to all candidates summarized. Still a separate section lists contributions over $100 by such organizations. In many cases, when a contribution is tracked down to this last list, there is no listing for the original candidate because the organization presumably did not give him more than $100.

Secretary of Senate's System

A microfilm system similar to that of the House Clerk was set up by the Secretary of the Senate, Frank Valeo, under the general direction of aides Orlando Potter and Burl Hays. Potter said about 15 persons work on administration and enforcement including four professional accountants obtained from the GAO.

Total administrative costs, including salaries and equipment, he estimated at $300,000 a year. All told, Potter said, 1,100 campaign organizations had been required to register under the law, but 200 were eliminated from the reporting requirements as too small, leaving some 900 organizations required to file reports. About 300 individual candidates also had to file reports in 1972 and from April 1972 to 1973 some 90,000 pieces of paper were processed.

All reports are investigated by quick office audit and violations or background information are investigated more extensively. "Our investigators have gone into the 33 states in which Senate elections were held in 1972" to verify information, Potter said.

The Secretary of the Senate's office set up the policy of referring all violations to the Justice Department. But like the House Clerk, the Senate Secretary does not make information on violators public.

The total of violations is "in the thousands," Potter said. "Every week they get a bundle. But some are minor—non-filing and lateness, inadequate or insufficient information. Others are more serious."

In 1972, the Secretary of the Senate reported 1,835 "types of apparent violations" to the Justice Department. These violations were discovered through desk audits of required committee and candidate reports. "The vast ma-

---

"The total of violations is in the thousands. Every week they (the Justice Department) get a bundle."
—Orlando Potter, office of the Secretary of the Senate

---

jority," the Senate Secretary said in his report on the 1972 election released Aug. 8, 1974, involved what might be considered technical violations of the statute rather than apparent willful attempts to avoid disclosure."

The Senate Secretary did not give the actual number of violations which he said amounted to "several thousand."

He also reported referring another 220 violations to the Justice Department after conducting field investigations. Again, he called most of the violations "technical."

General Accounting Office

The General Accounting Office, charged with administering the presidential campaign reporting provisions of the 1972 law, used a computerized system of record-keeping with xeroxes, at the same 10 cents a page charge as House and Senate, when a reporter or member of the public wanted a copy of any particular page of a raw report. Copies of the raw reports are kept in a huge file cabinet for public inspection.

McCoy said 2,715 organizations registered in 1972 but GAO waived further reports from 724, leaving just under 2,000 required to file quarterly and pre-election reports.

McCoy said under GAO rules reports filed the 15th day before the election need contain information on receipts and outlays only through the 7th day prior to filing of the report; and reports filed on the fifth day before election also carry only through the seventh day prior to that.

This means that the last two pre-election reports actually contain information from the 22nd and 12th days before the election.

"We've done field audits on 600 to 700 of the reporting agencies," he said. "To date we've received 16,524 reports, with 122,722 pieces of paper from April 7, 1972, to April 17, 1974. In 1972 alone we got 10,000 reports and 95,000 pieces of paper. After punching the information into a computer, we file the information in 10 to 12 five-drawer cabinets, with 25-30 added cabinets of duplicate reports for the press and public to examine."

"So far we have sold $22,437 worth of pages at 10 cents a page," McCoy said.

The GAO's Office of Federal Elections, McCoy said, had a staff of 28 and cost $1.376 million to run in fiscal 1974, which included $500,000 for a special set of studies.

The GAO put out a two-volume summary report on March 24, 1974, covering the 1972 spending reports.

Unlike the House Clerk and Secretary of the Senate, the GAO made a policy decision to release to the public the names of persons and organizations referred to the Justice Department as possible serious violators of the law. About six dozen had been referred by the start of May 1974. McCoy said late filings and incomplete reports were handled by the GAO itself through letters and investigations seeking compliance, and only very serious cases were referred to Justice. "We get fairly good compliance overall," said McCoy.

Enforcement Problems

Pre-April 7, 1972, Contributions

Before the new law's reporting provisions went into effect on April 7, 1972, the Nixon presidential campaign began collecting money from a large number of contributors with the expectation that their names would never be made public because their contributions would be made prior to April 7 and therefore would not have to be reported under the provisions of the expiring 1925 law.

In September 1973 Common Cause brought a lawsuit to force disclosure of pre-April 7 receipts. The Finance Committee to Re-elect the President contended that the contributions it sought prior to April 7 were not for Nixon's general election campaign but for possible primaries, and donations for primaries were not required to be disclosed under the old law.

Common Cause argued, however, that this was a patent trick, since the President was certain of renomination and had little or no primary opposition. The money, in fact, according to Common Cause, was actually being collected for Nixon's election campaign by a political committee operating in many states and therefore, even under the old law, was reportable.

The suit dragged on for many months in the course of which a list of many pre-April 7 contributors was discovered in the possession of presidential secretary Rose Mary Woods, obtained by Common Cause and turned over to the Watergate Special Prosecutor's office and many names were made public. It turned out that the pre-April 7 collection efforts had netted the Nixon campaign a minimum of close to $20-million including some huge contributions from individuals and industry and special interest groups—some illegal, as violating the ban on direct corporate contributions. *(Woods' list p. 65)*

Campaign Monitoring

From the beginning it was evident that unless the information filed with the GAO, House Clerk and Secretary of the Senate could be made known to the public, disclosure might have little impact. A number of organizations, because of the difficulties of taking the information off the microfilms and organizing it for use by reporters and the public, undertook their own campaign monitoring projects.

The most elaborate was that undertaken by Common Cause, which organized batteries of volunteers in more than 40 states to visit the offices of the secretaries of state and of the House Clerk and Senate Secretary to compile and collate the needed information and make it available immediately to reporters and other interested persons. The project cost about $250,000, even with volunteers, and eventually led to publication of a 13-volume series on all congressional campaign contributions. The aim, according to Wertheimer, was to make sure that the most flagrant contributions were made known in time to have some impact on the elections, while warning candidates that their receipts would not be ignored because of the difficulties of going over the reports.

Watergate Connection

The reports filed under the 1971 campaign law revealed for the first time the scope of some of the contributions by special interest groups. For example, the Common Cause monitoring project eventually revealed that three dairy groups alone (called C-TAPE, ADEPT and SPACE) had given $589,665 to congressional candidates. These revelations of huge contributions by special interest groups whom many of the public assumed were looking for legislative favors became part of the unfolding Watergate story of abuse of campaign funds.

At the same time, the GAO, investigating press reports of a mysterious $25,000 so-called "Dahlberg-Andreas" contribution to the Finance Committee to Re-elect the President, to determine if the 1972 reporting law had been violated, uncovered key violations which it reported on Aug. 26, 1972. This discovery was a crucial link in the chain of evidence which eventually opened up the whole Watergate scandal. "We never would have come up with the Dahlberg-Andreas contribution except for this act," said McCoy.

Moreover, the campaign reports made it evident that some legally questionable contributions had been made by corporations, and several came forward with confessions of their own guilt in making contributions from corporate funds, an act barred by statute since 1907 and carried forward in the 1972 law.

Compliance with the 1972 law, in turn was spurred by the burgeoning of the Watergate scandal, Potter said he had been receiving repeated requests on details of how to comply with the Senate filing requirements, in 1974, from candidates obviously frightened of being accused of footdragging on compliance.

Senators Bob Dole (R Kans.) and Lloyd Bentsen (D Texas) said their impression was that candidates were being extra careful to file reports accurately and on time and Dole said he had taken special precautions to rule out every faintly questionable outlay or practice.

James Duffy, counsel to the Senate Elections Subcommittee and one of the authors of the law of 1971, said he felt there was good compliance with it, as did Ken Davis, a key aide to Sen. Scott. But Duffy said the fear of being accused of wrongdoing and noncompliance engendered by the Watergate atmosphere of 1974 was undoubtedly a factor.

Problems, Loopholes and Proposals

The difficulties of organizing and distributing the information required in the 1972 law, to have maximum public impact, discussed above, were key problems with the 1972 law.

Duffy, Davis, Wertheimer, Rep. Hays, Potter, McCoy and others directly involved in administration said a substantial improvement in the use of the reports could be achieved by requiring each candidate to report through a single central financial committee. Such a committee, in its own report, would have to include in an organized form information about contributors and their own sources of funds which at present must be looked up separately. Under this method, instead of listing just a single entry "Receipt from Friends of Joe Smith," the candidate's report would have to include in the same listing all those who contributed to Friends of Joe Smith.

Another proposed reform, passed by the Senate early in 1974, was a requirement for administration of the law—and its enforcement with subpoena powers and the right to bring criminal actions against violators—by a single independent federal elections commission.

Wertheimer and several others said separate jurisdictions of the House Clerk, Senate Secretary and GAO made for lack of uniform rules (for example, on whether to make public names of accused violators) and weak enforcement, due to the political timidity in the two congressional administrative offices.

They also said the Justice Department, with a history of extreme timidity and inaction on prosecuting campaign law violations—and little evidence it was moving faster on the 1972 law despite thousands of violation referrals—was the wrong agency to enforce the law. "Justice is the only one with authority to go to court and they don't," said Wertheimer.

Virtually all interviewed said a ban on the use of cash for contributions was needed, since cash donations were too easy to conceal. Proposals for use of checks and money orders only for contributions over $50 or at most $100 were considered in 1974.

VARIATIONS ON A SINGLE THEME: FINANCE ABUSE

The single common denominator that ran through all of the scandals that have been grouped under the umbrella of Watergate was the abuse of campaign funds.

The many-faceted scandal included specific violations of campaign finance laws as well as violations of other criminal laws facilitated by the use of campaign funds. There were still other instances where campaign funds were used in a manner that strongly suggested influence peddling or at the very least gave the appearance of impropriety in the conduct of public office.

John Gardner, head of the citizens' lobby Common Cause, said in April, 1973: "The Watergate is not primarily a story of political espionage, nor even of White House intrigue. It is a particularly malodorous chapter in the annals of campaign financing. The money paid to the Watergate conspirators before the break-in—and money passed to them later—was money from campaign gifts."

Gardner's charge was dramatically acknowledged by former President Nixon on Aug 5, 1974, when he released a June 23, 1972, tape recording of conversations between himself and H.R. Haldeman, then Nixon's chief of staff. The recording revealed that Nixon was then told of the use of campaign funds in the June 17, 1972, Watergate break-in and agreed to an effort to help cover up that fact. The Aug. 5 disclosure was followed by Nixon's resignation Aug. 9. *(Excerpt of conversation, Box p. 10)*

1972 Campaign Finance Law

Some of the illegal Watergate activities came to light as a result of the comprehensive requirements for disclosure of political contributions and expenditures included in the Federal Election Campaign Act of 1971, which went into effect April 7, 1972. *(Chapter on 1972 law, p. 2; provisions of the 1972 law, p. 93)*

The new law enabled investigators to uncover some of the illegal purposes to which campaign contributions were put. For example, following press reports in July 1972 that money intended for President Nixon's re-election campaign was deposited in the Miami bank account of Bernard Baker, one of the men arrested at the Watergate, a General Accounting Office investigation traced the checks in Barker's account to a campaign contribution to the Finance Committee to Re-Elect the President. GAO official Larry McCoy said the link between the checks in Barker's account and the campaign contribution could not have been established without the 1972 law. *(p. 8)*

Investigations and Findings

The major Watergate investigations, other than those made by the press, were carried out by three official bodies—the Senate Select Committee on Presidential Campaign Activities (the Senate Watergate Committee), the office of the Watergate Special Prosecutor and the House Judiciary Committee in the course of its impeachment inquiry *(Box, p. 12)*. The Watergate investigations revealed

Scene of the June 17, 1972, break-in

eight areas where the use of campaign funds was either illegal or highly questionable. These eight areas are briefly described below, a more detailed discussion follows on pages 10 to 15. *(List of indictments, p. 90)*

Watergate Break-in and Coverup

Campaign funds donated to President Nixon's 1972 campaign were used to finance the actual break-in at the Democratic National Committee headquarters in the Watergate building and also were used to pay legal and other expenses of the defendants after the break-in. *(p. 10)*

Vesco case

A $200,000 cash campaign donation to Nixon's campaign by Financier Robert L. Vesco, who was under investigation for stock fraud, led to the trial of two former Nixon cabinet members (Attorney General John N. Mitchell and Commerce Secretary Maurice H. Stans) on charges that they obtained the contribution in return for promises to intercede with the government on behalf of Vesco. The two men were found not guilty. *(p. 11)*

Illegal Corporate Campaign Contributions

Several large corporations were found guilty of contributing corporate funds to the Nixon campaign and also to some Democratic presidential and congressional campaigns. Corporate contributions were prohibited originally under provisions of a 1907 act of Congress and were carried forward in the 1947 Taft-Hartley Labor-Management Act and by the Federal Election Campaign Act of 1971. *(p. 11)*

Milk Fund

Large contributions by dairy cooperatives following the Nixon administration's 1971 decision to raise federal milk price support subsidies raised questions about the possible relationship between the price support decision and the later contributions. Former Treasury Secretary John B. Connally was indicted in 1974 for allegedly receiving a bribe in exchange for his recommendation to increase the milk price supports. *(p. 12)*

Plumbers

Campaign funds were involved in financing the break-in at the office of Dr. Lewis Fielding, Daniel Ellsberg's psychiatrist, by agents of a secret White House investigative unit nicknamed the "plumbers." *(p. 14)*

Dirty Tricks

Political saboteur Donald H. Segretti, was hired by two White House aides to create dissension among the 1972 Democratic presidential contenders and received his expense money and salary from Nixon's chief campaign fundraiser. *(p. 15)*

Ambassadors

Large campaign contributions from persons seeking ambassadorships led critics to charge that the Nixon administration was brokering ambassadorships. Herbert W. Kalmbach, Nixon's personal attorney, pleaded guilty to a charge of promising federal employment in return for a campaign contribution. *(p. 15)*

"The Watergate affair reflects an alarming indifference displayed by some in high public office or position to concepts of morality and public responsibility and trust. Indeed, the conduct of many Watergate participants seems grounded on the belief that the ends justified the means, that the laws could be flaunted to maintain the present [Nixon] Administration in office."

—Senate Watergate Committee Report

International Telephone and Telegraph

A pledge to contribute $400,000 was made by the International Telephone and Telegraph Corporation (ITT) to help finance the 1972 Republican national convention. At the time of the pledge, ITT was involved in an anti-trust suit with the Justice Department; the suit was later settled in favor of ITT. *(p. 15)*

Watergate Break-in and Coverup

National attention was first focused on the misuse of Nixon's campaign funds immediately following the June 1972 Watergate break-in.

A police search of the five men arrested in the Watergate burglary produced $6,500 in new $100 bills, most

---

Watergate Break-in Money

H.R. Haldeman, President Nixon's chief of staff, told Nixon on the morning of June 23, 1972, that money paid to the Watergate burglars had been traced to the President's re-election committee by the FBI. Haldeman opened the conversation saying, "We're back in the problem area because the FBI is not under control...."

Transcript excerpts released Aug. 5, 1974, follow:

H. That the way to handle this now is for us to have Walters [Gen. Vernon A. Walters, deputy director of the CIA] call Pat Gray [acting director of the FBI] and just say, "stay to hell out of this—this is ah, business here we don't want you to go any further on it." That's not an unusual development, and ah, that would take care of it.

* * * * *

P. This is CIA? They've traced the money? Who'd they trace it to?

* * * * *

P. It isn't from the committee though, from Stans?
H. Yeah. It is. It's directly traceable and there's some more through some Texas people that went to the Mexican bank which can also be traced to the Mexican bank—they'll get their names today.

---

of which were serially numbered. In the process of tracing the bills, it was discovered that five checks which originally had been contributed to the Finance Committee to Re-Elect the President had later been deposited in the account of one of the burglars, Bernard Barker. The checks had been passed through numerous channels to obscure the original source of the contribution ("laundered") before reaching Barker's checking account.

It was later learned from testimony by finance committee treasurer Hugh W. Sloan Jr. before the Senate Watergate Committee that he had disbursed $199,000 to convicted Watergate burglar G. Gordon Liddy prior to the break-in when Liddy was counsel to the finance committee.

Further testimony before the Watergate Committee indicated that the Watergate break-in defendants received sizable sums of money from campaign funds following the break-in. The amount was estimated to exceed $400,000.

The General Accounting Office's (GAO) Office of the Federal Elections released a report Aug. 26, 1972, citing the finance committee for five "apparent" and four "possible" violations of the 1971 campaign act. The GAO report disclosed, among other things, that the committee did not keep a detailed account of $114,000 that eventually was deposited to Barker's bank account.

Following the GAO investigation, the Justice Department Jan. 11, 1973, charged the committee with eight violations of federal law in failing to record and report money given to Liddy. The committee pleaded *nolo contendere* (no contest) to the charges and on Jan. 26, 1973, was found guilty and given the maximum fine of $8,000.

Vesco Case

Another GAO report that charged the President's re-election finance committee with four more "apparent" violations was referred to the Justice Department on March 12, 1973, for possible prosecution. The chief subject of the report was a $200,000 cash contribution made by Robert L. Vesco, a New Jersey financier who had been accused by the Securities and Exchange Commission (SEC) of a $224-million stock fraud. Vesco's contribution was delivered to the committee April 10, 1972, three days after the 1972 campaign reporting law took effect. The contribution was never reported to the GAO and the finance committee was found guilty June 20, 1973, and fined the maximum penalty of $3,-000 for concealing a contribution. The committee argued that the money was not reportable under the 1972 election law, because it was pledged before the April 7, 1972 deadline. But District Court Judge George L. Hart ruled that, because the money was delivered on April 10, it should have been reported.

The $200,000 Vesco contribution, which later was returned by the committee, led to the indictment of John N. Mitchell (attorney general, Jan. 1969-Feb. 1972) and Maurice H. Stans (commerce secretary Jan. 1969-Jan. 1972), along with Vesco and Harry L. Sears, a lawyer who admitted delivering the $200,000 to Stans in $100 bills in a black briefcase. Mitchell was director of the Committee to Re-elect the President and Stans was chairman of the Finance Committee to Re-elect the President.

Mitchell and Stans, who later were found not guilty, were charged with obtaining the secret $200,000 Vesco contribution to the Nixon campaign in return for promises to intercede with the government on behalf of Vesco, who was being investigated by the SEC at the time.

Sears was granted immunity in the case for his testimony at the Mitchell-Stans trial, and Vesco was a fugitive residing in Costa Rica.

Illegal Corporate Contributions

Contributions from corporate funds, which were first-made unlawful in 1907 and have remained in the criminal code ever since, were among the offenses discovered in the wake of the Watergate investigation. The bulk of the illegal corporate contributions were made to the 1972 Nixon campaign, but some illegal contributions to Democratic presidential and congressional campaigns also were discovered.

As of mid-September 1974, the Special Prosecutor had brought charges against 14 corporations of which 13 pleaded guilty and one was acquitted for making illegal contributions to President Nixon's 1972 campaign. *(Status report, p. 90)*

These corporations contributed approximately $775,-000 to the Nixon campaign and most of it was delivered in cash.

In most cases the contributions were suggested, if not solicited, by top officials of the Nixon re-election finance committee. While the contributions were illegally made from corporate funds, the Senate Watergate Committee concluded from testimony it received that there was "no evidence that any fund-raiser who was involved in these contributions sought or obtained assurances that the contribution was legal at the time it was made."

The solicitations from the fund-raisers, the committee said, ranged from low key to vigorous.

One corporate executive, Claude C. Wild Jr., a former vice president of Gulf Oil Corporation, which pleaded guilty to making an illegal $100,000 contribution to the Nixon re-election effort, told the committee:

"I considered it considerable pressure when two cabinet officers [Mitchell and Stans] and an agent of one of the committees that was handling the election...[were] asking me for funds—that is just a little bit different than somebody collecting for the Boy Scouts."

The Watergate Committee pointed out in its report that the finance committee was, in the main, a White House controlled organization.

The charge to which Gulf pleaded guilty included separate campaign contributions of $10,000 for Sen. Henry M. Jackson (D Wash.) and $15,000 contribution for Rep. Wilbur D. Mills (D Ark.), both of whom were seeking nomination as the 1972 Democratic candidate for President.

"I considered it considerable pressure when two cabinet officers [Mitchell and Stans]...[were] asking me for funds—that is just a little bit different than somebody collecting for the Boy Scouts."

—Claude C. Wild Jr., Gulf Oil Corporation

In other testimony to the Watergate Committee William W. Keeler, chairman of the board of Phillips Petroleum Company, which pleaded guilty to making an illegal $100,000 contribution to the Nixon campaign, recalled a March 1972 discussion with Stans. He said Stans began by making "quite a speech" about the oil industry, in which he stated that the oil industry had done very poorly in the 1968 (Nixon) campaign. Stans, Keeler said, expected the oil companies to make substantial contributions to the 1972 Nixon campaign.

Clyde Webb, a vice president of Ashland Petroleum Gabon Inc., which pleaded guilty to an illegal $100,000 contribution to the 1972 Nixon campaign, told the committee he delivered the money in cash to Stans who "dumped it in his desk drawer and said 'thank you.'"

Methods of Corporate Contributions

There were various methods used in making the corporate contributions. Some were laundered through foreign subsidiaries. Other contributions were made through use of corporate expense accounts and corporate bonuses to reimburse corporate executives for making individual contributions.

For example, testimony before the Watergate Committee showed that executives of Braniff Airlines, which pleaded guilty to an illegal $40,000 contribution to Nixon's campaign, devised a scheme where the contribution would be laundered through Braniff's manager in Panama. Braniff sent a $40,000 check to a company owned by their Panama manager and entered it on the airlines' books as an advance for expenses and services. The check was cashed by

Three Separate Watergate Investigations

Investigations by three official bodies uncovered much of the information about abuses of campaign financing that emerged in the wake of Watergate.

Watergate Committee

The Senate Select Committee on Presidential Campaign Activities, known as the Senate Watergate Committee, was created Feb. 7, 1973, by a unanimously-passed Senate resolution. The committee was instructed to make a "complete" investigation and study "of the extent...to which illegal, improper, or unethical activities" occurred in the 1972 Presidential campaign and election and to determine whether new legislation was needed "to safeguard the electoral process by which the President of the United States is chosen."

Senators appointed to serve on the committee were: Sam J. Ervin, Jr. (D N.C.), chairman; Howard H. Baker, Jr. (R Tenn.) vice-chairman; Herman E. Talmadge (D Ga.); Daniel K. Inouye (D Hawaii); Joseph M. Montoya (D N.M.); Edward J. Gurney (R Fla.); and Lowell P. Weicker, Jr. (R Conn.).

In fulfilling its mandate, the committee held nationally televised hearings beginning May 17, 1973, which lasted almost without interruption until Aug. 7, 1973. The committee issued a final report July 12, 1974, eighteen months after it began the most intensive investigation into alleged political corruption in American history.

The three-volume, 2,217 page document detailed, for the first time, the comprehensive scandals lumped under the umbrella of Watergate. It laid out, among other things, the background of the Watergate break-in, the Watergate coverup, the campaign practices of the Committee for the Re-election of the President, and the financing of the 1972 presidential campaign. *(Report chapter p. 16)*

Special Prosecutor

In May 1973, Attorney General Elliot L. Richardson (May 1973-October 1973) established the office of the Watergate Special Prosecutor. The creation of the office was the result of an agreement between Richardson and the Senate Judiciary Committee, which was considering Richardson's nomination as attorney general.

The mission of the special prosecutor was to investigate and prosecute offenses arising out of the Watergate break-in, as well as all offenses arising out of the 1972 presidential election.

Archibald Cox served as special prosecutor from May 25 to October 20, 1973, and Leon Jaworski, was appointed Nov. 5, 1973 after Cox was fired at President Nixon's direction.

The special prosecutor's office brought numerous charges against persons or corporations that committed offenses falling under the prosecutor's mandate. *(List of indictments, p. 90)* Still ahead was perhaps the most important of all its cases, trial of White House and Nixon re-election aides charges with conspiracy to obstruct justice in the investigation of the June 17, 1972, Watergate burglary. The trial was scheduled to begin Oct. 1. 1974.

Judiciary Committee

On Feb. 6, 1974, the House of Representatives adopted by a 410-4 roll call vote a resolution directing the House Judiciary Committee to "investigate fully and completely whether sufficient grounds exist for the House of Representatives to exercise its constitutional power to impeach Richard M. Nixon, President of the United States."

After two months of evidence presentation by its impeachment inquiry staff, the committee began its nationally televised impeachment debate on July 24, 1974, and after six days had voted three articles of impeachment. The committee articles recommended to the House that President Nixon be impeached for obstruction of justice in the Watergate coverup, abuse of presidential powers and contempt of Congress.

Debate on the articles was to have begun in the House on Aug. 19, but the Aug. 9 resignation of President Nixon ended further House consideration of impeachment. The House Aug. 20 passed 412-3 a resolution accepting the Judiciary Committee Report (H Rept 93-1305) which explained the basis for its decision to recommend impeachment. By adopting the motion, the House put its stamp of approval on the committee's inquiry and its final report without impeaching the former president.

---

the Panama manager who returned the proceeds in U.S. currency to Braniff officials in Dallas, Texas. Subsequently, the Braniff officials delivered the $40,000 in cash to Stans.

Minnesota Mining and Manufacturing Company (3M), which made contributions to the 1972 presidential campaigns of Nixon, Sen. Hubert H. Humphrey (D Minn.) and Rep. Mills, devised a plan by which a Swiss consultant to 3M would submit false billings to the company for services and would, after payment, return the proceeds in cash to 3M officials. The money was kept in a separate account that was used for making political contributions.

Milk Fund

Campaign contributions by dairy cooperatives generated questions of possible influence peddling by Nixon administration officials. And, in a related matter, John B. Connally (treasury secretary, Feb. 1971-June 1972) was indicted for bribery in connection with an increase in federal milk price supports.

The three major dairy cooperatives, Associated Milk Producers, Inc. (AMPI), Mid-American Dairymen, Inc. (MAD) and Dairymen, Inc. (DI), set up "milk funds" or "trusts" that served as a means for making legal donations to political campaigns, and were among the largest political funds in the 1972 campaign.

The money in the "milk funds" or "trusts" was collected from farmers and was not actually corporate funds, thereby excluding it from the law prohibiting corporate campaign contributions.

National attention first was directed to the nation's leading dairy cooperatives in 1971. Then it was publicly reported that the Nixon administration's decision to raise the level of federal milk price support subsidies for dairy farmers was followed within six months by dairy contributions to Nixon re-election committees which amounted to about $250,000.

The July 1974 Watergate Committee report concluded that the milk producers, among the largest contributors to the 1972 campaign, "had actively sought favorable action from the Nixon administration throughout its first term on a number of matters of great financial importance to dairy farmers at the same time they were pledging hundreds of thousands, or even millions, of dollars to President Nixon's re-election campaign with the knowledge of President Nixon and with the encouragement of top presidential aides and fund-raisers."

AMPI delivered $100,000 in cash to fund-raiser Kalmbach in August, 1969 and had pledged another $2 million to Nixon's 1972 campaign by the fall of 1970.

Price Support Decision

On March 12, 1971, Agriculture Secretary Clifford Hardin set the milk price support for the April 1, 1971-March 31, 1972 year at $4.66, approximately 79 per cent of parity, and lower than the 85 per cent that the dairy cooperatives were seeking. (A report issued in July, 1974 by the House Judiciary Committee showed that a number of dairy cooperative attorneys and representatives met with officials of the Nixon administration following Hardin's decision, and urged that the President increase the milk support above the level set by Secretary Hardin.)

On March 23, 1971, the same day that Nixon met with representatives of the dairy cooperatives, Treasury Secretary Connally telephoned Nixon before the meeting and urged him to go along with the increase of the milk supports to 85 per cent of parity, according to a memorandum written by White House staff member John Whittaker. The memorandum later was turned over to the House Judiciary Committee by the White House.

AMPI General Manager Harold S. Nelson said, according to the Watergate Committee report, that he was notified on March 23 that a milk support increase was possible and that the milk producers needed to reaffirm their $2-million pledge to the Nixon campaign. Nelson said he was informed of the impending increase by AMPI lawyer Murray Chotiner, a former special counsel and long time aide to Nixon.

On March 24, Chotiner and Nelson met with Kalmbach. Kalmbach later testified before an executive session of the Watergate Committee that Chotiner told him at the meeting that the milk producers were reaffirming their earlier $2-million pledge to Nixon since a price support increase was to be announced the next day.

Kalmbach further testified that on March 25 he reported to John Ehrlichman, assistant to the President for domestic affairs, the reaffirmation of the pledge.

On March 25, Agriculture Secretary Hardin announced that the milk price support level for 1971-72 would be $4.93 for each one hundred pounds, or the approximate 85 per cent of parity that the dairy producers wanted. The increase was, according to the Watergate Committee report, worth "at least tens of millions of dollars to the milk producers."

Hardin testified in an affidavit that he reevaluated the evidence regarding the milk price support level and the decision to increase the price support was based entirely on a reconsideration of the evidence.

Nixon's Explanation: 1972 Politics

In a White House document released Jan. 8, 1974, while the Watergate Committee was investigating the price support increase, President Nixon asserted that his decision was influenced primarily by Democratic congressional pressure for the increase coupled with the President's fear of losing dairymen support in his 1972 re-election bid.

William Powell, president of MAD, wrote in a June 7, 1971 letter that was later filed with a court deposition: "I have become increasingly aware that the soft and sincere voice of the dairy farmer is no match for the jingle of hard currencies put in the campaign funds of the politicians...." He mentioned the March 23 meeting with the President and then said: "two days later an order came from the U.S. Department of Agriculture increasing the support price of milk...which added from $500-million to $700-million to dairy farmers checks. We dairymen cannot afford to overlook this kind of benefit. Whether we like it or not, this is the way the system works."

"I have become increasingly aware that the soft and sincere voice of the dairy farmer is no match for the jingle of hard currencies put in the campaign funds of the politicians...."

—William Powell, President,
Mid-American Dairymen

Nixon, according to the Watergate Committee report, was "well aware that at the time he considered the price support matter the milk producers had pledged $2-million to his campaign— but had not delivered one penny toward that pledge." At that time, the report said, the President's re-election campaign had just been organized and was seeking "early money" toward a campaign goal of $40-million. Meeting the goal was considered very important, the report said, because it appeared at the time that the President's re-election battle would be difficult. One leading poll showed Nixon trailed the Democratic frontrunner, Sen. Edmund S. Muskie (D Maine) by at least five percentage points.

The crux of its investigation, the committee report said, was not to determine whether the President's decision to raise the milk price supports was a correct one, but to determine whether the President made that decision for the wrong reason.

The report said: "Whatever the legal significance of the circumstances of the 1971 price support increase..., the fact is that the dual role played by many Nixon officials of both policymaker and fund-raiser gave, at the very least, the appearance of impropriety and provided circumstances that were ripe for abuse. Whether or not these two roles were directly tied, they *appeared* to be linked, and this had a significant impact on the approach taken by dairymen."

Connally Indictment

The events surrounding the milk price increase led to criminal charges against Connally, Jacobsen, and Nelson, with subsequent guilty pleas by Jacobsen and Nelson.

Connally, considered by Nixon as a nominee for vice president following Spiro T. Agnew's resignation in October, 1973, was indicted July 29, 1974, for receiving a $10,000 bribe in exchange for his favorable recommendation on the increase of the milk price supports, and also for conspiracy and perjury. He pleaded not guilty.

Jacobsen, who was indicted at the same time for giving the alleged $10,000 bribe to Connally, pleaded guilty. Nelson pleaded guilty to a one-count charge of conspiracy to pay the Connally bribe and to making numerous illegal corporate campaign contributions to both Democrats and Republicans.

The conspiracy charge to which Nelson pleaded guilty stated that $100,000 in AMPI funds were used, indirectly, to reimburse the co-op's political fund-raising affiliate, the Trust for Agricultural Political Education (TAPE), for the $100,000 that was delivered to Kalmbach in 1969. The money was paid to Kalmbach "for the purpose of securing access to White House officials" by AMPI officers and was reimbursed "to obviate the need for TAPE to report said payment publicly," the conspiracy charge said.

Milk Money to Democrats

Also lumped under the conspiracy charge against Nelson were the following political contributions:

• $63,500 to the Democratic National Committee for tickets to the Salute to the Vice President Dinner, a fund raiser for the 1968 election.

• $23,950 to the 1970 senatorial campaign of Hubert H. Humphrey (D Minn.).

• $5,000 in 1970 to the unsuccessful Senate bid by former Vermont Gov. Philip Hoff.

• $8,400 to committees organized in behalf of Maine Democrat Edmund S. Muskie's 1970 Senate race.

• $82,000 to a computer mail service concern, including $7,000 for services performed for James Abourezk's (D S.D.) 1972 Senate campaign, $25,000 for work for Humphrey's 1972 presidential primary campaign, and $50,000 for services to benefit "various Democratic Party candidates for federal elective office in the state of Iowa" in 1972.

In addition, Nelson admitted that he arranged for TAPE Secretary Bob Lilly to work in Humphrey's 1968 presidential primary campaign while continuing to pay Lilly's salary and expenses out of corporate funds.

According to the information, Lilly worked for Humphrey in seven states, and was authorized by Nelson to spend $38,000 to support Humphrey and other candidates in those states.

Another former AMPI official, David L. Parr, also pleaded guilty in July 1974 to criminal conspiracy involving repeated violations of federal election laws. Many of the illegal contributions cited in Nelson's case also were cited in the case against Parr.

Norman Sherman, Humphrey's former press secretary, pleaded guilty in July 1974 to charges arising out of the $82,000 in illegal AMPI funds that were paid to the computer mail service concern, Valentine, Sherman & Associates (VSA). Sherman's business partner, John Valentine, pleaded guilty to the same charges.

A criminal charge filed by the Watergate special prosecutor's office said Sherman and Valentine accepted the illegal money from AMPI to purchase computer-mail lists used in Humphrey's 1972 campaign for the Democratic presidential nomination and in a number of other campaigns, including that of Abourezk.

Of the total funds paid to VSA by AMPI, $25,000 allegedly was in part payment for services to Humphrey's campaign.

Both Humphrey and Abourezk said they were unaware of the nature of the contributions.

Mills, another contender for the 1972 Democratic presidential nomination, also was the recipient of dairy funds during 1971 and 1972.

"There is evidence," that the Senate Watergate committee report said, "that Congressman Mills' presidential campaign received the benefit of up to $75,000 from the corporate assets of AMPI, $15,000 from corporate assets of Mid-American Dairymen, Inc., and $40,000 in donations from members, employees and officers of AMPI, for a grand total of about $185,000 from dairy producer sources. This is equivalent to 38 per cent of his campaign revenues."

White House 'Plumbers'

$5,000 in AMPI funds, according to the Watergate committee report, was used to help fund the Sept. 3, 1971, covert entry by the "plumbers" into the Beverly Hills, Calif., office of Dr. Lewis Fielding, Daniel Ellsberg's psychiatrist.

The "plumbers," a secret White House investigative team set up at Nixon's direction to plug security leaks, were investigating Ellsberg, who had leaked the Pentagon Papers, a secret Defense Department study of U.S. involvement in the Vietnam war, to the press. The investigation extended to matters such as uncovering and publicizing certain aspects of Ellsberg's background and private life including his psychiatric records.

The burglary came to light in testimony given by convicted Watergate conspirator E. Howard Hunt to a federal grand jury in April 1973. The testimony was released by the U.S. District Court in Los Angeles.

The AMPI money that indirectly funded the break-in at Fielding's office was acutally paid to a Nixon re-election committee after the break-in. It was used to reimburse Joseph Baroody, a Washington public relations man who had been working with presidential counsel Charles W. Colson on certain projects while being paid by AMPI. Baroody had supplied $5,000 to the "plumbers" just prior to the break-in. There was no evidence that AMPI officials knew the money went to fund the break-in.

Dirty Tricks

Another covert White House-connected group hired to create confusion and dissension among the 1972 Democratic presidential contenders was the apparent recipient of some campaign contributions made to the 1972 Nixon re-election effort.

Donald H. Segretti, who headed the group, said he received $45,336 from Kalmbach during the period from September 1971 to March 1972, which paid for his bi-weekly salary of $667 and expense money.

Segretti, one of three men charged and found guilty in connection with the so-called "dirty tricks," testified before the Watergate Committee that he had been hired in the summer of 1971 by two former classmates, Dwight L. Chapin, President Nixon's appointments secretary, and Gordon Strachan, staff assistant to presidential aide H.R. Haldeman.

Chapin, Segretti said, was Segretti's boss while the "dirty tricks" were carried out.

Ambassadors and Money

A list of eight Western European ambassadors and their contributions to Nixon's 1972 re-election campaign follows:

Country	Ambassador	Contribution
Great Britain	Walter H. Annenberg	$250,000
Switzerland	Shelby Davis	$100,000
Luxembourg	Ruth L. Farkas	$300,000
Belgium	Leonard K. Firestone	$112,600
Netherlands	Kingdon Gould	$100,900
Austria	John F. Humes	$100,000
France	John N. Irwin II	$50,500
France	Arthur K. Watson	$300,000
Ireland	John D. Moore	$10,442
Total		**$1,324,442**

One of Segretti's most successful tactics, according to the Senate Watergate report, was to distribute false and misleading literature in nearly every primary state. For example, Segretti and his operatives had about 300 posters distributed throughout Florida which said, "Help Muskie in Bussing [sic] More Children Now." The poster was signed by the "Mothers Backing Muskie Committee," a nonexistent committee, and the intent of the poster was, according to the Watergate Committee report, to identify Muskie with a strong pro-busing position which was very unpopular in Florida.

Ambassadors

Large campaign contributions from another group, ambassadors and persons seeking ambassadorships, led critics to charge that the Nixon administration was brokering ambassadorships.

In a Feb. 25, 1973, news conference Nixon denied such accusations and said: "Ambassadorships have not been for sale, and I would not approve an ambassadorship unless the man or woman was qualified clearly apart from his contribution."

Exactly one year later, Nixon's personal attorney, Kalmbach, pleaded guilty to a charge of promising federal employment as a reward for political activity and for support of a candidate.

A condition of Kalmbach's guilty plea was that he be granted immunity from further prosecution in connection with "contributions from persons seeking ambassadorial posts."

Kalmbach entered his guilty plea to having promised, in 1971, then-ambassador to Trinidad and Tobago, J. Fife Symington (June 1969-1971), a more prestigious European ambassadorship in return for a $100,000 contribution to be split between Republican senatorial candidates and Nixon's campaign.

Symington did not in fact receive a European appointment. In an interview with the Watergate Committee staff, Symington stated that there was no "direct linkage" between his contribution and his desire for another post.

After his 1972 re-election, Nixon appointed 13 non-career ambassadors, eight of whom had donated a minimum of $25,000 and in aggregate, $706,000.

According to the Senate Watergate Committee report, over $1.8-million in presidential campaign contributions was attributable in whole, or in part, to persons holding ambassadorial appointments from Nixon.

The committee report stated further that about 30 per cent of all foreign envoy posts were held in July 1974 by non-career appointees. The largest concentration of non-career ambassadors was in Western Europe, where there was also a high concentration of persons contributing $100,000 or over. (Box, this page)

While White House officials maintained they told persons seeking ambassadorships that no quid pro quo could follow contributions, the Senate Watergate committee report concluded that, "at the very least, a number of persons saw the making of a contribution as a means of obtaining the recognition needed to be actively considered."

ITT's $400,000 Pledge

A pledge made by International Telephone and Telegraph Corporation (ITT) to contribute as much as $400,000 to help finance the 1972 Republican national convention also raised questions as to the propriety of the company making such a pledge while it was involved in an anti-trust suit with the Justice Department.

The office of the special prosecutor investigated a possible connection between an anti-trust settlement considered favorable to ITT and the contribution, but Special Prosecutor Leon Jaworski announced in May 1974 that his investigating force had failed to uncover any criminal conduct by ITT executives in the case.

Nevertheless, two persons, former Attorney General Richard G. Kleindienst, (June 1972-April 1973) and California Lt. Gov. Ed Reinecke (R), were convicted on charges arising from the investigation.

Kleindienst pleaded guilty May 16, 1974, to one count of failure to testify fully, a misdemeanor, and was sentenced to one month of unsupervised probation and given a suspended sentence of one month in jail and a $100 fine.

The charge filed by the special prosecutor's office said that during the Senate Judiciary Committee's confirmation hearings following Kleindienst's nomination to become attorney general that Kleindienst had failed to tell the committee that Nixon had, at one point, ordered him to drop the ITT case.

Reinecke was found guilty July 27, 1974, in the U.S. District Court in Washington, D.C., on one count of lying to the Senate Judiciary Committee during the Kleindienst hearings. He was accused of lying April 19, 1972, when he told the committee that on Sept. 17, 1971, he had informed Attorney General Mitchell of the $400,000 pledged by ITT for the Republican national convention if it were held in San Diego. The government charged that Reinecke had informed Mitchell of the pledge four months earlier in a May 21, 1971, phone call. Reinecke acknowledged during his trial that he had informed Mitchell of the pledge in May 1971 and that he had made "a mistake" when he testified before the Senate Judiciary Committee. The significance of the dates was that in May the negotiations between the Justice Department and ITT over the anti-trust were still in progress, but by September the case had been settled. ∎

FINANCE ABUSES DETAILED; 35 REFORMS PROPOSED

Eighteen months after it began the most intensive investigation into alleged presidential corruption in American history, the Senate Select Committee on Presidential Campaign Activities (Watergate Committee) issued its final report. The scene in the Senate caucus room July 12, 1974, when the 2,217-page document was handed out was almost anticlimactic, because most of the committee's preliminary findings had been leaked to the press over the preceding months.

Yet the impact of the three volumes was significant. The report laid out all together, for the first time, the details of the comprehensive scandals lumped under the umbrella of Watergate. It started with the background of the Watergate break-in—Tom Charles Huston's intelligence plan, the "enemies" list and the White House "plumbers" unit—and moved on to the coverup, the campaign practices of the Committee for the Re-election of the President, the Nixon administration's "responsiveness program," the financing of the 1972 presidential campaign and the Hughes-Rebozo investigation.

The findings, adopted unanimously by the seven members of the select committee, were couched in laconic prose, devoid of almost any indignation or emotion, and they scrupulously avoided assessing whether President Nixon was implicated in the Watergate coverup. The committee said it purposely refrained from making any judgments because of the House Judiciary Committee's impeachment inquiry and the Watergate-related trials either scheduled or already in progress.

The report included "general observations based on the evidence." "The Watergate affair," the committee said, "reflects an alarming indifference displayed by some in high places to concepts of morality and public responsibility and trust. Indeed, the conduct of many Watergate participants seems grounded on the belief that the ends justified the means, that the laws could be flaunted to maintain the present administration in office." The report exonerated the chairmen of the Republican and Democratic National Committees in 1972—Republican Sen. Robert Dole (Kan.) and Democrat Lawrence F. O'Brien—of any involvement in the scandal.

"Watergate was a conglomerate of various illegal and unethical activities...."

—Sen. Sam J. Ervin Jr. (D N.C.), chairman of the Watergate committee

The select committee was created by the Senate by a vote of 77-0 on Feb. 7, 1973. The resolution establishing the committee (S Res 60) gave it full investigative powers and wide latitude to examine the 1972 presidential election, the Watergate break-in and coverup and any other matters found to be relevant to those subjects.

The committee's high point came in the spring and summer of 1973, when it heard testimony from 62 witnesses in three months of public sessions. Those sessions, televised nationally, provided the first detailed public account of how the Watergate break-in and subsequent coverup were conceived and conducted.

Break-In and Coverup

The report recounted the familiar story of the break-in at the Democratic national headquarters in the Watergate office building on June 17, 1972, seeing the break-in as growing out of the White House domestic intelligence activities that had started two years earlier. "The Watergate break-in cannot be understood unless viewed in the context of similar White House activities," the report said. "The evidence presented...shows that, from the early days of the present administration, the power of the President was viewed by some in the White House as almost without limit. Especially when national or internal security was invoked, even criminal laws were considered subordinate to presidential decision or strategy."

The Senate committee considered the Committee for the Re-election of the President (CRP) to be the creature of the White House, especially of Nixon's closest aides. "The evidence accumulated by the Select Committee demonstrates that CRP was a White House product, answerable to top White House leadership. It appears that H.R. Haldeman, the President's Chief of Staff, was principally responsible for organizing CRP, and John Mitchell (the former attorney general) has stated that Haldeman was the moving force," the report said.

Campaign Practices

Political intelligence-gathering played an important part in the Nixon re-election drive, along with the use of federal agencies to harass Nixon's opponents, the select committee found. The report focused on those activities, which, it said, began almost 3½ years before the 1972 presidential election.

"The campaign to re-elect President Nixon in 1972 was expensive, intense and long," the report said. "It began in late March 1969, soon after the President's inauguration, when John Ehrlichman, Counsel to the President, hired Jack Caulfield to gather political intelligence and derogatory information on individuals considered to be unfriendly to the new administration."

The investigations were carried out by Anthony T. Ulasewicz, a former New York City policeman who had been hired by Caulfield and Ehrlichman. Ulasewicz was paid secretly by Herbert W. Kalmbach, Nixon's personal attorney, from an unused reserve of 1968 campaign funds.

The Caulfield-Ulasewicz operation, the report said, raised "serious questions...as to what the President knew, approved or condoned and what his ethical and legal responsibilities should be for the campaign conduct of his subordinates."

The committee said the White House political activities raised serious questions about campaign practices in a free society. "The 1972 presidential campaign was replete with abuses of positions, power, and prerogatives, particularly by White House personnel. ...A corollary to the abuse of presidential incumbency for political gain is the considerable extent to which objectionable campaign practices were conceived, encouraged, and controlled by high-level presidential aides.

"Another important theme," the report added, "is the misuse of large amounts of money, especially difficult-to-trace cash that was held in secret places in the White House and elsewhere."

As part of the administration's "attack strategy" aimed at putting Democrats on the defensive, White House officials, according to the report, used the Internal Revenue Service (IRS), the FBI and the Secret Service to obtain sensitive or derogatory information about their opponents.

The report called the IRS "a preferred target of the White House staff in its attempts to politicize independent agencies.... The Political Enemies project, White House efforts to have the IRS focus on left wing organizations, White House efforts to get IRS information for political purposes, and the White House concern with tax exemptions given to liberal foundations all attest to the serious efforts made by the White House to use an independent agency for political purposes."

The FBI was used by administration aides such as former White House Counsel John W. Dean III as a source of information that they could "leak" to the press to smear political opponents, the committee found. It was also used by the White House, according to the report, to investigate alleged critics such as CBS correspondent Daniel Schorr.

While the report did not find anything "improper in itself" in the White House strategy of trying to undercut Sen. Edmund S. Muskie (Maine) in the Democratic presidential primaries and to divide the Democratic Party, it charged that that strategy ultimately led to the dirty tricks carried on by the re-election committee.

"The absence of primary opponents for the President allowed his political strategists to target their efforts on the Democrats," it said. The abundance of money in the CRP allowed the political operatives to set up a concerted effort to infiltrate and interfere with the Democratic primaries. "The result," the committee found, "was a campaign to re-elect President Nixon that was filled with illegal, improper, and unethical activity...."

Donald H. Segretti conducted dirty tricks operations in the Florida presidential primary, and the re-election committee was behind vote-siphoning operations in the Democratic primaries in Illinois and New Hampshire. The Senate committee uncovered improper campaign activities directed against the Nixon re-election drive. But the report said that "except for a few isolated examples..., there is presently no evidence indicating that these improper activities were directly or indirectly related to the campaign of any Democratic candidate."

'Incumbency-Responsiveness Program'

Beginning in the spring of 1971, top White House officials began drawing up plans to use federal agencies to bolster the President's re-election campaign, the report charged. "Documents obtained by the committee indicate that this effort—which had as its main vehicle a White House devised plan known as the Responsiveness Program—was an organized endeavor 'to politicize' the executive branch to ensure that the administration remained in power."

The program, the report said, included "plans to redirect federal monies to specific administration supporters and to target groups and geographic areas to benefit the campaign. It entailed instructions to shape legal and regulatory action to enhance campaign goals. It comprised plans to utilize government employment procedures for election benefits."

The committee was especially critical of the use of federal funds for Spanish-speaking groups and the Federation of Experienced Americans, a pro-Nixon organization of elderly persons, calling the grants "flagrant abuses of proper governmental procedures.

"In fact," the report continued, "a question exists whether the planning and implementation of the Responsiveness plan rises to the level of a conspiracy to interfere with the lawful functioning of government, conduct prosecutable under 18 U.S.C. section 371 as a conspiracy to defraud the United States, as that term has been interpreted by the Supreme Court."

The report noted the argument that the administration's responsiveness program was nothing more than politics as usual, as practiced by earlier administrations. But the committee dismissed that argument, saying that "to some degree, the contention that other administrations have done the same thing misses the point. For...certain of the activities...not only appear to contravene the notion that our nation's citizens are entitled to equal treatment under the law, but also raise questions as to the applicability of specific federal civil and criminal statutes.

"It is also relevant," the report added, "that the major documents promulgating Responsiveness plans were classified 'Confidential,' 'Extremely Confidential' and/or 'Eyes Only' and noted that secrecy in the implementation of the proposal was of paramount necessity in order to avoid adverse publicity."

Campaign Financing

The Senate committee devoted one 838-page volume to the financing of the 1972 presidential campaign. The report focused primarily on the Nixon re-election drive. It also examined contributions to former New York Mayor John V. Lindsay's short-lived campaign for the Democratic nomination and the campaigns of Sen. Hubert H. Humphrey (D Minn.) and Rep. Wilbur D. Mills (D Ark.), and on Democratic nominee George McGovern's settling of campaign bills after his defeat.

Investigators found evidence that McGovern was settling bills with creditors at 50 per cent face value—while making substantial transfers to his 1974 senatorial campaign. The investigators learned that Lindsay had accepted a $10,000 cash contribution from a group of contractors who later won a $1.7-million New York City asphalt contract. And the investigators charged that Humphrey and Mills had received thousands of dollars in illegal corporate contributions for their unsuccessful primary campaigns.

The Nixon campaign, according to the report, received allegedly illegal contributions from at least 13 corporations.

The contributions totaled $780,000 in corporate funds, the report stated.

"While there is no evidence that any fund-raiser for President Nixon directly solicited a corporate contribution," the committee said, "there is evidence that a number of them either were indifferent to the source of the money or, at the very least, made no effort whatsoever to see to it that the source of the funds was private rather than corporate. In any event, there is no evidence that any fund-raiser who was involved in these contributions sought or obtained assurances that the contribution was legal at the time it was made."

The committee's investigators explored the sources of money for the corporate contributions. The largest source was foreign subsidiaries, but corporate expense accounts and corporate bonuses to reimburse executives for their contributions were also used, they found. Most of the contributions were given in untraceable cash to the Finance Committee to Re-elect the President, headed by former Commerce Secretary Maurice H. Stans.

The corporate contributions were not disclosed until July 6, 1973, "—or 15 months after almost all of them were made," the report stated. The disclosure was forced by a lawsuit by Common Cause, the so-called citizens' lobby, to compel disclosure of contributions to the Finance Committee to Re-elect the President made before April 7, 1972 (the date the Federal Election Campaign Act of 1971 became effective, requiring disclosure of contributions).

The report was a primer of questionable contribution practices. It detailed how $1.8-million was collected in contributions from ambassadors appointed by Nixon, and the apparent relationship between campaign contributions and ambassadorial appointments. It also examined the role of Herbert W. Kalmbach, the President's personal attorney, as a chief Nixon fund-raiser.

Kalmbach began raising money for the 1972 campaign in late 1970, and investigators gave an insight into some of his techniques. "Kalmbach sought out friends in an effort to obtain what amounted to commitments for campaign contributions," the committee reported. "Kalmbach states that he never asked for a commitment in so many words, but rather approached people, suggested an amount to them and asked if they would accept a 'goal figure.'

"Kalmbach acknowledged that he told contributors that there were different classes of contributors, and he had different 'cut-off points,' for example at $25,000, $50,000 and $100,000. Kalmbach said that on occasion he referred to a '100 Club'—meaning contributors who gave $100,000. He indicated that he told contributors that there were a lot of people in the $25,000 class, and if one wanted to be known as a major contributor, he should give more."

One of the major areas of the committee's investigation was the $2-million pledge to the Nixon re-election campaign in 1971 from the Associated Milk Producers Inc., a dairy cooperative, at the time it was seeking an increase in milk price supports.

White House aides and dairy industry representatives denied there was a *quid pro quo* of dairy contributions in exchange for the presidential increase, and the report noted that "much of what the President says is supported by surrounding events: the dairy lobby had successfully gathered the support of about a quarter of each House in support of bills to raise the support level and at least some dairy leaders had considered boycotting further Republican fundraising efforts because of the administration's position on price supports."

But investigators found strong links between Nixon's decision on milk price supports and dairy industry political influence. "The crux of the committee's investigation was...not whether it was the correct decision but whether the President made the decision for the 'wrong' reason," the report said.

After reviewing the dealings between Nixon aides and dairy industry officials on the eve of the price support decision, the report concluded, "Whatever the legal circumstances of the 1971 price support increase and these and other matters, the fact is that the dual role played by many Nixon officials of both policymaker and fundraiser gave, at the very least, the appearance of impropriety and provided circumstances that were ripe for abuse. Whether or not these two roles were directly tied, they *appeared* to be linked, and this had a significant impact on the approach taken by the dairymen."

Hughes-Rebozo Investigation

Investigators broke new ground in their examination of a $100,000 campaign contribution by billionaire Howard R. Hughes to Charles G. Rebozo, Nixon's close friend, and Rebozo's expenditures for Nixon that pointed toward possible financial corruption by the President.

The money had been delivered to Rebozo in cash in $50,000 installments by a Hughes emissary in 1969 and 1970. Nixon and Rebozo claimed the money was intended for the 1972 presidential campaign, and had been placed in a safe deposit box at a bank owned by Rebozo. Rebozo testified that the money remained at his bank until it was returned to the Hughes organization three years later. But the Watergate Committee report cited circumstantial evidence to the contrary.

The committee staff constructed an elaborate series of charts, taking up five pages in the report, tracing an array of Rebozo transactions and intended to show that some of the cash actually was diverted to pay for improvements to Nixon's properties. The expenditures included $18,435 for a swimming pool, $6,508 to extend a roof, $11,900 to convert a garage into living quarters, $3,586 for a fireplace and $3,335 for architect's fees. Rebozo allegedly paid for these expenses in several ways—with cash, with checks drawn on his personal account at the bank he headed, and, most importantly, with checks drawn on trust accounts in the name of his attorney, Thomas H. Wakefield.

Rebozo deposited $20,000 in $100 bills—the currency denominations used by Hughes for his contributions—into two of the trust accounts in November 1972, shortly after the presidential election, according to the report. Besides these, two other trust accounts also figured in the complex transaction by which campaign funds remaining from 1968 apparently were used to pay for a pair of diamond earrings for Mrs. Nixon.

As the committee saw it, that jewelry purchase tied presidential purchases most closely to the campaign cash under Rebozo's control. Rebozo, after the 1968 election, kept an account in his bank in the name of the Florida Nixon for President Committee. In April 1969, he shifted $6,000 from that account to the Thomas H. Wakefield special account. The Wakefield special account remained inactive until June 28, 1972, the day a series of four money-laundering transactions—involving transfers of funds among three accounts at two Miami banks—"concealed the fact that the funds (for the earrings) originated from contributions to the 1968 campaign and were ultimately used by Rebozo on behalf of President Nixon," the report said.

Committee Recommendations: Toward Tighter Regulations

To guard against future Watergate scandals, the Senate Watergate committee made 35 specific recommendations for preventing abuses of government power. The proposed reforms would curb the President's authority, bring federal intelligence agencies under closer congressional scrutiny and establish a permanent special prosecutor. The recommendations were scattered through the seven-member select committee's 2,217-page final report. The document, made public July 13, outlined the committee's exhaustive findings of its 18-month investigation of the Nixon administration scandals, known collectively as Watergate.

The committee said it was "careful to recommend only where the need is clear." Its recommendations "relate to the creation of new institutions necessary to safeguard the electoral process, to provide the requisite checks against the abuse of executive power and to ensure the prompt and just enforcement of laws that already exist."

Noting that "legislation is, at best, a blunt weapon to combat immorality," the committee members cautioned that they were "mindful that revelations of past scandals have often failed to produce meaningful reform. Too frequently there is a tendency to overreact in the wake of a particular scandal and burden the penal code with ill-considered laws directed to the specific—perhaps aberrational—conduct exposed."

Differences

Most of the proposals were adopted unanimously, but some committee members had ideas of their own. Sen. Howard H. Baker Jr. (R Tenn.), committee vice chairman, opposed an independently appointed special prosecutor. Instead, he favored one named by the president who would serve in the Justice Department. Sen. Edward P. Gurney (R Fla.) rejected the idea of a special prosecutor.

Senators Daniel K. Inouye (D Hawaii) and Joseph M. Montoya (D N.M.), in a joint statement, supported the public financing of federal elections, a reform rejected in the committee report. "...Public financing can...move us one step closer toward...open, fair, honest elections in which the ideas of citizens and candidates compete regardless of the size of their pocketbooks," they said.

Sen. Lowell P. Weicker Jr. (R Conn.) included 17 recommendations for constitutional or legislative action in his own Watergate report. He backed the committee's proposals for a central campaign committee for presidential and vice presidential candidates, tightening of federal wiretapping laws and financial disclosure by the president and vice president. He also proposed that the attorney general be made elective, that the Supreme Court be granted original jurisdiction in executive privilege cases, that top White House aides be subject to Senate confirmation and that a joint congressional committee with rotating membership be created to oversee federal law enforcement and intelligence agencies.

Other committee recommendations included a federal election commission, limits on campaign contributions and spending, annual financial disclosures by the president and vice president to the General Accounting Office, restrictions on campaign dirty tricks, severe restrictions on all communications between the Internal Revenue Service and the White House and a ban on intelligence-gathering by the White House.

Legislative Outlook

Prospects for early enactment of many of the proposals appeared dim, for 1974 at least. One member of the Watergate committee, Weicker, conceded the day after the report was released that action on most of the recommendations would have to wait until 1975.

Despite President Nixon's Aug. 9 resignation because of his involvement in the Watergate coverup and the House Judiciary Committee's impeachment debate July 24-30, some Capitol Hill aides felt they would have many problems getting the committee's recommendations adopted.

Others, however, saw the impeachment debate and President Ford's sudden pardon of Nixon as reviving Watergate as an issue and improving legislative prospects.

The Nixon pardon, according to an aide to a Republican Senator, showed that "the shadow of Watergate still looms over the White House. The Nixon holdovers are still there and you'll be having the Watergate coverup trial."

Several Senate aides saw little support for the committee's proposals. "First, you've got the usual election-year pressures that work against any major legislation," said Kennedy E. Davis, administrative assistant to Minority Leader Hugh Scott (R Pa.). "But I think the Watergate committee was kind of stretching it. Most of the senators I've talked to are not impressed with these recommendations."

Another Senate Republican staff member doubted that the impetus for passage of the Watergate committee's recommendations could be carried over to the next session of Congress because of the retirement of Chairman Sam J. Ervin Jr. (D N.C.). "I didn't sense that any of the other Democratic senators on the committee had much invested in the recommendations," he said.

Proposals given the best chance of passage by Senate observers would grant the Supreme Court original jurisdiction in executive privilege disputes, establish a joint congressional committee to oversee the intelligence and law enforcement agencies, and require annual financial disclosure by the president and vice president.

The proposal for a special prosecutor, however, was reported to have only a slight chance of passage. "The Senate is a little bit leery of this," said an aide to a senior Democratic senator. "There's concern about institutionalizing too many special agencies like the special prosecutor. I don't think it would stand the test of debate."

Recommendations by two Watergate Committee members—Weicker and Baker—for stricter regulation of government access to federal tax data and increased congressional oversight of government intelligence agencies stood better chances of passage because of the impeachment debate and the disclosures in September of Central Intelligence Agency activities in Chile that led to the downfall of that country's Marxist government, according to Senate sources.

Report Recommendations

Following is a complete listing of the Senate Watergate committee's recommendations:

Watergate Break-In and Coverup

1. A permanent office of public attorney [special prosecutor] should be created "which would have jurisdiction to prosecute criminal cases in which there is a real or

apparent conflict of interest within the executive branch." The public attorney would have "access to executive records" and would be able to act on "complaints and criminal charges concerning federal departments and regulatory agencies." He would be confirmed by the Senate for a five-year term and chosen by the Chief Justice of the Supreme Court from a list drawn up by three retired members of the U.S. Court of Appeals "to ensure his independence from executive control or influence."

The committee said it proposed the permanent special prosecutor's office because "in each of the nation's two major scandals during the past half century, Teapot Dome and Watergate, the appointment of a special prosecutor was essential to preserve the integrity of the criminal justice system and public confidence in the rule of law."

The committee envisioned the public attorney's role as "preventative." "Because of this preventative role," the report said, "it is unwise to wait until another national crisis to reinstitute the office of Special Prosecutor. It is far better to create a permanent institution now than to consider its wisdom at some future time when emotions may be high and unknown political factors at play."

The public attorney would also be an "ombudsman," the report said, having the power to respond to complaints from the public, the Congress or the courts, conduct investigations on his own and prosecute criminal cases referred to him by the proposed federal election commission.

2. Crimes such as burglary and larceny, committed with the intent of interfering with or affecting a federal election or nominating process, should be treated as federal felony offenses.

The committee said it proposed the change from state to federal jurisdiction because the Watergate burglary and the break-in at the office of Daniel Ellsberg's psychiatrist could not be tried in a U.S. District Court under a burglary indictment. "It would allow the prosecution of crimes in which there is a federal interest in federal courts," the report said.

3. White House officials should be barred from authorizing or engaging in "any investigative or intelligence gathering activity concerning national or domestic security not authorized by Congress." This proposal would prohibit the establishment of another White House "plumbers" unit.

4. Congressional committees should intensify their oversight of federal intelligence and law enforcement agencies such as the FBI, the Central Intelligence Agency and Internal Revenue Service.

5. The false declaration prohibition in the federal criminal code (18 U.S.C. section 1623) should be amended to cover testimony before congressional committees. Section 1621 of Title 18, another perjury statute, should also be amended to require a witness, who had already been sworn in, to give truthful testimony before a congressional committee that did not have a quorum or when a member was present.

6. Congress should not pass pending proposals in two bills (HR 10047 and S 1) that would broaden existing defenses to criminal charges of official mistake of law and execution of public duty. The committee supported the existing common law defense that "any reliance on a mistake of law or superior orders must be objectively reasonable to constitute a valid defense."

7. Title III of the Safe Streets Act of 1968, which covered electronic surveillance, should be tightened. According to the report, "The committee's investigation has revealed incidents of unlawful violations of privacy through electronic surveillance...."

Campaign Practices

8. Congress should enact criminal legislation to prevent the infiltration of presidential and federal campaigns by persons "under false pretenses...or other fraudulent means for the purpose of interfering with, spying on or obstructing any campaign activities." This proposal was specifically aimed at preventing a repetition of the kind of activities conducted by Donald H. Segretti and other Nixon re-election committee employees who infiltrated and disrupted Democratic presidential primary campaigns in 1972.

9. Legislation should be enacted barring individuals from requesting or knowingly disbursing campaign funds that would be used to violate federal election laws. Under this proposal, for example, Herbert W. Kalmbach, Nixon's personal lawyer and fund-raiser, would not have been able legally to fund the political spying conducted by Anthony T. Ulasewicz for the White House or Segretti's political pranks.

10. A larceny statute should be enacted to prohibit the "theft, unauthorized copying, or taking by false pretenses" of private campaign materials in a federal election. Several Nixon re-election committee employees stole confidential campaign material from Democratic presidential contenders in 1972, and the committee found such theft not covered by "larceny by false pretense" statutes in many states. Those laws require the object taken to be a "thing of value." "Since papers are generally not thought to have value in the sense that the term is used in the existing statute, a new federal election larceny statute is necessary to prosecute such violations," the report said.

11. The federal criminal code should be amended to make illegal fraudulent telephone calls, door-to-door canvassing and campaign literature that interfere with an election. This provision was specifically aimed at outlawing tactics used in the 1972 presidential primaries, such as the distribution of scurrilous campaign literature attributed to one candidate and late-night, harassing telephone calls made in the name of an opposition candidate

Use of Federal Agencies

12. The public attorney should have authority to prosecute violations of federal criminal statutes covering federal elections.

13. The federal election commission should be given the authority to investigate and act against violations of federal election laws.

14. Congress should enact legislation making it a felony for campaign officials, government personnel and others to "defraud" the government by using federal agencies or funds to influence a federal election. This recommendation stemmed from the committee's findings that Nixon administration and re-election committee officials used federal policy and government funds to help the President's campaign.

15. The federal criminal code provision (Title 18, Section 595) making it illegal for a government official involved in the awarding of federal grants or loans to influence an election should be made a felony. The committee proposed that the provision "be expanded to include misuse of official authority in connection with the dispensing of other federal funds as government contracts, payments and federal subsidies."

Provisions in three bills before Congress to revise the federal criminal code—S 1, S 1400, and HR 10047—would either "seriously limit" or "remove" that provision from the law, the committee said.

16. Two other sections of the federal criminal code, 611 and 602, should be retained and strengthened. Section 611 bars political contribution by or solicitations to government contractors, while Section 602 bars solicitation for political contributions to persons receiving federal funds for "services rendered." The proposed revisions of the criminal code would weaken those sections, the report warned.

The committee said it uncovered evidence that the Nixon administration planned to ask for campaign contributions from minority groups that received federal grants or loans and from minority businessmen dependent on government contracts.

17. All Justice Department officials, including the attorney general, should be placed under the Hatch Act. The Hatch Act prohibits activity by federal employees.

18. Congressional committees, "in accordance with their constitutional responsibilities, [should] maintain a vigilant oversight of the executive branch in order to prevent abuses of governmental processes to promote success in a federal election."

Campaign Financing

In its introduction to its campaign financing proposals, the committee called full disclosure of contributions and expenditures and strict government enforcement of election laws "the critical minimum of campaign financing reform." However, the report warned against "the temptation to overregulate" for that could reduce the willingness of citizens "to participate voluntarily in the electoral process."

The committee urged enactment of campaign reform legislation well before the election it was supposed to regulate, in order to prevent a recurrence of what happened just before April 7, 1972. The 1971 Federal Election Campaign Act went into effect on that date, and the Nixon re-election organization engaged in "a frantic effort," according to the report, to obtain secret contributions before the deadline. The new law required the disclosure of campaign contributions. "Any significant change in the law with respect to campaign financing late in the campaign creates the potential for abuses such as occurred in the 1972 Presidential election," the report said.

Following were its recommendations:

19. Congress should establish an independent, nonpartisan federal election commission to enforce federal election laws. The committee endorsed the proposed commission, included in the Senate-passed campaign finance reform bill (S 3044). The House Administration Committee proposed a congressionally dominated supervisory board.

The report called an independent election commission "probably the most significant reform that could emerge from the Watergate scandal.... Such a body—given substantial investigatory and enforcement powers—could not only help insure that misconduct would be prevented in the future, but that investigations of alleged wrongdoing would be vigorous and conducted with the confidence of the public."

20. Cash contributions and expenditures over $100 in political campaigns should be barred. This prohibition was included in S 3044 and the House Administration Committee's proposal bill. The ban was needed, the report said, because the use of cash in political campaigns was not regulated by federal law.

21. Presidential and vice presidential candidates should be required to designate one political committee as their central campaign committee to handle their contributions and expenditures. This proposal was included in S 3044 and in the House Administration Committee bill.

During the 1972 presidential campaign, the committee said, the campaign disclosure law was undermined by the "hundreds of committees" the candidates established to handle their contributions and spending. That permitted funds to be laundered by contributing and transferring them from committee to committee to conceal the source.

22. Over-all spending for each presidential candidate in the general election should be limited to 12 cents per voter. The committee also recommended that spending in presidential primary elections be limited to twice the amount a Senate candidate in that state was permitted to spend.

Both recommendations were part of S 3044, although that bill would publicly finance general elections and use public matching grants to partially finance presidential primaries. The bill set the primary spending limit at an over-all $11.4-million or 8 cents per voter. *(p. 31)*

The House Administration Committee legislation would publicly finance presidential general elections through the presidential campaign fund check-off. The limit for each candidate would be $20-million. The presidential primary spending limit would be $10-million for each candidate. Part of the funds would come from public matching of some contributions (up to $250) once a candidate qualified by raising $100,000 in matchable contributions. *(Tax check-off, p. 40)*

Noting that the 1972 presidential election cost more than $100-million, the committee warned that "if presidential candidates are permitted to raise unlimited amounts of money, campaign spending will continue to soar leading to uneven access to the electorate and surpluses in the hands of certain candidates."

23. Individual contributions should be limited to $3,000 for each presidential candidate before the nominating conventions and $3,000 during the general election.

S 3044 included a $3,000 contribution limit that covered the entire primary and general election campaign. The House Administration Committee measure would limit contributions to a candidate to $1,000 for the primary and general election combined.

24. The internal revenue code should be amended to provide a credit "in a substantial amount" on individual federal income tax returns for political contributions—federal, state and local.

S 3044 included a provision (Title V) that was detached from the committee version and sent to the Senate Finance Committee to double the tax credit for contributions to $25 from $12.50 for individual returns and $50 from $25 on joint returns. The Finance Committee had not acted on Title V. The House Administration Committee bill did not include any language on tax credits for political contributions.

25. The committee opposed the public financing of federal elections that was the major provision of S 3044. The House Administration Committee bill had public financing of presidential general elections. The report said that public financing, in any form, violated the First Amendment to the Constitution and led to "inherent dangers" by creating a federal bureaucracy that would fund "and excessively regulate political campaigns."

The campaign financing abuses of the 1972 presidential election were not due to private financing, the committee said, but to "the absence of any effective regulation of the

(Continued on p. 33)

WATERGATE FUELED PRESSURE FOR NEW LEGISLATION

As of mid-September 1974, Congress appeared to be nearing passage of the second major campaign reform bill in less than three years. In 1972, Congress cleared the Federal Election Campaign Act, the first significant reform bill since the 1925 Corrupt Practices Act. But with the Watergate scandal revelations of campaign contribution and spending abuses in the 1972 presidential campaign, pressure mounted for passage of campaign reform legislation that would go beyond the disclosure requirements and tentative spending limitations included in the law signed by President Nixon in early 1972. *(1972 spending law p. 2; provisions p. 93)*

The 1972 law set spending limits on media political advertising, required candidates to file reports with the Clerk of the House, Secretary of the Senate, and federal General Accounting Office detailing all campaign contributions and expenditures in excess of $100, and set limits on the amount of money a candidate could contribute to his own campaign. However, it did not change the way political campaigns were financed and money was spent. It did not establish over-all spending limits, and it did not move away from the existing system of private financing of campaigns to public financing.

Those reforms were included in bills that passed the Senate and House in April and August 1974. The measures, which would establish the first public financing of American election campaigns and an independent agency to oversee and administer the new law, went to conference in late August to iron out major differences between them. *(Action on 1974 legislation p. 29)*

The pressure that led to the passage of campaign finance reform legislation in 1974 was a direct result of the Watergate scandal. The disclosures of widespread campaign contribution and spending abuses made by the Senate Watergate Committee fueled a searching debate on campaign financing and how it could be reformed to prevent future Watergate-type abuses.

Calls for reform had multiplied since the Senate Watergate committee in 1973 began exposing abuses in the collection and spending of huge sums of money in the 1972 Nixon re-election campaign. The Gallup Poll in September 1973 found that 65 per cent of those surveyed favored public financing and a ban on private contributions, a significant increase over previous years. Many members of Congress also took up the cry for reform, particularly in the wake of a January 1974 Harris Survey which showed Congress ranking even lower than the President in public esteem (21 per cent, compared with Nixon's poll ratings of around 27 per cent).

Public Financing: A New Approach

While no one could be sure just what the effects of public financing would be, it was apparent that they would be profound—on candidates, both challengers and incumbents; on individuals and groups accustomed to giving money and other assistance to candidates; on the political parties, both major and minor; on the taxpayers; and perhaps most of all, on the process of government itself.

Debate tended to center on the need to end specific Watergate-type abuses, on various formulas for setting up public financing and on its effect on individuals and groups. To some observers on both sides of the issue, it was apparent that the greatest long-range effect could be on the system itself—the close relationship, more than 100 years old, between big money and the American government.

Changing the System

"Don't kid yourself that you back public financing to prevent Watergates and corruption," Walter Pincus, executive editor of *The New Republic,* put it bluntly to a conference on money and politics Feb. 27, 1974, in Washington, D.C. "You do it to change the system."

Under the existing system, 90 per cent of contributions came from 1 per cent of the people, according to William H. Vanderbilt, chairman of the Citizens Research Foundation, which sponsored the conference and which had studied campaign financing longer than any other group. Candidates were dependent on big givers—big business interests, big labor committees and "fat cats" (wealthy individuals)—often with a direct stake, certainly with a special interest in who won elections and in influencing their policies after they won.

Few proponents of public financing really dwelt on the possibilities for changing the system, probably because the members of Congress who would have to approve any new system were part and parcel of the old one, and thus probably not inclined to overthrow it.

Sen. Edward M. Kennedy (D Mass.), a leader in the fight for public financing, was one who did attack the old system head on. He charged on Feb. 27 that "for at least a generation, few major pieces of legislation have moved through the House or Senate, few major administrative agency actions have been taken, that do not bear the brand of large campaign contributors with an interest in the outcome.

"Who really owns America?" Kennedy asked. "Is it the people or is it a little group of big campaign contributors?" He cited as examples "the connection between the energy crisis and the campaign contributions of the oil industry,...America's reluctance to enforce effective price controls and the campaign contributions of the nation's richest corporations,...America's health crisis and the campaign contributions of the American Medical Association and the private health insurance industry,... the crisis over gun control and the campaign contributions of the National Rifle Association,...the transportation crisis and the campaign contributions of the highway lobby,...the demoralization of the foreign service and the sale of ambassadorships for private campaign contributions."

Only through public financing of campaigns, Kennedy claimed, could the nation "guarantee that the political influence of any citizen is measured only by his voice and vote, not by the thickness of his pocketbook."

Candidates: Incumbents and Challengers

Although most financing proposals discussed in 1974 required candidates to raise some funds privately (in strictly regulated amounts), a major portion of that burden would be lifted from their shoulders. They might have to raise a certain "threshold fund" in small private contributions to become eligible for public funds (to show they had some support), or half their primary campaign funds, with the government providing the other half on a matching basis.

Most proposals would permit candidates to use some or all private funds in the general election, too, if they chose; voluntary participation was believed to be a necessary requirement for constitutionality of any public funding plan. Such candidates would be subject to the same spending limits as fully subsidized candidates, however, and contributions would be limited.

Under those conditions, if public funding were available, it was generally conceded that most candidates would use it. Most of them, it was thought, probably would be glad to be freed from what Sen. Hubert H. Humphrey (D Minn.) once called "the most demeaning, disgusting, depressing and disenchanting chore" in the elective process—fund-raising.

So would their fund-raisers. Henry Kimelman, finance chairman of South Dakota Sen. George McGovern's 1972 Democratic presidential campaign, ventured the guess that "if you asked any finance chairman, Democrat or Republican, he'd be for public financing."

Incumbent members of Congress would be among the first to feel the impact of any public-financing system, which no doubt accounted for the reluctance of many of them to approve such a system. Rep. Wayne L. Hays (D Ohio), chairman of the House Administration Committee, which had jurisdiction over federal elections, was often charged by critics with bottling up campaign reform proposals; he said Feb. 27 that he did not think the majority of members of Congress favored public financing. Hays gave one slightly tongue-in-check clue to his own opposition; in one city alone in his district, he said, there were probably 1,000 people who would run against him just for the $90,000 (one proposed amount of public financing for House candidates).

More seriously, others suggested that if public funding were available, many incumbents might be challenged effectively in districts in which it had been virtually impossible for opponents to mount an adequate campaign in the past. Minority candidates, women or candidates representing consumer or environmentalist views, for example, who might be unable to attract large private contributions, would be better able to challenge an entrenched incumbent or better-heeled competitors. The advantages of an incumbent already were so overwhelming, critics pointed out, that fewer than 5 per cent of them had been unseated in recent years, and it often took well over $100,000 to do it.

In addition to the many publicized advantages of incumbents—franked (free) mail, office staffs, free broad-

casting and photographic services, auto and access to the news media—many incu campaign chests on a year-round basis. under the Federal Election Campaign Act of 19 that candidates already had $24-million in cash on hand for their next campaigns, some of them years off, at the beginning of 1974.

With such built-in advantages for incumbents, public financing advocates were advised not to set campaign spending limits too low, in order to ensure that little-known challengers would have adequate resources to make themselves and their positions known. A single all-voter mailout in a district, for example, could cost $12,000 to $15,000. Television costs were high. So, while not wishing to saddle the taxpayers with excessively high expenditures for campaigns, reformers were finding it difficult to define how much was enough. Low limits, favored by Hays and many others, were criticized by reformers as ensuring that incumbents would remain in office.

Hays' fear that rafts of candidates might appear for every office if federal funds were available was shared by a number of other observers. Despite plans for "threshold funds" or signatures on petitions to ensure that only candidates with some degree of backing could qualify for public funds, Pincus of *The New Republic* pointed out that, for example, 100 doctors (or any other group) could put up $100 each (or some similar formula) and run their own candidate. "You will see frivolous candidates," he said. "You could see 15 to 20 candidates in a race and a minority candidate winning."

Contributors and the Constitution

Some people who had been giving to politicians would welcome public financing. Corporation executives who said donations were extorted from them, labor committees and many wealthy individuals who contributed heavily had said it was time for a change.

But others saw an infringement of their constitutional rights in any attempts to prohibit or limit their giving to candidates of their choice. Ralph K. Winter, a Yale University law professor, said Feb. 27 that he believed the media spending limits imposed by the 1971 Federal Election Campaign Act were unconstitutional and that limits on individual and group campaign contributions would be, too, as violations of the First Amendment, guaranteeing freedom of speech.

Speaking as a "fat cat," Stewart R. Mott, General Motors heir who had given hundreds of thousands of dollars to liberal candidates in recent years and wanted to go on doing so, said the constitutional questions of placing limits on candidates or donors "boggle my mind. Giving is a form of advocacy," Mott said, and should not be shackled.

Lawyers for Common Cause produced a 26-page legal brief setting guidelines for and defending the constitutionality of the proposed campaign finance reforms. The Supreme Court had upheld other limitations on the conduct of elections, the brief pointed out, and "it is clear from the Court's own language in numerous cases that the preservation of the integrity of the electoral process from the corrupting effect of money is a 'compelling and overriding' state interest."

In addition, Common Cause contended, campaign finance reforms would have "an important positive impact on the exercise of the First Amendment rights of many citizens who are now prevented from effectively participating in the political process. Many lack the good fortune to possess a good fortune, and this handicaps both their ability to run for office...and their ability to communicate their views to their elected representatives on an equal basis with large contributors."

Both advocates and opponents of public financing expected court tests of any reforms. Alexander Heard, chancellor of Vanderbilt University and author of a pioneering study of campaign financing, suggested Feb. 28 that a constitutional amendment be considered if reforms were legislated and ruled unconstitutional.

Organizations of various political persuasions had their own worries about the effects of proposed limits on their activities and influence. Limiting their contributions to $1,000 or $3,000 per candidate, or prohibiting in-kind services, as Nixon proposed, would render these groups ineffective, they feared.

If many small contributors chose to pool their resources through a single organization that represented their point of view, and channeled funds to candidates in selected districts, they should be allowed to do so, argued Russell D. Hemenway, whose National Committee for an Effective Congress had worked that way for years. Ideologically oriented interest groups would be "an endangered species," and their members' rights would be infringed upon, Hemenway said.

Marion Edey, coordinator of the League of Conservation Voters, said environmental groups such as hers, which often back challengers against incumbents, could be "put out of business" if proposed restrictions on group giving and unrealistically low campaign spending limits were enacted, leaving incumbents virtually unbeatable.

In-kind contributions, such as manpower, office space, transportation and services, were of crucial interest to both friends and foes of campaign reform. Some persons felt that if private money contributions were banned or severely limited there would be a healthy rise in volunteer help in politics. Others felt that removing private money from the scene would leave a disproportionate amount of influence with large organizations, such as labor unions, which could provide countless dollars' worth of manpower and services to candidates.

Nixon's plan would ban such help, and require individual volunteers to report the monetary value of their help as contributions. Some persons, including David K. Wilson, chairman of the Republican National Finance Committee, suggested that "quasi-political" groups, which did not endorse candidates but lobbied for issues, such as Common Cause or the American Civil Liberties Union, also should be regulated if other groups were, since they also influenced public opinion and policy.

Political Parties

In most of the foreign democracies that had public financing of elections (usually 30 to 60 per cent public, with private contributions permitted) distributed the money to political parties, which then disbursed it to their candidates. That was how Theodore Roosevelt suggested it be done in the United States. But between 1907 and 1974, political parties declined in power and influence, and money in politics usually flowed to individual candidates rather than to parties. The pending bills for public financing would continue that trend. Whether that would contribute, to the decline of the parties or strengthen them was being debated. *(Campaign finance in Europe, p. 57)*

In earlier hearings, spokesmen for the Democratic Party, which often had debts and seldom had a surplus, tended to support public financing. The Republicans, whose party was traditionally better financed, opposed changing the system. The parties themselves would be able to raise and spend money independently under most public-financing proposals; the Senate bill would even require party approval before a candidate could make an expenditure of more than $1,000. However, many observers felt that giving public money directly to candidates could make the parties even less influential than they already were. Candidates could "thumb their noses at their parties if they had enough personal charisma," said Sen. Wallace F. Bennett (R Utah). George Agree, who studied public financing in other countries for the Twentieth Century Fund and advocated it for the United States, conceded that candidate-oriented public funding proposals could damage the parties.

David S. Broder, political reporter for *The Washington Post* and author of several books on U.S. political parties, foresaw development of a multi-party system, with parties growing up around successful candidates. Such a system would result in less accountability to the voters, Broder warned Feb. 27. He said public campaign funds should go to the parties, but added that there was no chance Congress would devise such a system, because "most office holders are enemies of their parties; they're not interested in raising money for their parties, but for themselves."

Strengthening of the parties was foreseen by Robert E. Weiss, deputy finance chairman of the Democratic National Committee. He thought public funding of candidates would free contributors to support their parties instead.

It appeared that the two major parties stood to gain the most from the pending proposals, despite formulas to give minor- and new-party candidates funding proportional to their parties' strength in previous or (retroactively) in current elections.

Court challenges were expected on grounds of discrimination. Gov. George C. Wallace (D Ala.), for example, would not be eligible for public funds as a minor-party presidential candidate in 1976, because his American Independent Party did not get 5 per cent of the votes in the 1972 election. If Wallace ran and polled more than 5 per cent of the vote in 1976, he could be reimbursed retroactively for a proportion of his campaign costs.

Cost to the Taxpayers

While opponents of public financing argued that it was wrong to force the taxpayers to subsidize campaigns, proponents pointed out that indirectly they already were paying billions of dollars a year for the existing system—in higher prices as a result of policies "bought" by industries with big campaign contributions (oil, milk and wheat prices were frequently cited); unfair tax laws that benefited wealthy individuals and corporations at the expense of ordinary taxpayers, and other hidden costs.

Philip M. Stern, president of the Center for Public Financing of Elections, cited milk price increases alone of $500-million to $700-million a year as a result of dairy industry campaign contributions—two to three times the estimated cost of public financing of elections, he said. Stern figured that even if three times as many candidates ran in federal elections as in 1972, the cost of the entire campaign under the most generous proposed public financing plan would be about $262-million, or $1.88 per voter per year. The Senate Rules Committee estimated costs of $358-million over a four-year period, or $89-million a year—"as wise an investment of tax dollars as a democracy can make."

Presidential consultant Patrick J. Buchanan, in an article in *The Los Angeles Times*, doubted the taxpayers would be so excited about their "bargain" when they learned that "not Clement Stone, not Stewart Mott, but they themselves are footing the bill for $200-a-day political consultants, two-inch-thick carpets for junior campaign staffers, Bloody Mary parties for the campaign gang and traveling press corps, and millions of dollars for unnecessary polling or idiotic campaign ads that contradict their political beliefs and insult their intelligence.

"The waste and folly in a presidential campaign are gargantuan in scale," Buchanan wrote. "The taxpayer is already subsidizing enough nonsense without adding politics to his tab."

Lobbying Pressures

The debate was resolved in favor of comprehensive public financing of all federal elections in the Senate in late March and April 1974. The Senate passed S 3044 by a wide margin after Senate backers and pro-public financing coalition mounted an intensive lobbying effort. *(1974 legislation, p. 29)*

The House approved a more limited public financing bill in August. Unlike the Senate measure, it restricted public financing only to presidential general and primary elections. But public financing proponents saw it as a breakthrough since it did establish the precedent of using federal funds to pay for campaign costs. *(House bill, p. 31)*

Aside from a warning March 8 by President Nixon that he would veto any public financing bill, the White House kept its distance from the major campaign reform issue in the second year of Watergate. So had most groups like the U.S. Chamber of Commerce that opposed public financing legislation.

The debate in the House and Senate was dominated by those legislators and outside lobby groups that supported major changes in the way political campaigns were financed. And that created a very deceptive picture of how Congress handled this legislation.

For public financing legislation did not generate typical lobbying patterns. It was one of the very few issues that directly involved the self-interest of a member of Congress. Thus, much action was centered in Congress itself.

It might best be characterized as an iceberg issue, difficult to be against publicly, where most of the opposition, both in and out of Congress was hidden from direct view.

"Public financing today is like the motherhood issue," said John Gabusi, an aide to Rep. Morris K. Udall (D Ariz.), cosponsor of a public financing bill in the House. "Voting against it is like voting for the evils of Watergate, yet there are many guys who would do that if their votes were not made public."

The Senate April 11 passed its own comprehensive bill that would provide public financing for all federal elections. The landmark measure (S 3044) would limit the financing of primary campaigns for the House, Senate and the presidency to a hybrid system of small private contributions and matching public grants and would fully cover general election campaign costs with public money.

The House Aug. 8 passed its own bill that would provide for the public financing of presidential elections and party nominating conventions. It would establish an independent supervisory board to oversee and administer the law and set low spending limits for Senate and House campaigns.

Public Financing Supporters

Most of the backing for public financing legislation came from a broad coalition of groups and legislators that cut across party lines.

The coalition included:

● Common Cause, the 323,000-member self-styled national citizen's lobby that made public financing of elections one of its main legislative goals in 1973.

● The Center for Public Financing, an umbrella lobbying organization founded by philanthropist Philip M. Stern in 1973.

● The League of Women Voters, the women's public policy study and lobbying group that in March mounted a petition drive to get two million signatures supporting public financing.

● Unions, including the AFL-CIO and the United Auto Workers.

● In the Senate, Majority Leader Mike Mansfield (D Mont.), Minority Leader Hugh Scott (R Pa.) and Senators Edward M. Kennedy (D Mass.), Howard W. Cannon (D Nev.), Walter F. Mondale (D Minn.), Alan Cranston (D Calif.), Philip A. Hart (D Mich.), Charles McC. Mathias Jr. (R Md.), Robert T. Stafford (R Vt.) and Richard S. Schweiker (R Pa.).

● In the House, Anderson (Ill.) and Udall, cosponsors of the Clean Elections Act (HR 7612), along with more than 180 other representatives who cosponsored or signed statements of support for legislation to establish some form of public financing of federal elections.

Public Financing Opponents

Aside from the White House, opponents of public financing legislation included:

● The U.S. Chamber of Commerce, the businessmen's lobbying organization.

● In the Senate, an unorganized coalition of southern Democrats and conservative Republicans led by James B. Allen (D Ala.).

● In the House, Hays and the House Democratic leadership, who opposed all but the public financing of presidential elections, and a large number of representatives who were uneasy about any change in campaign financing practices.

Senate Lobbying

Public financing forces had the field to themselves early in 1974 as the Senate took up its campaign finance reform bill in late March.

The U.S. Chamber of Commerce had sent a letter Feb. 8 to its members warning them that "some in Congress now want to begin controlling our political freedom" by taking "a portion of our tax dollars and dividing the spoils among all federal candidates." Arch N. Booth, then the chamber's chief executive officer, called that "the height of arrogance."

But neither the chamber nor the White House, which successfully fought the public financing rider four months earlier, followed up their denunciations with any lobbying activity.

In contrast, Common Cause and the Center for Public Financing worked actively in public and private to lay the groundwork for passage of a bill to provide public money for federal elections.

"Campaign finance reform has been our top priority since we started," said Fred C. Wertheimer, Common Cause's chief lobbyist. "When we started to monitor the 1971 disclosure law two years ago, we saw a progression that led us to public financing.

"We saw that disclosure made clear what the source of the campaign money was but that it didn't provide a system of alternative campaign funding."

"Last year," Wertheimer added, "we decided to make public financing one of our prime legislative goals on the Hill."

Backers' Strategy

Common Cause went public as the Senate began taking up a public financing bill that had been reported by the Rules Committee Feb. 21. It ran an ad March 21 in *The Washington Post* accusing House Democrats of dodging campaign reform legislation. And it held a news conference March 28 to release figures on the political warchests special interest groups already had assembled for the 1974 congressional elections. At the news conference, Common Cause singled out members of Congress who had received large special interest contributions in the past.

"The key was to get senators and representatives out in the spotlight on public financing," said Neal Gregory of the Center for Public Financing.

The privately funded Center for Public Financing, headed by Gregory and Susan B. King, worked mainly within the Senate, dealing with the backers of the public financing bill and trying to coordinate the lobbying activities of various member groups like the League of Women Voters and the union organizations that supported public financing.

These groups as well as Senate backers planned their Senate strategy with an eye to the situation in the House. As they saw it, the chances of passing a tough public financing bill in the House were slim. If a bill that established the principle of public financing for all federal elections were to be enacted by Congress, the Senate would have to adopt a strong bill by a wide margin to let it bargain with the House from a position of strength.

"We had to go into conference with the House with the strongest possible hand," said Kenneth E. Davis, an aide to Minority Leader Scott and one of the public financing strategists.

Senate Votes

Before the bill was passed, over 50 roll-call votes were taken on amendments and procedural motions. What occurred behind the scenes on three of those votes provided a good picture of how the public financing measure was adopted.

The first vote was on March 27 on an amendment introduced by Sen. James B. Allen (D Ala.), the leading public financing opponent, to effectively kill the bill by striking its public financing provisions. The amendment, the second to be considered, was viewed as a test of support for the measure by the its backers.

The other two votes were April 4 and April 9 on cloture motions to limit debate on the legislation. Opponents resorted to the tactic of delaying the bill by introducing over a score of amendments, and Majority Leader Mansfield considered that a form of a filibuster.

The bill eventually passed on a 53-32 vote on April 11.

Allen acknowledged that he purposely set up the first test the day after the Senate took up the bill to get a public count of how many senators opposed it.

"I put my first amendment in to get a vote to weigh the situation," the Alabama Democrat said. He quickly learned where he stood; it failed on a 33-61 vote.

After the first cloture vote April 4 that fell four votes short of the two-thirds majority required to limit further debate, "I saw it would pass whenever they wanted it to," Allen said. Cloture was invoked by a one-vote margin, 64-30, April 9.

Labor Role

The AFL-CIO, the United Auto Workers, and the League of Women Voters joined with Common Cause and the Center for Public Financing to push for cloture.

"The unions didn't play a public part working for the bill," said one pro-public financing lobbyist. "They have such a diverse calendar they can't work as hard for everything they want."

"But they were active at key points," he added. They did cloture work on (Frank) Church (D Idaho) and (Gale W.) McGee (D Wyo.). They also talked to (Alan) Bible (D Nev.) and (Ted) Stevens (R Alaska)."

"Senators' offices were clearly aware of labor's interest in getting the bill through," another lobbyist agreed.

Kenneth Young of the AFL-CIO got the head of the AFL-CIO in Idaho to call Church to ask him to appear for the second cloture vote April 9. "He didn't have much success since Church wasn't in the Senate then, but labor let McGee and Church know they were upset by their absence and that led them to arrange a pair with Bible so they could cover themselves," one lobbyist said.

And Jack Beidler of the UAW had a long talk with Adlai E. Stevenson III (D Ill.) about his amendment to replace full public financing with a matching public-private system at the time it appeared that amendment might pass. "He tried to get Stevenson to water down his amendment but didn't have much success," according to a lobbyist who followed the Senate action. The amendment failed.

The labor-Common Cause relationship was tense, however, particularly after Common Cause's March 21 newspaper ad that included labor among the special interests using campaign contributions to buy influence.

Neither Common Cause nor labor spokesmen would speak on the record about the problem. But, as one pro-public financing lobbyist explained it, "There's a great deal of antagonism between Common Cause and labor. A lot of the labor hostility came out after Common Cause's full-page ad in the Post. They resented Common Cause lumping them with the special interest groups."

"There's a certain elitism among Common Cause," this observer continued. "They can be very effective in the districts, but their style is much different than labor's. They don't like Hays. But labor gets along with Hays and doesn't want to get in a...contest with him."

League of Women Voters

The League of Women Voters concentrated on doubtful senators to persuade them to vote for cloture. Mrs. Lucy Benson, league national president, called William V. Roth Jr. (R Del.), Robert Taft Jr. (R Ohio), Robert Dole (R Kan.) and J. W. Fulbright (D Ark.), said Lesley C. Gerould, staff director of the league's legislative action department.

Roth opposed cloture on the first vote but backed it on the second try; Dole supported cloture both times; Taft opposed it on the two votes; and Fulbright, who was absent for the first vote, showed up to vote for cloture on the second attempt.

League presidents in 14 states including Connecticut, Delaware, Kansas, Kentucky, Alaska, Colorado and Vermont also called their senators, Gerould said.

Bipartisan Coalition

But the key activity that led to the bill's eventual passage took place within the Senate, where a bipartisan coalition headed by Scott, Mansfield, Kennedy and Cranston pushed S 3044. "The key was the bipartisan approach," Common Cause's Wertheimer said.

Scott, aided by Senators Schweiker, Mathias and Stafford and their staffs, worked the Republican side. "Scott was very important," said one Senate staffer, "because he worked for a strong bill and his backing made it difficult for the White House to work here. After all, he's the Republican leader in the Senate."

"Scott and Mansfield did a hell of a job on cloture," Wertheimer said. Cranston also played an important role in lining up the votes to limit debate April 9 as did Carey Parker, Kennedy's legislative assistant, and Kenneth E. Davis, Scott's administrative assistant in his minority leader office.

Neal Gregory called Cranston the "key senator on the second cloture vote. He's an ace counter, a key member in doing cloakroom work."

Allen Opposition

Unlike the senators working for the bill, the opponents were unorganized and only had Allen as their leader because no other senators stepped forward to work with him.

"Allen is an excellent legislative tactician," said Davis, Scott's aide. "He knows the rules, and is very smart, shrewd and respected."

Allen tried a new approach to filibustering to delay action on the bill. Instead of talking for hours, he introduced a large number of amendments and then agreed to vote on several each day.

But Allen did little lobbying for his amendments. "I did very little work on behalf of my amendments other than offer them," he said. It showed. All but two of them were rejected.

Assessing Allen's actions, Davis said, "He knew he didn't have a majority. He needed a minority plus one and he knew he was outvoted after we took the first cloture vote."

Davis called Sen. Robert P. Griffin (R Mich.), the assistant minority leader, "the closest you'd come to a Republican counterpart to Allen." But Griffin "operated independently. He didn't talk with Allen," said Cecil Holland, Griffin's administrative assistant.

And, unlike Allen, who stayed on the floor as long as S 3044 was being considered, Griffin missed the second and crucial cloture try that succeeded by one vote. He was in Michigan's 8th Congressional District campaigning with President Nixon.

House Lobbying

The House offered a much tougher problem than did the Senate for backers of public financing legislation.

In the Senate, the Republican and Democratic leadership backed a comprehensive public financing bill, and Cannon, chairman of the Rules Committee which was responsible for election legislation, worked hard to report a strong bill out of his committee and to pass it on the floor.

The House has the reverse situation. The Republican and Democratic leadership and Rep. Wayne L. Hays (D Ohio), whose House Administration Committee had jurisdiction over election bills, opposed the public financing of congressional elections and only supported using public money to finance presidential elections.

Beyond that, many House members were wary of any election legislation they thought would make it easier for them to be challenged. "Most members of the House are a bit gun shy," said the Center for Public Financing's Gregory. "They don't see public pressure except for public financing at the presidential level."

Campaign finance reform legislation remained locked in the House Administration Committee through late July when the bill was reported. At first, public financing supporters had tailored their strategy to avoid Hays' panel and concentrate on the House floor to push a bill through. That was the strategy from late March, when the committee began its mark-up sessions, through early June. By then, however, it became clear that Hays was working seriously on a bill and the emphasis shifted to the committee to try to get as comprehensive a bill as possible.

The lobbying groups had set their sights lower in the House than in the Senate and were prepared to accept a financing bill there much more limited than the Senate version.

"Our sights are lower in the House," said Wertheimer, Common Causes' lobbyist, two months before the committee's bill reached the floor. "There, the fight is over a matching system that would finance campaigns with a mixture of public and private money."

As it turned out, the main fight was over including public financing of presidential elections in the House bill. "We lobbied the committee all the way through realizing they wouldn't buy public financing of congressional elections," explained Gregory. "We concentrated on full public financing of presidential elections."

The key lobbying groups with the House Administration Committee were the Center for Public Financing and the labor unions, especially the AFL-CIO and the United Auto Workers. Labor had great influence in the House Administration Committee since five of its Democratic members also served on the House Education and Labor Committee and other members came from strong labor House districts.

They concentrated on pushing for presidential campaign public financing after it became clear that Hays adamantly opposed any public financing for congressional campaigns and would refuse to compromise.

Common Cause, whose influence in the committee was severely diminished by its March 21 newspaper advertisement castigating particularly Hays who was also chairman of the Democratic Congressional Campaign Committee, worked to generate public pressure to force the House Democratic leadership to act.

They had no choice but to work on the outside. "Common Cause was completely negative in working with Hays' committee," according to a Hill source. "Their ad really burned the Democrats in their attitude toward Common Cause. They were thoroughly denounced at the weekly Democratic whip meetings."

When the campaign finance reform bill reached the House floor, only Common Cause pushed hard for an amendment to include public financing of congressional elections in the measure.

Labor laid low. "When the Anderson-Udall amendment for congressional public financing came up for a vote," said one lobbyist, "none of the labor lobbyists left the House gallery to go down to the doorways to let the representatives know they were behind it. Labor didn't push the amendment because they realized its chances of passage were remote and they felt that it might endanger the whole bill. They didn't want to antagonize Hays."

White House Role

With all the pressures for a public financing bill, the Nixon White House remained inactive. Three months before the bill came up in the House, Vern C. Loen, special assistant to the President for legislative affairs, said the White House would "do pretty much the same thing we did in the Senate. This is an area where the legislative branch doesn't take kindly to being told."

"This is an exceedingly difficult area for the administration to have much influence except through the veto threat," he added.

However, David Stockman, staff director of the House Republican Conference, attributed the White House's lack of influence directly to Watergate. "The White House won't be an influence in the House among middle-of-the-road Republicans because it has totally lost credibility," he said.

As it turned out, the White House was in no position to have any influence over House action since the Watergate crisis reached a climax the week the House debated the bill. In fact, the House passed the measure at about 7 p.m. on Aug. 8, two hours before President Nixon went on television to announce his resignation. *(Legislative action 1973-74, p. 29)* ∎

CONGRESS NEARED PUBLIC FINANCE ACT IN 1974

The unfolding Watergate scandal made campaign finance reform a major issue in both the 1973 and 1974 sessions of the 93rd Congress and led to conference approval of a landmark campaign finance reform bill in October 1974. *(p. 33)*

The 92nd Congress in 1972 had cleared the Federal Elections Campaign Act, which required disclosure of campaign contributions and expenditures and set limits on the amount of money candidates could spend in media advertizing. But with the revelations of serious money abuses in the 1972 election, pressure increased on Congress to deal with the problem of how to limit the influence and abuse of money in politics. *(Chapter on 1972 law, p. 2; provisions of 1972 law, p. 93.)*

1973 Action

In 1973, the Senate passed two bills on campaign financing. The first was S 372, which was passed July 30. It was essentially regulatory, imposing over-all spending and contribution limits on federal election campaigns, establishing an independent elections commission to oversee the new law and repealing the "equal time" broadcast provisions of the 1934 Federal Communications Act. As reported, S 372 was the result of months of work by the Senate Commerce Committee and Rules and Administration Committee. It was debated for five days, during which nearly 50 amendments were considered. One of the most important of these, providing for complete public financing of general elections, was rejected.

The House Administration Elections Subcommittee held hearings on S 372 at a slow pace during the fall of 1973. John H. Dent (D Pa.), subcommittee chairman, and Wayne L. Hays (D Ohio), chairman of the full committee, made it clear that they intended eventually to rewrite the bill. They favored lower spending limits, opposed the proposed enforcement commission and indicated lukewarm enthusiasm for contribution limits. And Hays was strongly opposed to public financing of campaigns—an idea that appeared to be gaining favor in the Senate, where the Rules and Administration Committee held hearings in September 1973.

Frustrated by lack of action in the House, Senate supporters later in the fall voted a major overhaul of the system of campaign financing when they attached a rider to a debt ceiling bill providing for public financing of presidential and congressional general elections and primary campaigns. The rider to HR 11104 included the text of S 372 as well as the public financing provisions. When the bill was returned to the House, the leadership agreed to schedule a House vote on the provisions affecting presidential elections if the provisions on congressional elections were dropped.

The bill was returned to the Senate to allow this change to be made. But once there, it was caught in a filibuster by James B. Allen (D Ala.). The Senate took two unsuccessful cloture votes, then gave in and approved the debt ceiling bill to become law without any campaign finance provisions.

1974: New Move

The failure of campaign reform legislation in 1973 did not mean that it was dead in the second session. Soon after it reconvened in 1974 after its Christmas recess, the Senate Rules Committee, chaired by Howard W. Cannon (D Nev.), began work on a comprehensive public financing bill. Cannon had pledged Dec. 3, 1973, to report out a public financing bill within 30 days after the opening of the second session of the 93rd Congress.

Cannon was several days overdue on his pledge, but his committee reported out its campaign finance reform bill (S 3044) on Feb. 21 by an 8-1 vote. The bill contained most of the provisions offered in HR 11104 and also conformed to the eight "basic principles" endorsed by 31 senators and several major groups supporting public financing in September 1973, the committee report said.

The bill was designed to provide "complete control over and disclosure of campaign contributions' and expenditures," both public and private, in elections for federal office, according to the committee, and was of "historic significance" in its thrust to reduce the influence of wealthy campaign contributors and give citizens without access to such sources equal opportunity to run for public office.

Under the bill, candidates for president, the Senate and the House of Representatives would be able to receive public funds for their primary as well as general election campaigns. General election campaigns would be fully funded with public money. Candidates, however, would have to first raise a qualifying minimum amount from private contributions for their primary campaigns to show that they had some base of support and were not frivolous candidates in order to qualify for public matching grants for primary campaigns.

Spending would be strictly limited in all campaigns, with primary costs held below general election campaign costs. In primaries, the House limit would be $90,000; for the Senate or for a House seat in a one-district state, the limit would be $125,000 or eight cents times the voting age population, whichever was greater; for president, the limit would be two times the amount the Senate candidate would be permitted to spend in each state, but with a nationwide limit of no more than 12 cents times the voting age population.

In the general election, spending limits would be $175,000 or 12 cents times the voting age population for the Senate and $90,000 for the House. Unopposed candidates could spend no more than 10 per cent of these amounts.

Candidates could choose whether to use all public, all private or a mix of both types of financing. The spending limits would encompass outlays by the candidate and his campaign committee, but would not cover spending for candidates by national or state parties, independent groups or individuals. Spending by those groups was strictly limited. For example, individual contributions were limited to $3,000 for each election, with an aggregate limit of $25,000 for all federal election campaigns. Independent groups could spend no more than $1,000 a year to advocate the election or defeat of any one candidate.

Senate Passage

After 13 days of debate, the Senate April 11 passed landmark election reform legislation that would radically change the existing system of campaign financing. Instead of relying on large private contributions to finance their campaigns, candidates for the House, the Senate and the presidency would be limited to a hybrid system of small private contributions and matching grants from the federal government to pay for their primary contests and to full public financing to cover their general election campaign costs.

The measure was passed on a 53-32 vote two days after the Senate voted April 9 to shut off the filibuster of southern Democrats and conservative Republicans, led by Allen, against the public financing provisions. The Senate took two votes on cloture—April 4 and April 9. The first try failed when the Senate fell four votes short of obtaining the two-thirds vote required to limit further debate. The vote was 60-36.

The second attempt succeeded by 64-30—one vote over the two-thirds majority required.

Cloture was invoked only after Minority Leader Hugh Scott (R Pa.), Edward M. Kennedy (D Mass.) and Alan Cranston (D Calif.) and labor union representatives conducted intensive lobbying among senators. Common Cause worked on the outside to build up pressure for S 3044.

Debate began March 26 with Allen promising "extended discourse" to kill the public campaign subsidies. The first test of strength of public financing support came March 27, when the Senate voted on Allen's first amendment, to delete entirely the public financing provisions from the measure. It lost 33-61, and the vote set the pattern on other amendments that would have weakened the measure. Most of them were easily defeated.

Throughout the debate, Allen charged that the bill was a "raid" on the public treasury for the benefit of politicians. Other opponents, such as Lowell P. Weicker Jr. (R Conn.), opposed public financing because they said it did not deal with the problem of controlling campaign costs. That was one of the prime lessons of Watergate, and that was not dealt with in S 3044, he said.

Supporters, such as Kennedy, said the public financing bill would remove the influence of big money in politics and would return integrity to campaign financing.

The Senate fended off attempts to significantly weaken the public financing provisions in the measure. Only two major changes were adopted. The federal subsidy for primary and general campaigns was reduced by 20 per cent, and the private fund-raising requirements for presidential candidates to receive public funds in primary elections were tightened.

During the 13 days of debate on the bill, the Senate took 51 roll-call votes. It adopted 23 amendments and rejected 28. Other changes and additions to the bill included an anti-vote fraud provision with a heavy jail sentence and fine, prohibiting foreign contributions, requiring that polling stations close at the same time on election day regardless of the time zones, reducing over-all contribution limit to a candidate to $3,000 for an individual and $6,000 for an organization, deleting from the bill spending limitations for candidates who did not face primary opposition, requiring financial disclosure by top federal employees including members of Congress, and an anti- "dirty tricks" provision with a heavy jail sentence and fine.

House Action

After 21 mark-up sessions between March 26 and July 1, the House Administration Committee reported its version of campaign finance reform legislation.

The bill, ordered reported July 24 by a 21-2 vote, was sponsored by Chairman Hays of Ohio, along with 11 other Democrats and three Republicans. Bill Frenzel (R Minn.), chairman of the House Republican task force on campaign reform, did not cosponsor the bill and severely criticized it in a minority report.

The bill would provide for public financing of presidential general and primary elections and national nominating conventions, set strict limits on campaign contributions and expenditures and bar foreign contributions and cash contributions of over $100. It would create a seven-member supervisory board dominated by Congress to oversee and administer the law, limit the honoraria elected and appointed federal officials could accept and require every candidate for federal office to establish one central campaign committee to report all receipts and expenditures.

The measure was much more limited in scope than the comprehensive campaign financing bill (S 3044) passed by the Senate April 11. The major differences were in campaign financing and enforcement. S 3044 provided for full public financing of presidential, Senate and House general election campaigns and partial public financing of primary campaigns. It also would establish an independent federal election commission of seven members appointed by the president and confirmed by the Senate to administer and enforce the election law.

Seven committee Republicans filed minority reports criticizing the bill's provisions for publicly financing presidential elections, its failure to limit even more severely campaign contributions by special interests, its lack of an independent enforcement agency and the absence of a ban on campaign "dirty tricks."

Committee Republicans had tried unsuccessfully to prohibit all contributions by special-interest groups, prevent the pooling of individual contributions by organizations (union political action funds, for example) and ban in-kind contributions (such as volunteer help and loans of equipment). The moves were blocked by the Democratic majority led by Hays.

Hays' Delay

The committee's action fulfilled a pledge by Hays to report a campaign reform bill out of his committee. The committee began work on a bill in October 1973, three months after the Senate passed its first campaign reform bill (S 372).

During the following months, many backers of campaign finance reform doubted that Hays would permit the panel to seriously draft a bill. Hays kept pushing back the date for his promised bill. The elections subcommittee held hearings on election reform legislation in October and November 1973. The full committee waited until March 26 to begin mark-up sessions and worked slowly through April and May before quickening its pace in June. Meanwhile, the Senate had approved S 3044, superseding S 372. The House panel tentatively approved its reform bill July 1, but its staff took until late July to rework the legislation and complete the committee report.

(Continued on p. 32)

1974 Campaign Finance Reform Bills

S 3044, the Senate-passed bill

HR 16090, the House-passed bill

Contribution limits on contributors

$3,000 per individual for the entire campaign. $6,000 per organization or political committee for the entire campaign. Aggregate limit of $25,000 per year for organizations and individuals. Candidate's and his family's contributions: $50,000 for President; $35,000 for Senate; $25,000 for House. Unsolicited individual expenditures on behalf of a candidate without his permission limited to $1,000 a year. Cash contributions of over $100 barred. Foreign contributions barred.

$1,000 per individual for each primary, runoff and general election, and an aggregate contribution of $25,000 to all federal candidates annually, $5,000 per organization, political committee and state party organization for each election. Candidate's and his family's contributions: $25,000. Individual expenditures on behalf of a candidate with his permission limited to $1,000 a year. Cash contributions of over $100 barred. Foreign contributions barred.

Spending limits on candidates

Presidential primaries—$11.4-million or eight cents times the voting-age population for all primaries. Presidential general elections—$17-million or 12 cents times the voting-age population. Senate primaries—$125,000 or eight cents times the voting-age population, whichever was higher. Senate general elections—$175,000 or 12 cents times the voting-age population, whichever was higher. House primaries—$90,000. House general elections—$90,000. Repealed the media spending limitations in the Federal Elections Campaign Act of 1971.

Presidential primaries—$10-million for all primaries. Presidential general election—$20-million. Presidential nominating conventions—$2-million. Senate campaigns—$75,000 or five cents times the voting-age population, whichever was greater, for each primary and general election. House campaigns—$60,000 for each election. Repealed the media spending limitations in the Federal Election Campaign Act of 1971.

Exemptions

None

Exempted from contribution and spending limits: expenditures of up to $500 for food, beverages, invitations, use of personal property and spending on "slate cards" and sample ballots. Fund-raising costs of up to 25 per cent of the candidate spending limit exempted from spending limits, thus effectively raising House campaign spending limits to $75,000 from $60,000.

Public Financing

Full, voluntary public funding for presidential and congressional general elections, with candidates having the option of selecting public or private financing; matching public funds in primaries after meeting fund-raising requirement. Proportional funding for minor-party candidates.

Full mandatory public funding for presidential general elections; public funding of national party nominating conventions voluntary; matching public funds in presidential primaries after meeting fund-raising requirement. All federal money for public funding of campaigns would come from the Presidential Election Campaign Fund. Proportional funding for minor-party candidates. Congressional campaigns not publicly financed.

Disclosure and Reporting Dates

Candidates required to establish central campaign committee; bank loans treated as contributions; government contractors, corporations and unions permitted to maintain separate, segregated political funds. Disclosure filing dates: 10 days before primary and general election, on Dec. 10 in an election year, and quarterly reports each year.

Candidates required to establish a central campaign committee; bank loans treated as contributions; government contractors, unions and corporations permitted to maintain separate segregated political funds. Disclosure filing dates: 10 days before an election (postmarked no later than 12 days before the election), 30 days after an election and quarterly, unless the committee received or spent less than $1,000.

Enforcement

Independent federal election commission comprised of seven members appointed by the president and confirmed by the Senate. Power to prosecute.

A six-member supervisory board controlled by four voting public members appointed by the speaker of the House and president of the Senate. Cases referred to the Justice Department for prosecution. House and Senate veto power over regulations issued by board.

While the committee worked on the bill, Hays steadfastly refused to buckle under to public pressure from Common Cause, the self-styled citizens' lobby, to quickly report out legislation. The chairman, who had a well-publicized feud with John Gardner, Common Cause chairman, was backed by the House Democratic leadership, who said they were confident Hays would finish work on a bill.

Republicans, as expected, attacked the bill. They charged it favored incumbents by setting spending limits which were unrealistically low. Most Democrats appeared to back it. "We have no problems with large portions of it," said John Gabusi, an aide to Rep. Morris K. Udall (D Ariz.), a leading public financing supporter.

Public financing lobbying groups split on the bill. Common Cause criticized loopholes that it said would permit campaign spending to exceed the ceilings set in the bill, the lack of an independent election commission and the failure to publicly finance congressional elections. The Center for Public Financing of Elections, however, backed the measure. "The bill is better than the existing situation," said Neal Gregory, the center's codirector. "It's a very good bill. But it could be made better by adding congressional public financing."

House Passage

A few hours before President Nixon resigned Aug. 8 as a consequence of his involvement in the Watergate coverup, the House approved by a 355-48 vote its campaign reform bill (HR 16090).

The bill would limit political contributions, restrict candidate spending, establish an independent supervisory board to enforce the legislation and finance presidential general elections and party nominating conventions and, to a limited degree, presidential primary campaigns with public funds.

President Nixon had strongly opposed public financing of federal elections. On March 8, he vowed to veto any bill that included that provision.

As Vice President, Gerald R. Ford had also voiced opposition to public financing of federal election campaigns.

Both the Senate- and House-passed versions of the campaign reform legislation provided for public financing of presidential campaigns.

Public financing of House and Senate campaigns, however, was in doubt. It was included in the Senate bill but rejected by the House Aug. 8 on a 187-228 vote.

Major Differences

The major provisions on which the two bills differed involved public financing of congressional campaigns, the type of federal body that would administer the new controls, campaign spending ceilings for House and Senate races, Senate language setting aside election day as a national holiday, requiring financial disclosure for top federal employees, imposing a uniform closing time at all polling booths and banning campaign dirty tricks and House restrictions on acceptance of honoraria.

One aide predicted that the House bill's limits on acceptance of honoraria by federal employees, including senators and representatives, would be dropped from the final bill. "That was put in clearly for a trade-off," he said.

During House debate Aug. 7-8 on the campaign finance legislation, Hays announced that the Senate would have to accept the $60,000 spending limit for House races, adopted on the floor, and the House's six-member supervisory board if he were to approve the campaign reform bill. Hays in the past had singlehandedly blocked campaign legislation he opposed or forced changes to meet his objections.

House Version Praised

The House-passed version generally won praise by those backing campaign finance reform. Common Cause, which lobbied hard for the measure, said it "will revolutionize the financing of American elections." But Common Cause accused the House of opting for a double standard by adopting public financing for presidential races but not for congressional races.

The Center for Public Financing of Elections called the bill "a significant beginning" toward public financing, adding: "A good campaign bill may be the only decent legacy for this sordid chapter in American politics. Any hint of a veto of this crucial legislation...would be a cruel slap in the face of the American people."

House Minority Leader John J. Rhodes (R Ariz.) had said he would recommend a veto on grounds that it was biased in favor of the Democratic Party.

House Floor Changes

As passed, the House bill closely resembled the committee version. The only major changes were:

● A six-member supervisory board controlled by four voting public members appointed by the House speaker and the president of the Senate (the vice president of the United States) to oversee and administer the election law. The clerk of the House and the secretary of the Senate would be ex-officio members. The committee version had a seven-member board made up of four public members appointed by the House and Senate presiding officers and three congressional employees.

● A $60,000 spending limit for House races. The committee version had a $75,000 expenditure ceiling.

● Expenditures of up to $500 for food and beverages, invitations, personal property and travel expenses would have to be disclosed, although they would still be exempted from the spending limit. The committee version did not require them to be reported. Both versions covered expenditures over $500.

● Bank loans to candidates would be treated as contributions. This provision was not included in the committee version.

The Senate bill provided for full public financing of presidential and congressional general election campaigns, partial public financing through matching grants of presidential and congressional primary campaigns, a $90,000 spending limit for House races and an independent, seven-member federal election commission appointed by the President and confirmed by the Senate to enforce the law. S 3044 did not include public financing of presidential nominating conventions, limits on the amount of honoraria a member of Congress could accept or campaign spending exemptions for fund-raising or food and beverages, invitations, personal property or travel expenses under $500.

House debate was dominated by Hays who, in his bluff, blunt-talking manner, fended off all of the major challenges to the bill his committee reported out.

Hays Compromises

In a last-minute move to stave off amendments with strong House backing, however, Hays Aug. 7 called together the House Administration Committee to approve a compromise supervisory board amendment and an amendment closing a loophole that would have exempted several campaign expenses of less than $500 from the bill's reporting requirements. Hays had pushed for the adoption of a "modified closed rule" by the House Rules Committee to prevent the introduction on the floor of certain amendments to some sections of the bill.

The key issue was the supervisory board provision. In the original committee version, the board was composed of seven members—four public members appointed by the House speaker and the president of the Senate—and three congressional employees—the clerk of the House, the secretary of the Senate and the comptroller general. The House Administration Committee and the Senate Rules Committee had veto power over the board's regulations.

Under the Hays compromise, the House clerk and Senate secretary were made ex-officio members of the board, and the four public officials became the only voting members. The comptroller general was dropped, and the House and the Senate, rather than the committees, were given the power to review and veto the board's regulations.

Frenzel, a member of Hays' committee, and Dante B. Fascell (D Fla.) had already introduced an amendment to establish an independently appointed federal elections commission, a body Hays was strongly opposed to.

Conference Agreement

After meeting five times over a three week period in late September, House-Senate conferees Oct. 1 reached agreement on the major provisions of a campaign finance reform bill.

The main sticking point had been the public financing of congressional elections, a provision backed by Senate conferees. But at the Oct. 1 meeting, Senate members agreed to drop their demand for congressional campaign public financing in exchange for provisions to create a strong independent elections commission and increase spending limits for congressional races.

The bill agreed to by the conferees would:

● Set a $70,000 spending limit for House primary and general elections separately. The Senate spending limit would be $100,000 or eight cents per eligible voter, whichever was greater, in primaries and $150,000 or 12 cents per eligible voter, whichever was greater, in general elections. Candidates could spend an additional 20 per cent for fund-raising expenses.

● Create a full-time independent six-member elections commission with its own civil enforcement powers. Two members would be appointed by the House Speaker, two by the Vice President and two by the President.(The Senate Secretary and House Clerk would be ex-officio members.) They would be confirmed by Congress. The commission would be able to go into court to seek injunctions against candidates who, among other things, accepted corporate contributions, exceeded the spending limit or failed to disclose their contributions and expenditures. Criminal prosecutions would be handled by the Justice Department.

● Require full public financing of presidential general elections and partial public financing of presidential primaries. Spending limits would be $10-million for the primary and $20-million for the general election. Presidential conventions could be publicly financed up to $2-million.

● Permit the two major parties to spend $10,000 in House elections, $20,000 or two cents per eligible voter, whichever was greater, in Senate elections, and two cents per eligible voter in presidential elections in addition to what individual candidates themselves could spend.

● Set contribution limits of $1,000 for individuals and $5,000 for organizations for each election.

(Watergate report continued from p. 21)

source, form, or amount of campaign contributions. In fact, despite the progress made by the Federal Elections Campaign Act of 1971, in requiring full public disclosure of contributions, the 1972 campaign still was funded through a system of essentially unrestricted, private financing."

Instead of abandoning private financing of elections, the committee urged that the system be reformed "to vastly expand the voluntary participating of individual citizens while avoiding the abuses of earlier campaigns."

26. Foreign contributions should be prohibited. Both House and Senate bills included this provision.

27. The committee recommended that federal officials confirmed by the Senate or who served in the White House be prohibited from soliciting or receiving campaign contributions while serving in the government or for a year after they left.

The recommendation was aimed at preventing abuses the committee uncovered in the 1972 campaign when it found former high Nixon administration officials who had been transferred to the re-election committee soliciting campaign contributions from the people they previously had regulated. "Particularly in view of the likelihood that many of these officials would return to the government," the report said, "solicitation by them may well have had undesirable coercive aspects."

28. Stringent limitations should be placed on the right of organizations to contribute to presidential campaigns. S 3044 would limit contributions from organizations to $6,000. The House Administration Committee bill would set a $5,000 limit for organizations.

29. Violations of the financing law by corporations, unions and foreign nationals should be felonies.

30. Requests, "direct or indirect," for information from the Internal Revenue Service (IRS) made by White House officials, "up to and including the President," should be recorded by the person making the request and by the IRS. Responses by the IRS should be disclosed to Congress.

31. "Sensitive case reports," which cover special IRS cases, should be disclosed to White House officials only in general terms.

32. All White House officials, including the President, should be prohibited from receiving directly or indirectly any federal income tax return.

33. All requests for information or action and all IRS responses should be disclosed periodically to congressional committees overseeing the agency.

34. Congress should enact legislation requiring full financial disclosure annually by the president and vice president to the General Accounting Office "of all income, gifts, and things of value that they or their spouses received during the year or expenditures made for their personal benefit or the benefit of their spouses by other individuals."

35. State and local bar associations should review the lawyer-client privilege in the light of the abuses of the privilege uncovered during the Watergate committee's investigations. The committee said the lawyer-client privilege was used four times during its investigation in an attempt to cover up illegal or questionable activities "that had nothing to do with the rendering of legal advice." ▮

WATERGATE SPURS FINANCE REFORM IN THE STATES

State legislatures, feeling the reverberations of the Watergate scandal, have responded with a flurry of measures to reform campaign finance laws.

"The most interesting fact of political life today is that the states have been far more responsive than the Congress to citizens' concern for a housecleaning in politics," noted Jack T. Conway, president of Common Cause, the Washington-based citizens' lobby.

Conway traced the beginning "wave of reform" to the 1972 elections, when two states, Washington and Colorado, passed "open government" initiatives. The Washington law survived a court challenge when the state supreme court upheld it and the U.S. Supreme Court refused to hear an appeal. In 1973 and 1974, as many as 40 state legislatures enacted 67 measures dealing with limiting campaign contributions and spending and monitoring ethical standards for politicians.

The resulting laws reflected a variety of approaches to improving campaign finance practices.

"There is an element of experimentation at the state level that you do not find at the federal level," said Herbert E. Alexander, director of another monitoring group, the Citizens' Research Foundation.

Among the reform measures adopted were:

● Open meetings. In 1973-74, 18 states took steps to open state legislative processes to the public, according to Common Cause. Comprehensive measures were adopted in such states as Oregon, Texas and Kentucky. New rules increased public access to committee meetings in New Jersey, New York and Pennsylvania.

● Lobbyists. Twelve states enacted laws aimed at disclosing the activities of lobbyists. In California, for example, registered lobbyists were prohibited from making political contributions. Texas and California required lobbyists to file detailed expenditure reports regularly. Massachusetts enacted a statute requiring disclosure by lobbyists of the executive branch.

● Personal finances. Fourteen states had set up independent ethics commissions to monitor personal finance statements filed by public officials. In 1973 and 1974, 11 states passed legislation toughening the laws. According to Common Cause, over half of the states require public officials to disclose their personal finances.

● Campaign financing. Some states moved toward public financing through various tax incentives. Five states adopted the $1 checkoff in effect at the national level. Two states approved $1 and $2 tax surcharges. Two states allowed tax credits for contributions, and 10 states approved deductions ranging from $25 to $100. *(Chart p. 36)*

● Campaign expenditures. Over half of the states placed some kind of limits on how much candidates could spend in different races. Some states used fixed ceilings, while others scaled limits based on population figures or past voter turnout. California held incumbents' expenditures to 90 per cent of that allotted to challengers, and three states—Massachusetts, North Carolina and Utah—restricted the amount a candidate could spend on a media campaign.

Disclosure

By July 1974, campaign finance disclosure statutes were law in 46 states. The trend was to "tighten up a great deal disclosure requirements, lower thresholds for disclosure and have more timely filings," according to Tom Belford, who monitors state campaign finance reform progress for Common Cause. Belford cited the setting up of enforcement commissions with powers to subpoena records and prosecute potential violators. In California, Washington and Texas, he said, lawsuits could be brought by citizens to force compliance.

Opposition

But stringent disclosure laws have provoked bitter opposition in some quarters. The American Civil Liberties Union in California contemplated bringing suit to challenge parts of that state's campaign reform initiative, Proposition 9, which was passed by a 2-to-1 margin in June 1974.

The ACLU objected to the initiative's requirement that all donors of over $50 be identified by name, address, occupation and employer. "At some point the public's right to know outweighs the right to privacy," said staff counsel Joe Remchow, "but the $50 (threshhold) may be too low." Remchow gave an example of a clerk at a large grocery chain who might donate to the United Farmworkers' Union, sponsors of the grape and lettuce boycotts. The clerk's donation would be listed under his employer's name, possibly jeopardizing his future there. California law prohibited firing an employee for political reasons, but Remchow thought few persons could challenge an employer in court.

ACLU board member Howard Jewel said the disclosure requirement "punishes unpopular political activity. It doesn't harm anybody doing the right thing for his own group. But what about a black who supports [Alabama Gov. George C.] Wallace or a closet gay who supports a candidate for sheriff who's for legalizing consenting acts in private?" Jewell added that small, highly controversial parties such as the Socialist Workers Party or Communist Party of America would find their fund-raising efforts "chilled" by the reluctance of potential donors to be identified.

Another area of concern, Jewel said, was the Fair Political Practices Commission created by Proposition 9 to enforce reporting requirements. Jewel feared the commission would become a "repository of political information," giving its five members "access to all kinds of political records."

Alexander of the Citizen's Research Foundation defended the independent enforcement commissions. "The trend is toward commissions that are bipartisan in nature, as compared with the old system of reports filed with secretaries of state who were partisan—elected or appointed, they achieved their positions through partisan activity. It is hard to get enforcement of an even-handed nature," he said. Alexander cited the New Jersey Election Law Enforcement Commission, comprised of two Democrats and two Republicans appointed for staggered terms: "You don't avoid entirely political influence, but they can blow the whistle on each other."

Loopholes

Despite the tougher disclosure laws, some loopholes did exist. In Georgia, Lt. Gov. Lester E. Maddox (D), a candidate for governor in 1974, voluntarily released a list of co-signers on bank loans totaling $155,000 after his critics charged that keeping his backers secret was a way of circumventing the state's disclosure laws. Gubernatorial candidate Charles D. (Pug) Ravenel (D) encountered similar controversy in South Carolina in 1974 and also released the names of co-signers on his campaign bank loans.

Limiting Contributions

Another area of dispute in drawing up campaign finance reform legislation arose in setting limits on contributions. Tom Belford of Common Cause said it was the area where proponents of campaign finance reform "fell apart on partisan grounds." Their disagreement reflected the traditional sources of money of each party. Republicans, Belford noted, frequently received large gifts from individuals through the party structure and were "very anxious to have low disclosure floors and restrictions on committees in an earmarking situation." This prompted Republicans to oppose such political committees as the AFL-CIO's Committee on Political Education (COPE).

Democrats, Belford said, did not raise most of their money through individual donations to the party, but relied on political committee activity. They favored lower individual donation ceilings and high limits on donations from union and other political fund-raising committees.

Proponents of political committee donations argued that permitting small givers to aggregate their money encouraged some small contributors who would not have donated otherwise. Opponents of pooling donations contended that the committees were interest groups that should be allowed to function but not contribute funds.

Three states moved in 1974 to limit the activities of political committees: California, Connecticut and Wyoming. A 1973 law prohibits corporate and union giving in New Hampshire, and a similar 1969 statute was in force in North Dakota.

Wyoming

Wyoming's new provisions were voted by a Republican-dominated state legislature in the form of an amendment offered by Republican State Rep. Robert W. Frisby. The Frisby amendment required political committees to use only those funds collected from members living within the candidate's district. Committees were required to show that they had the approval of the membership by a vote of at least 66.3 per cent before contributing to any candidate. The amendment allowed out-of-state contributions by individuals but limited all donors, in or out of state, to contributing no more than 5 per cent of a candidate's spending limit.

The Frisby amendment was upheld by a Cheyenne court after the Wyoming Education Association and the AFL-CIO brought suit. U.S. Rep. Teno Roncalio (D) told

Congressional Quarterly the Frisby amendment was affecting his re-election campaign "harshly and adversely." He estimated by late July he had returned between $5,000 and $6,000 in contributions from labor and education groups, "crippling" his fund-raising efforts.

"I'm running against a wealthy, tough, Republican oilman who's running at full speed," Roncalio said. His Republican opponent, State Sen. Tom Stroock, was a Casper oil leasing executive with supporters among Wyoming's oil industry, who donated as individuals.

Roncalio told CQ he did not intend to violate the Frisby amendment deliberately to test it in court. He hoped a higher Wyoming court would overturn the decision against the teachers and AFL-CIO. He added that he had accepted "a couple of little checks" from groups who held membership meetings in full compliance with the Frisby amendment.

Connecticut

In Connecticut, a Republican legislature enacted a law in 1974 barring all "non-natural" contributions—defined as those not coming from individuals. According to Evon Kochey of the Connecticut chapter of Common Cause, the statute had been sponsored by State Sen. Lewis B. Rome (R) and the Republican leadership in the legislature and passed by "very partisan voting." Democrats said it was an attack on labor."

The law prompted a variety of lobbies and other associations to ask the elections commission to rule on its provisions. A formal complaint was filed by Bridgeport Mayor Nicholas A. Panuzio against the Bridgeport Taxpayers Association, which criticized him in its newsletter. Panuzio, who lost a convention contest in 1974 for the Republican gubernatorial nomination, complained that the association violated the law by spending money to oppose him. The ACLU represented the Bridgeport Taxpayers Association.

Common Cause prepared questions on the law, and the League of Women Voters reportedly was planning to ask for declaratory judgment on provisions.

Kochey of Common Cause told CQ she thought a liberal interpretation of the Connecticut law would require groups to organize as political committees each year for specific elections, dispose of their funds and reorganize. A stricter view could bar them from any activity. Some feared the law would prohibit corporations from contacting stockholders on bond issues, based on the political nature of the issue.

The Connecticut law required labor unions, for example, to set up separate political committees to collect voluntary gifts from individual members. It would be a cumbersome process, said Kochey, but easier for business lobbies and unions to accomplish than for small groups only peripherally involved in politics and lacking the resources to set up separate offices for political purposes. The law backfired on the Republicans who supported it; the Connecticut Key Club, a Republican organization which traditionally contributes to its state party's housekeeping funds, was also seen as needing to reorganize each year for each election.

Some of the groups opposed to the Connecticut law hesitated to bring a court action, Kochey said, because the statute had no savings clause. Throwing out language restricting committees would mean the loss of controls on cash contributions and disclosure sought by several of the groups seeking liberal interpretations of the restrictions on committees.

California

The California initiative required business and labor groups to separate their political activities—including donations—from their lobbying of officials in the legislature and executive agencies. The initiative was vehemently opposed by the AFL-CIO, which withdrew its support of Democratic gubernatorial candidates supporting it. But it passed overwhelmingly on the June 1974 primary ballot.

Unfair?

Some who urged reform of campaign finance practices thought restricting political committees was unfair. "It's utterly obnoxious to exclude from the political process interest groups like that," said Herbert Alexander. "It's one thing to put limits on the amounts of contributions...but in a pluralistic society, all kinds of voices should be heard. I don't like the politics of exclusion—I think people should be encouraged to participate in the political process, including with money." Alexander drew the line at contributions made by contractors with government ties.

Belford of Common Cause defended restrictions on political committees: "Pooling has a reasonable and important purpose in a private [campaign] financing system, but as we move toward public financing, we can cut back on pooling.... Only parties play a pooling function."

Four States

By August 1974, all but four states had enacted some kind of campaign finance disclosure legislation. Four states—Idaho, Illinois, Louisiana and North Dakota—had no campaign finance disclosure laws, but an Illinois statute requiring periodic reporting of donations over $150 was awaiting signature by the governor. A Common Cause-sponsored "Sunshine Initiative" was planned for the November 1974 ballot. It would require reporting of campaign contributions above $50, but would not limit spending or fund-raising.

Reports of contributions were filed in most states either with the secretary of state or with a separate elections commission. In addition, some states set up ethics commissions to monitor disclosure of the personal finances, and potential conflicts of interest, of candidates and officeholders.

In two states, Georgia and Texas, efforts to create separate election commissions failed. Georgia's 1974 financial disclosure act provided for such a commission, but the state supreme court ruled the commission unconstitutional. The Texas commission was invalidated by the state attorney general.

Those commissions with enforcement powers could issue subpoenas, investigate violations and hold hearings, but prosecution usually was handled by the state attorney general. Commissions in California, New Jersey and New York also were able to assess penalties.

In the following chart, limits on contributions or expenditures apply to statewide offices unless noted otherwise. When limits for governor are specified, there could be different limits for other statewide offices.

State	Tax Provisions	Individual Donation Limits	Expenditure Limits	Reporting Provisions	Elections Commission	Ethics Commission
Alabama	None	None	Gov., U.S. Sen.: $50,000—primary and general: U.S. Rep.: $10,000—primary and general	After election	None	Depository, investigations
Alaska	None	$1,000	Gov.: 40 cents multiplied by total population (40% primary, 60% general)	Before and after election	Depository, investigations	None
Arizona	None	None	10 cents multiplied by total population of election area	Before and after election	None	Enforcement only; reports filed with secretary of state
Arkansas	Deduction: $25	None	None	After election	None	Personal financial disclosure by officials
California	Deduction: $100	None	Gov.: Primary—7 cents multiplied by voting age population; general—9 cents multiplied by voting age population	Before and after election	Depository, enforcement	Receives disclosure of personal financial assets
Colorado	None	None	None	After election, within 48 hours if over $500	None	Personal financial disclosures by candidates
Connecticut	None	Gov.: $2,000 primary; $5,000 general	Gov.: 15 cents per resident	Before and after election	None	None

State	Tax Provisions	Individual Donation Limits	Expenditure Limits	Reporting Provisions	Elections Commission	Ethics Commission
Delaware	None	$1,000	Primary: 25 per voter; general: 50 cents per voter	Before and after election	None	None
Florida	None	$3,000	Gov.: $250,000 primary; $350,000 general	Before and after election	Enforcement only	Personal financial disclosure by officials
Georgia	None	None	None	Before and after election	Depository, enforcement	None
Hawaii	Deduction: $25	None	Primary: 50 cents per voter qualified in last election; general: same as primary	Before and after election	Depository, enforcement	None
Idaho	None	None	None	None	None	None
Illinois	None	None	None	Before and after election*	None	Personal financial disclosure by officials
Indiana	None	None	Gov.: U.S. Sen.: $25,000; U.S. Rep. $10,000 (primary and general)	After election	Depository, enforcement	Rules of conduct, investigations
Iowa	Deduction: $100; $1 checkoff	None	30 cents per each vote cast for president in last election	4 times per year	Enforcement only	None
Kansas	None	Gov.: $2,500 primary; $2,500 general	Gov.: $500,000 (primary and general)	Before and after election	Enforcement only	Depository, enforcement (effective 1975)
Kentucky	Deduction: $25	$3,000	None	Before and after election	Depository, enforcement	None
Louisiana	None	None	None	None	None	None
Maine	$1 Surcharge designated to preferred party	None	Primary: 25 cents per voter; general: 50 cents per voter	After election	None	None
Maryland	$2 Surcharge (effective 1978)	Private gifts (in denominations under $50) matched: $30 public to $1 private. No more than 75% from public funds.	10 cents per voter	Before and after election	None	Enforcement of personal worth disclosure law
Massachusetts	None	$1,000	None (media limits: Gov.— $500,000)	Before and after election	Depository, enforcement	None
Michigan	Deduction: $25	None	Primary: $40 per 1,000 votes cast for gov. in last election; at least 25% of one year's salary; general: same as primary	After election	None	None
Minnesota	Credit: half of political donations up to $25; deduction: $100; $1 checkoff to party or general account	None	Gov.: $600,000 or 12½ cents per capita, whichever is greater	Before and after election	Depository, enforcement	Disclosure of economic interest
Mississippi	None	None	None	Before and after election	None	None

* Bill pending governor's signature, source Common Cause.

State	Tax Provisions	Individual Donation Limits	Expenditure Limits	Reporting Provisions	Elections Commission	Ethics Commission
Missouri	Deduction: $50	None	$25 per 100 votes cast in last presidential election	After election	None	None
Montana	Deduction: $50 $1 checkoff to gub. campaign fund.	None	Primary: 15% annual salary; general: 10% annual salary	After election	None	None
Nebraska	None	$1,000	None	Before and after election	None	None
Nevada	None	None	State legislature only: greater of $15,000 or 50 cents per voter for for largest vote-getter in last election	After election	None	None
New Hampshire	None	$5,000	15 cents per voter	Before and after election	None	None
New Jersey	None	$600 (may borrow up to $50,000 from banks to be repaid 30 days before election)	50 cents per voter Gov.: maximum $1.5-million per candidate	Before and after election	Depository, enforcement	None
New Mexico	None	None	None	After election	None	None
New York	None	$150,000	Primary: 50 cents per voter or $2,500, whichever is greater; general: same as primary	Before and after election	Depository, enforcement	Fair campaign practices code enforcement
North Carolina	None	$3,000	None (media limits: 10 cents per voter)	Before and after election	Depository, investigations	None
North Dakota	None	None	Primary: 15% of year's salary or or $500, whichever is greater; general: same as primary	None	None Depository, investigations	None
Ohio	None	None	Gov., U.S. Sen., U.S. Rep.: 10 cents per capita	Before and after election	Investigations only	None
Oklahoma	Deduction: $100	$5,000	None	After general election	None	None
Oregon	Credit: half of political contributions up to $25	None	Statewide races: 15 cents per voter; lesser races: 25 cents per voter or $1,000, whichever is greater	Before and after election	None	None
Pennsylvania	None	None	None	After election	None	None
Rhode Island	$1 checkoff to party or general account	None	Gov.: $400,000 general; $100,000 primary	Before and after election	Depository, enforcement	None
South Carolina	None	None	None	Before and after election	None	None
South Dakota	None	None	Primary: 50% annual salary: general: same as primary	After election	None	None
Tennessee	None	None	None	After election	None	None

State	Tax Provisions	Individual Donation Limits	Expenditure Limits	Reporting Provisions	Elections Commission	Ethics Commission
Texas	None	None	None	Before and after election	None	None
Utah	Deduction: $25; $1 checkoff to party	None	25 cents per voter; up to 70% spent after primary (media limit: Gov.—$100,000)	Before and after election	None	None
Vermont	None	$1,000	Gov.: $40,000 primary; $40,000 general	Before and after election	None	None
Virginia	None	None	None	Before and after election	None	None
Washington	None	None	Gov.: 10 cents per voter; $5,000; or twice annual salary; whichever is larger, not to exceed $100,000	Before and after election	Depository; investigations	Depository, investigations
West Virginia	None	$5,000	Primary: $75 per county; general: same as primary	Before and after election	None	None
Wisconsin	None	None	Gov.: $10,000 primary; $10,000 general	Before and after election	None	Depository; enforcement
Wyoming	None	5% of total allow-able expenditures	75 cents per vote cast for same office in last election	After election	None	None

Source: Citizens Research Foundation

CAMPAIGN FUND TAX CHECK-OFF GAINS IN USERS

In 1973, only 3.1 per cent of the nation's taxpayers earmarked $1 of their federal income taxes for the new presidential election campaign fund on their 1972 tax returns.

Most supporters agreed at the time that the $4-million thus set aside provided an abysmal start for the experiment to have the public finance presidential general elections.

They had thought that an overwhelming number of taxpayers would support the supplanting of political contributions from interest groups and wealthy individuals—especially since the $1 designated would come from taxes already paid and would not be taken from tax refunds or added to tax payments.

But actual first-year response fell so far short of expectations that the plan had nowhere to go but up—and it did.

Five-Fold Increase

In 1974, with the check-off in its second year, the Internal Revenue Service (IRS) reported that taxpayer response on the 1973 income tax return had increased five-fold to 15 per cent. This added another $17.5-million to the fund, plus $8.4-million collected retroactively from taxpayers who had missed the first year of the check-off.

By July 1, $29.8-million had been collected of the $72-million that the General Accounting Office (GAO) expected to be amassed for the 1976 presidential election.

If the presidential nominees of both major parties chose to use the fund, campaign spending would be held far below the more than $100-million that presidential candidates spent in 1972. The GAO, which would administer the fund once Congress appropriated it, projected that $42-million would cover the 1976 election costs of the Democratic and Republican nominees.

Congress had enacted the check-off in 1971 to finance the 1976 presidential election. It first appeared on the 1972 income tax forms. *(Box on check-off system, p. 42)*

Assessments

Even though the process had demonstrated an ability to raise money, it still was a matter of debate whether the check-off proved successful in 1974, which many persons considered to be the year of its first real test.

Did the 15 per cent taxpayer response mean public support, apathy or rejection of the idea of public financing of elections?

Political observers closely watched how the campaign fund fared on the 1973 returns because the fund's financing depended upon taxpayers' voluntarily marking the check-off box on their tax returns. In a sense, the check-off was a public opinion poll of the nation's 81 million taxpayers.

Most political observers interviewed by Congressional Quarterly agreed with the assessment of Sen. Russell B. Long (D La.), considered the father of the check-off since he sponsored the original legislation in 1966 to establish it.

"I think it's moving along fine," Long told CQ. "At the rate people are marking the check-off, it will provide enough money to pay for the Democratic and Republican presidential campaigns in 1976."

But there were dissenters. One was Thomas F. McCoy, a Washington political consultant who was executive director of the bipartisan Committee for the Presidential Election Campaign Fund Thru the Dollar Checkoff. Funded by philanthropist and public financing backer Philip M. Stern, the committee spent $18,000 publicizing the check-off in the media and workers' pay envelopes during the 1974 tax preparation season.

"I wish I could report that we had great success," McCoy said. "But, unfortunately, the results do not back up that kind of assessment."

He agreed with Long that the check-off would generate "more than enough" money to finance the 1976 presidential election, the objective for which it was created. But he was

Form **1040**	**US**	Department of the Treasury—Internal Revenue Service **Individual Income Tax Return**	**1973**

For the year January 1–December 31, 1973, or other taxable year beginning ...., 1973, ending ...., 19........

Name (If joint return, give first names and initials of both) ... Last name ... COUNTY OF ... Your social security number

...... line 24 to be ...... on 1974 est........
mated tax . . . . ▶ | 26 |

Note: 1972 Presidential Election Campaign Fund Designation.—Check ☐ if you did not designate $1 of your taxes on your 1972 return, but now wish to do so. If joint return, check ☐ if spouse did not designate on 1972 return but now wishes to do so.

Under penalties of perjury, I declare that I have examined this return, including accompanying schedules and statements, and to the best of my knowledge and belief it is true, correct, and complete. Declaration of preparer (other than taxpayer) is based on all information of which he has any knowledge.

Taxpayers were given a second chance on their 1973 tax returns to check off the presidential campaign fund

looking at the taxpayer response—not at the dollar figures as Long was.

"It is difficult to believe that the majority of the taxpayers were unaware of the opportunity to use the check-off," McCoy said. "I believe that a majority of the 85 per cent who did not use the check-off made a positive judgment against doing so."

He said he based his judgment on "discussions with numerous tax preparers who report a considered rejection (of the check-off) by a vast majority of their clients."

Other factors that had to be taken into account in assessing the response to the check-off included the existing political climate, how extensively and adequately the check-off was publicized and explained, the problems it encountered in its first year and what its maximum level of public support could realistically be projected to be.

Impact of Watergate

McCoy said the widespread distrust of politicians resulting from the Watergate scandal was responsible, in part, for what he judged to be the check-off's poor showing.

"We had a line in our television spots saying that the check-off wouldn't cost the taxpayer a cent," he said. "But taxpayers didn't appear to be buying that. They saw it as the politicians getting their hands in the till a different way."

The Wall Street Journal reported March 14 that many taxpayers were refusing to "give any money to politicians" as a result of bitterness about President Nixon's use of large deductions to keep his own income taxes minimal. Nixon's tax problems were a major issue while taxpayers filled out their 1973 tax returns.

IRS Action

The Internal Revenue Service stepped up its publicity of the check-off in 1974 and moved it onto the front page of the 1040 income tax form of the 1973 return. It set the box off in red print, produced public service ads explaining what the check-off did, and had the ads placed in newspapers, magazines and on television. It also placed a second box on the front page of the 1973 tax return to permit taxpayers who missed the 1972 check-off to mark it retroactively for 1972.

Controversy Over Performance

Compared with its performance in 1973, the IRS gave the check-off banner treatment in 1974.

For the 1972 return, the IRS had provided a separate form for the check off—4875—on which a taxpayer designated which party his $1 would go to, as the check-off law then required.

"IRS had two reasons for putting the check-off on a separate form," said Philip L. Rothchild, assistant to the IRS commissioner for public affairs. "There was an ethical question of letting the IRS know a taxpayer's party preference since he had to designate a party. We didn't want that on the 1040. And then there was no room on the front of the 1040 for the check-off. We had new revenue-sharing information that had to be included."

IRS also conducted a low-key publicity program on the check-off. "It was brand new. We were feeling our way," said Rothchild.

Criticism

But others saw it as IRS foot-dragging or worse. "When the check-off was on a separate form," said Mitchell

Rogovin, who was IRS general counsel in 1964-65, "a tax preparer was required to type in the name and address of the taxpayer. He felt obliged to charge an extra fee to fill it out and many taxpayers saw no reason to pay it."

Sen. Long accused the IRS of sabotaging the check-off on the 1972 return. "People had to use a separate form and most didn't know the form was in their tax packet," he said. "It was also difficult for people to get extra 4875 forms at IRS offices or post offices."

"The President said he was against the check-off although he signed it," Long added. "He threatened to veto it if it applied to the 1972 presidential election, and he wanted it repealed. Against that kind of animus, it's not surprising what the IRS did."

Rogovin said that Johnnie M. Walters, IRS commissioner when the check-off went into effect, "had denied that IRS received any White House pressure on how to handle the check-off. My view is that you don't have to find pieces of paper saying 'do something.' You sometimes assume things—for instance, that the White House didn't want the check-off prominently displayed. That's what Walters probably did."

Long and Common Cause, the self-styled citizens lobby, pressed the IRS in early 1973 to change its handling of the check-off. Long, who chairs the Senate Finance Committee, extracted a promise from Donald C. Alexander—at the Finance Committee's hearings on his nomination as IRS commissioner—to put the campaign fund box on the front page of the 1040 form.

And Common Cause successfully sued the IRS in the U.S. District Court for the District of Columbia to force it to include the check-off on the 1040 form, to publicize it adequately, and to permit taxpayers to file the $1 checkoff after they had filed their tax returns.

Changes Praised

Long and Rogovin praised the IRS for its handling of the check-off in 1974. "The IRS did the right thing in putting the check-off on the front page of the 1040 form, and allowing taxpayers to designate retroactively for 1972," said Long.

Said Rogovin, who handled the Common Cause suit against IRS, "The IRS streamlined the check-off and put it on the front page of the return. Things are working out well now on the check-off.'

Outlook

Long, Rogovin and McCoy said they expected between 25 and 30 per cent of the nation's taxpayers to mark the presidential election campaign fund box once it was fully understood.

"We had hoped to reach a 25 per cent response to the check-off this year," said McCoy. "But I feel now that if we can get the percentage up to 25 to 30 by 1976, we'll be doing well."

Rogovin said he expected the check-off response "to increase to 30 per cent before it levels off." Long talked of 25 per cent as the response he eventually expected on the check-off.

H & R Block Approach

That response already had been reached in tax returns prepared by H & R Block Inc., the nation's largest tax preparation firm, which did 10 per cent of the federal income tax returns in 1974. "Our sample shows that 35 per cent of our customers told us to mark the check-off on their

Check-Off Money: Only Paper Until Congress Acts

The money checked off by taxpayers on their federal income tax returns for the presidential election campaign fund stood to remain only a bookkeeping entry at the Treasury Department until Congress passed legislation converting the paper designations into a cash campaign chest.

Congress was expected to do that in time for the 1976 presidential campaign. When Congress activated the fund by appropriating an amount equal to the total of $1 designations, each candidate would be free to choose between public or private funds for his campaign.

How the Fund Would Work

If a candidate opted for public financing, he would be limited in the general election to spending no more than 15 cents for each voting age person in the United States, under terms of the 1971 law (PL 92-178) that established the check-off. Candidates relying on check-off money would solicit private contributions only if there was not enough money in the special fund to cover their campaign costs under the spending formula. Under those circumstances, they could raise only enough money to make up the difference between the amount they received from the fund and the campaign spending limit.

Republican and Democratic presidential nominees would receive money from the check-off fund in advance for their campaigns. The 1971 law contained a formula that would determine the amount of money for presidential candidates of minor parties who received between 5 and 25 per cent of the vote. They would be given money after the election.

Spending limits have not been placed on candidates relying on private financing.

The General Accounting Office would administer the fund once Congress appropriated it for the 1976 election. The Internal Revenue Service's role was only to collect the money.

Turbulent Beginnings

The check-off had a tempestuous history. Congress first passed it in 1966, but then suspended it in 1967. It was resurrected in 1971 and approved by Congress again. But the campaign funding plan could become effective only in time for the 1976 presidential election. House-Senate conferees, faced with President Nixon's threat to veto the bill (HR 10947) to which the check-off had been attached in the Senate as a rider (non-germane amendment), delayed the effective date of the campaign financing provision until Jan. 1, 1973. *(Background, Congress and the Nation, Vol. III, p. 410)*

The check-off as passed in 1971 required taxpayers to designate which political party would receive their $1 designation. However, at the suggestion of Sen. Hubert H. Humphrey (D Minn.), Congress amended the law in 1973 to eliminate the separate party designations and have the check-off contributions collected for a single fund to be shared by all presidential candidates. *(1973 CQ Almanac, p. 548)*

returns," said William F. Toevs, the firms' director of advertising and public relations.

The reason for the check-off's higher success rate with Block customers was publicity. "We took no position on the check-off," Toevs said. "But we realized very early in January that most people were unaware that the check-off wouldn't cost them any money. We made it our policy to explain the check-off to our customers. That explanation was the only positive step we took and that might account for the increased percentage of people marking the check-off on returns we prepared."

Even with Block's policy of creating "additional awareness" of the checkoff, Toevs said that "two-thirds of our customers said, 'I don't want to do it.' "

Proposals

The Senate Finance committee had before it in 1974 a proposal to double the check-off to $2 per person and $4 per couple and make it automatic unless a taxpayer said no. That change had been included in the Rules Committee version of S 3044, the comprehensive public financing of elections bill passed by the Senate in April, but it was removed before the Senate took up the bill and the proposal was sent to the Finance Committee.

Sen. Long, who would have a major say about any changes in the presidential election campaign fund, said he had "no objection" to doubling the check-off. But he clearly was not enthusiastic about the proposal.

"I wonder whether we're getting ahead of ourselves with that," he said. "You have to be careful not to go overboard on the check-off. You have to get people to accept it."

Long said he would be "willing to expand the check-off to cover presidential primaries." But again he cautioned that "you have to be very careful."

One change he accepted without reservation would have check-off funds used to finance the national party presidential nominating conventions. The House Administration Committee added that provision, setting aside $4-million from the check-off fund for the Democratic and Republican conventions, to its campaign reform bill (HR 16090) which the House passed Aug. 8.

Selling the Check-Off

Looking ahead to the 1975 tax season, Long said he wanted the IRS to boost its publicity program for the check-off. "I'd like IRS to explain even more what the check-off is and urge people to consider marking it," he said.

The check-off still suffered from the public misconception that "it means an extra $1 on their income tax," said Robert C. Higgins, counsel to the GAO's Office of Federal Elections.

The only way to solve that problem and increase public acceptance, according to some check-off backers, including McCoy, was to have the check-off turned into a political issue. "It can't be sold in five lines on the front of the income tax packet." McCoy said. "You've got to make it an issue between candidates. You've got to get them to explain their stands on it, turn it into an issue like Proposition Nine in California [a campaign and lobbying reform proposal approved by the voters]. Then you might be able to get broader public support for it." ∎

BOTH PARTIES USE A VARIETY OF TECHNIQUES

National party fund-raising and distribution activities are similar for both the Democratic and Republican Parties, but each has developed individual methods and procedures to suit its particular needs and opportunities.

Republicans

For the Republicans, the Republican National Finance Committee is the recipient and depository for most funds. In the period Jan. 1 through May 31, 1974, the committee raised nearly $3.5-million, of which almost $3.4-million was from individual contributors, according to figures compiled by the Citizens' Research Foundation from records filed with the General Accounting Office. Individual contributors include both individual persons and organizations. *(Box, this page)*

The individual persons contributing ranged up to $5,000, with numerous contributions of $1,000 each. The largest organization contribution during this period was $10,000 from the Minnesota Republican Finance Committee. Committees for political candidates also contributed: the Winn for Congress Committee, set up for Rep. Larry Winn Jr. (R Kan.), gave $5,110 during the first five months of 1974, the records showed.

The main methods of fund-raising for the Republicans consist of direct mail appeals; sustaining members, who agree to give a certain amount each year; a quota system for state parties, and a miscellaneous category that includes a certain percentage of the take from party speeches, dinners and other money-raising functions.

In turn, the finance committee transfers its funds to the other major Republican committees, chiefly the Republican National Committee. The national committee provides a wide variety of services to candidates. These services mainly include expertise—such as advice on how to run a campaign, use of news media and polling techniques. Special attention is given to candidates who have a close race or an opportunity of pulling an upset.

On the congressional level, the National Republican Congressional Committee for the House and the Republican Senatorial Campaign Committee raise and distribute funds to help Republican candidates. Each consists of a committee of members from the respective houses, which makes the over-all policy decisions. The chairman of the National Republican Congressional Committee is Rep. Robert H. Michel of Illinois; the chairman of the Senate group is Sen. Bill Brock of Tennessee.

Direct-mail solicitation is the main fund-raising method of these committees, plus an annual joint dinner in March. The committees provide both cash and services to candidates. Only incumbents are aided by the House committee. A separate committee was established to help challengers: the Republican Congressional Boosters Club. As an aid to the Boosters Club, the House campaign committee meets all the club's overhead costs (rent, salaries, etc.) so that all funds coming in to the Boosters may be used for the benefit of the candidates.

Mailing and computer services paid for by the National Republican Campaign Committee are contracted out to commercial firms, keeping to only four persons the committee staff working directly on funds.

Democrats

Democrats at the national level have three major fund-raising methods: telethons, direct-mail solicitation and a givers' program under which persons pledge to donate a certain amount over a specified period of time.

A relatively new device, the telethon has proven to be a major asset for Democratic fund-raisers, competing with celebrity dinners and computerized letters. In fact, the telethon has at least temporarily replaced the dinners, the last one being held in 1971. During the latest nationwide telethon, in June 1974, $7.1-million was pledged, with actual receipts of $6.3-million, according to the Democrats.

National Party Finances

Receipts and Expenditures, Jan. 1-May 31, 1974

Receipts	DNC[1]	DFC[2]	RNC[3]	RNFC[4]
Individual contributions	$ 753,578	$83,892	$ 11,009	$3,375,093
Sales and collections	2,629	0	214	121
Loans received	165,000	0	0	0
Other (refunds, rebates, interest, etc.)	74,805	0	18,943	1
Transfers in from other committees	94,020	6,674	2,279,027	88,563
Total	**$1,090,032**	**$90,566**	**$2,309,194**	**$3,463,779**

Expenditures				
Communications media	0	0	0	0
Personal services, salaries, etc.	3,123	0	742,021	0
Loans made	0	0	0	0
Other expenditures	761,623	48	1,427,759	0
Transfers out to other committees	1,481,925	85,500	129,139	3,350,000
Total	**$2,246,672**	**$85,548**	**$2,298,920**	**$3,350,000**

[1]*Democratic National Committee*
[2]*Democratic Finance Committee*
[3]*Republican National Committee*
[4]*Republican National Finance Committee*

Source: Citizens Research Foundation

Income and Outgo of House, Senate Committees

Jan. 1—May 31, 1974

	Democratic National Congressional Committee	Democratic Congressional Campaign Committee	Democratic Senatorial Campaign Committee	Democratic Congressional Finance Committee	National Republican Congressional Committee	National Republican Senatorial Committee	Republican Congressional Boosters Club
Receipts							
Individual contributions	$ 8,475.00	$ 52,383.41	46,965.00	$ 3,000.00	$ 971,502.18	$421,858.60	$323,811.36
Sales and collections	0	0	0	11,418.90	0	0	0
Loans received	0	0	0	0	0	0	0
Other (refunds, rebates, interest, etc.)	0	0	91.27	0	58,339.54	7,470.40	0
Transfers in (from other committees)	453,000.00	221,750.00	236,750.00	0	145,340.68	511,044.86	101,000.00
Total	$461,475.00	$274,133.41	$283,806.27	$14,418.90	$1,175,182.40	$940,373.87	$424,811.36
Expenditures							
Communications media	0	0	0	0	0	0	0
Personal services, salaries, etc.	$298,770.86	101.27	54,506.84	0	220,633.38	98,286.80	0
Loans made	0	0	0	0	0	0	0
Other expenditures	0	202.57	37,645.49	11,899.13	502,636.95	538,576.78	201,000.00
Transfers out (to other committees)	8,000.00	112,930.44	149,200.00	5,000.00	196,836.97	129,158.97	28,700.00
Total	$306,770.86	$113,234.28	$241,352.33	$16,899.13	920,107.30	$766,022.55	$229,700.00

Source: Citizens Research Foundation

Advantages of the telethon, besides the amount of money raised, include getting large numbers of people involved in the political process and obtaining massive publicity for the Democratic Party. A major disadvantage is the overhead cost (about $2.5-million for Telethon III in June).

Funds from the telethons are divided during the national and state Democratic parties. The national committee made exclusive claim on money from the first telethon in 1972, but there was a 50-50 split with the states in 1973, and the state parties received two-thirds of the funds in 1974.

The Democrats have no state party quota system similar to that of the Republicans for contributions to their national committee. Besides the telethon, individual contributions and loans are the main sources of revenue. As with the Republicans, both individual persons and organizations contribute. Union funds are important; one of the largest givers in the first five months of 1974 was the Machinists Nonpartisan Political League, which gave $15,000.

The Democratic Finance Committee, unlike the Republican National Finance Committee, functions on a small scale, with most of its funds used to pay operational expenses and debts incurred during past campaigns.

Similarly to the Republican National Committee, the Democratic National Committee provides a variety of services to party candidates, including help in polling and fund-raising techniques and in research. Campaign schools or seminars are held for candidates from time to time around the country.

The Democrats established in 1974 a new committee to help raise funds for congressional candidates. It is a joint Senate-House venture called the Democratic Congressional Finance Committee. The main emphasis in fund-raising is on the development of a sustaining membership program and a dinner solicitation.

Funds from the new committee were to be divided on a 55-45 basis, 55 for the House. No direct-mail operations were under way; they were left to the Democratic Congressional Campaign Committee in the House and the Democratic Senatorial Campaign Committee.

The Democratic campaign committees for the House and Senate, like their Republican counterparts, provide services and cash for candidates. The provisions are made strictly on the basis of political need—the opportunity for capturing or holding a seat.

The chairman of the Democratic Congressional Campaign Committee is Rep. Wayne L. Hays (Ohio), the Senate Committee is headed by Sen. Lloyd Bentsen (Texas). ∎

DESPITE WATERGATE A TIGHTER SQUEEZE IN 1974

The 1974 campaign season should have been, according to some predictions, a fat time for liberal political fund-raising groups. Their *bete noire* for the past quarter century, Richard M. Nixon, faced possible impeachment. Republicans at all levels were on the defensive because of the Watergate scandal.

Yet the organizations that normally provide a large part of the money to finance the campaigns of liberal House and Senate challengers and incumbents hit lean times in 1974.

Most of them had the same problems—their contributions were off, their large contributors were giving less or not giving at all, and they had to scale down their fund-raising goals. The case of the National Committee for an Effective Congress, the grandfather of liberal money-raising groups, was typical. "In good years, our average contribution has run as high as $26 to $27," said the committee's V. Marie Bass. "But this year, our average contribution has dropped to $17."

The money shortage was not limited to liberal organizations. Democratic and Republican congressional fund raising dinners in Washington in early 1974 recorded lower receipts than usual. And many politicians reported that it was harder than usual to raise campaign funds.

But some liberal political operatives were worried by the fund-raising groups' woes. They feared that liberal candidates would suffer because of the unusual role these organizations play in campaign financing.

Richard P. Conlon, staff director of the House Democratic Study Group, warned, "We'll be in a bad bind this year. It's more than likely that we'll have less money this year, yet we'll have twice as many candidates in marginal districts to back."

Organizations and Their Roles

The main liberal political money-giving organizations are the National Committee for an Effective Congress, the Council for a Livable World, the Democratic Study Group, the Congressional Action Fund, George E. Agree's Campaign Fund, John R. Wagley's biennial committees and the League of Conservation Voters.

In 1972, they gave almost $1.1-million in direct campaign contributions and claimed to give another $640,000 in indirect contributions to candidates. An indirect contribution is one that an organization advises a contributor to give to a candidate but does not pass through the organization's treasury.

According to a Common Cause study of 1972 campaign contributions, liberal fund-raising groups gave 29 per cent of their contributions to incumbents, 44 per cent to challengers and 27 per cent to candidates in non-incumbent races. Ninety-one per cent of their contributions went to Democrats and only nine per cent to Republican candidates, the study found.

The groups reported giving contributions to more than 100 Democrats running for the House and Senate, but only a few Republicans. Among the Republican winners were Representatives Paul N. McCloskey Jr. (Calif.) and Joel Pritchard (Wash.) and Senators Edward W. Brooke (Mass.), Clifford P. Case (N.J.) and James B. Pearson (Kan.).

Several groups such as Agree's 1974 Campaign Fund, Wagley's committee and the Democratic Study Group have given exclusively to liberal Democrats. Others, such as the National Committee for an Effective Congress, the League of Conservation Voters, the Congressional Action Fund and the Council for a Livable World, contribute to liberal Republicans as well as Democrats. Yet they tend to concentrate on the Democrats because of ideological preference, the Democratic Party structure and candidates' money needs.

"The Republican Party is better financed and more homogeneous than the Democratic Party," explained political consultant Tom McCoy. "The Republican Party itself raises much more money, and it gives to all Republican candidates. The Democrats, on the other hand, are factionalized, and that tends to be reflected in their fund-raising. The party itself does not raise as much money, and thus there is a need for non-party fund-raising organizations for liberal Democrats."

George Agree, former director of the National Committee for an Effective Congress, called non-party fund-raising groups "inevitable in a heterogeneous party like the Democrats. Liberals are much more selective about which candidates get their money. They don't want to give to the party per se, because they don't want conservatives to get any of their money. Since the Democratic Party has such a diverse constituency, many liberals want to make sure their money reaches only liberal Democratic candidates. That's a major reason why you have these non-party fund-raising groups."

Aside from the Democratic Study Group, an organization of about 170 moderate and liberal House Democrats, the liberal fund-raisers have no ongoing lobbying programs and do not lobby for specific economic interests, as do labor unions, which also contribute heavily to Democratic and liberal candidates. Representatives of these groups occasionally testify before congressional committees or meet with members of Congress on issues such as campaign finance reform. Many of them, such as Wagley's committee, George Agree's Campaign Fund and the Congressional Action Fund, close down during non-election years.

Two New Competitors

While the fund-raising organizations are soliciting money, two newer groups that tend to be nonpartisan and issue-oriented are competing in the same basic constituency—Common Cause and the Women's Campaign Fund.

Some liberal fund-raisers are worried that Common Cause might be attracting new members and contributions at the expense of their organizations because of the effect of Watergate. "We might be seeing a shift of people from making political contributions to making contributions to issue-oriented groups like Common Cause," said Agree.

Common Cause's membership jumped in 1973, the year that the Watergate story unfolded, to 323,000. "We got 150,-000 new members that year for a net membership increase of 100,000," said Fred M. Wertheimer, a Common Cause official. However, he said he found "no indications that we're cutting into liberal fund-raising."

Common Cause was established in 1970 to serve as a nonpartisan citizens lobby on issues such as campaign finance and congressional reform. It does not make political contributions.

The Women's Campaign Fund was organized in February 1974 "for the sole purpose of raising funds to elect highly qualified, progressive women to federal and statewide offices." Its executive director is Maureen S. Aspin, wife of Rep. Les Aspin (D Wis.), and it operates out of a first-floor room in the Aspin townhouse in Washington's Georgetown section.

The fund supports "progressive" women candidates, but it purposely does not define what is a "progressive." "We didn't come up with a list of 10 issues to give us flexibility in making our choices," Aspin said. "We wanted to be able to take regional differences into account." The fund canvassed some liberal fund-raisers, the Republican Ripon Society and the congressional Republican Wednesday Group in search of women candidates to back.

Plans for 1974

As the 1974 fall elections approached, the liberal fund-raising groups were selecting candidates to support and were raising money. Following were their tentative plans:

● National Committee for an Effective Congress hoped to raise more than $1-million that would go to at least 80 candidates, said Russell D. Hemenway, its director. The committee's contributions to candidates were expected to average between $15,000 and $20,000 for Senate races and $2,000 to $3,000 for House contests, he said.

The committee contributed to candidates in four of the special congressional elections in early 1974. It gave $1,000 each to Representatives John P. Murtha (D Pa.), Richard F. Vander Veen (D Mich.), Thomas A. Luken (D Ohio) and Bob Traxler (D Mich.).

The committee started a new service to candidates it supports—subsidized political consulting headed by David Brunel, former administrative assistant to Rep. Donald W. Riegle Jr. (D Mich.). "We've set up a professional consulting service in-house for House challengers to help them in all facets of campaigning like media, budgeting and scheduling," said Hemenway. At least $200,000 was allocated to offer this special aid to about 40 of the candidates that would receive contributions.

● The Council for a Livable World planned to back at least 15 Senate incumbents and challengers, including Senators Adlai E. Stevenson III (D Ill.), Abraham A. Ribicoff (D Conn.), Frank Church (D Idaho) and Birch Bayh (D Ind.) and challengers William L. Guy (D N.D.) and Rep. Wayne Owens (D Utah). Charles E. Bosley, the council's Washington director, reported that the fund-raising response from the group's mailing list of 30,000 "is on the up side."

● The Congressional Action Fund hoped to raise $36,000 from its 1,200 members to give to 12 liberal House incumbents and challengers, its spokesman said. It already had contributed to three candidates: Rep. Patricia Schroeder (D Colo.), Floyd Fithian (D Ind.) and Julian Camacho (D Calif.).

● The 1974 Campaign Fund's response from mailings was "uneven," said Agree, its director. He had not yet selected which candidates to support.

● The Democratic Study Group had netted between $16,-000 and $18,000 from direct mail, which it contributed to Democratic candidates in the four House special elections in Ohio, Michigan and Pennsylvania. It also raised $50,000 at a fund-raising dinner in Washington in May. According to Conlon, the organization was eyeing at least 100 marginal races to give money to.

● John Wagley selected 16 non-incumbent Democratic House candidates to help for his Committee for Fifteen (he said he expected to drop one of the 16 later): Camacho of California, Fithian of Indiana, Hess Dyas (Neb.), Jim Florio (N.J.), Tom Harkin (Iowa), Kyle Hubbard (Ky.), John Krebs (Calif.), Andrew Maguire (N.J.), Abner Mikva (Ill.), Robert Mondragon (N.M.), Nina Miglionico (Ala.), Fran Ryan (Ohio), Philip Sharp (Ind.), Paul Simon (Ill.), Jack Weiland (S.D.) and Tim Wirth (Colo.). Wagley's number varies with elections.

● Marion Edey, the League of Conservation Voters' director, planned to raise $70,000 to contribute to federal and statewide candidates.

● The new Women's Campaign Fund, started with a $15,-000 loan from General Motors heir Stewart R. Mott, borrowed the direct-mail lists of several other organizations. Its first mailing went out in April and May, and Maureen Aspin reported contributions of nearly $12,-000 by mid-May. The money would go to five or six women candidates, both Republicans and Democrats, she said.

The Year's Peculiar Problems

The liberal fund-raising organizations reported running into serious problems raising money for the 1974 campaigns. While mailing costs had risen because of increased paper prices and postage rates, the average contribution to the groups had dropped off—in some cases by more than 25 per cent—and the number of large contributions had fallen significantly.

"Our average contribution in 1972 was $17," said the Democratic Study Group's Conlon, who relies heavily on direct mail to raise money. "It's $13 in 1974. For whatever reason, direct mailing is not producing this year what it has produced in the past."

According to political consultant Tom McCoy, "The $15 to $20 contribution has been coming in, but not the $500 to $1,000 contribution. It's those large contributions that raise the size of the average contribution in a direct mail campaign." Some fund-raisers said the number of small contributions had fallen off, too.

The fund-raisers cited several reasons for the dearth of political contributions: the supersaturation of the direct mail liberal constituency; Watergate and a pervasive public disillusionment with politicians in general; lack of an overriding issue; liberal overconfidence about the outcome of the fall elections; the sagging economy, and the 1973 Arab-Israeli war.

Supersaturation

Tom McCoy, finance director of the 1968 McCarthy presidential campaign, and Keith Haller, political director of Americans for Democratic Action (ADA), estimated the potential liberal fund-raising constituency at between one million to two million Americans.

These people are concentrated in the Northeast and on the West Coast, home of many contributors to the National Committee for an Effective Congress, and in what McCoy called the "export states for liberal money"—California, New York, Massachusetts, Connecticut and New Jersey.

It was to these people that the mailings went from the National Committee for an Effective Congress, the Democratic Study Group Campaign Fund, the Committee for Fifteen, the Council for a Livable World and other liberal fund-raising groups. Several fund-raisers were worried that the mailing lists had been overused, especially after the high point of direct mailing to liberals in George McGovern's 1972 presidential drive. "When you swap lists with magazines and other organizations, there are only a certain number of people in that base constituency," said the ADA's Haller.

Conlon of the Democratic Study Group complained that "everybody's gotten into direct mail today. Without any question, there's an awful overlap now with direct mail fund-raising, since there's an incestuous relationship between the groups. They share each other's mailing lists. We've reached the point where we're having super-saturation. There are just too many groups."

At least one organization—the Council for a Livable World—was trying to avoid this problem. "In the past year and a half," said McCoy, "the council has spent a lot of money expanding its list. It made a concerted effort to build up its mailing list in the off year beyond its original 12,000 names to at least 30,000."

Political Disorientation

The money-raising difficulties, however, went beyond the overuse and duplication of mailing lists. They became entangled in Watergate and its accompanying political malaise. "This whole Watergate thing has disoriented the political patterns of the country," complained George Agree. "To some degree, it has turned off some liberals from politics and political giving."

The Nixon administration's fund-raising scandals also hurt liberal fund-raisers. The Congressional Action Fund's Fleischaker found "a real stigma attached to political contributions now. Some people are hesitant about anything related to the notion of political contributions."

Some larger liberal contributors reportedly withheld their usual political contributions in 1974 to try to force Congress to enact a law for public financing of federal election campaigns. "The expectation that we'll have some sort of public financing and the propaganda against private financing has tended to turn off some people who'd give," said Agree.

And some liberals felt there was no great need to contribute because of their expectations of liberal successes at the polls. "Some of our long-time loyal contributors are saying this year, 'Well, all liberal candidates are going to win, so we don't need to give any money,' " said Bass.

The Economy

The slumping economy had also cut liberal political contributions by leaving people with less money to give. "With the stock market in terrible shape," said McCoy, "some of the large contributors don't have their stock dividends or stock gains to give away."

Arab-Israeli War

A sizable share of contributions to liberal political fund-raising organizations usually comes from Jews, many liberal fund-raisers reported. A great deal of that money was given to Israel after the October 1973 Yom Kippur War, "draining much of the traditional liberal money," according to Marie Bass.

No Overriding Issue

With the end of the Vietnam war, liberal fund-raising organizations lost their main issue of the late 1960s and early 1970s. "A major issue like Vietnam was a great catalyst for fund-raising," said ADA's Keith Haller.

Liberal organizations were casting about but were having a difficult time finding new issues, and some fund-raisers doubted whether groups set up primarily to raise money for anti-war liberals could survive the 1974 campaign. "The malaise in Congress isn't an issue you can sell people on," said Haller. "It's very hard to sell people on a positive issue. The problem with direct mail is that its success depends on picking the right issue with appeal."

Impeachment was one of the issues before the country as election day approached. Yet liberal fund-raisers tended to shy away from using it to raise money. "Impeachment would be the major issue for the liberal community," said Conlon. "But we don't even mention it in our mailings. We don't want impeachment to become a partisan issue."

1972 Spending

Of the seven liberal fund-raising groups that Congressional Quarterly surveyed for 1972, the National Committee for an Effective Congress was the largest fund-raiser and contributor to candidates. Common Cause reported that the committee gave after April 7, 1972 (the date that the 1971 Federal Election Campaign Act became effective), $393,888 to 88 House and Senate candidates—80 Democrats, five Republicans, two independents and one Liberal; 15 Senate and 73 House candidates; 31 incumbents, 26 challengers and 21 candidates in non-incumbent races. More than $232,000 went to Senate races and $161,650 to House races, Common Cause stated.

The Groups and Their Leaders

Organization	Date Founded	Director
National Committee for an Effective Congress	1948	Russell D. Hemenway, national director
Democratic Study Group	1959	Richard P. Conlon, staff director
Council for a Livable World	1962	William Doering, president Charles E. Bosley, Washington director
Campaign Fund	1968	George E. Agree, director
League of Conservation Voters	1969	Marion Edey, director
Committee for Fifteen	1970	John R. Wagley, director
Congressional Action Fund	1970	Pam Fleischaker, director
Women's Campaign Fund	1974	Maureen S. Aspin, executive director

In a report issued at the end of 1972, the committee said it gave $525,000 directly as well as funneling another $440,500 indirectly to candidates. The committee's figures included contributions made between Jan. 1 and April 7, 1972, which the organization was not required to include in its campaign spending reports filed with Congress.

The Council for a Livable World contributed $31,250 of its funds to six Democratic Senate candidates, according to Common Cause. They were Senators Floyd K. Haskell (Colo.), Joe Biden (Del.), Dick Clark (Iowa), William D. Hathaway (Maine) and James Abourezk (S.D.) and William E. Davis, an unsuccessful candidate in Idaho. However, the council reported in December 1972 that its members had indirectly contributed almost $201,000 in additional funds to the six candidates and to another seven candidates, including Senators Lee Metcalf (D Mont.), Pearson of Kansas and Case of New Jersey.

The Congressional Action Fund gave $37,430 to 20 House candidates (17 Democrats, two Republicans and one Liberal), Common Cause reported.

George Agree's 1972 Campaign Fund contributed $97,000. The Common Cause study showed 10 Democratic Senate candidates receiving contributions of $5,000 to $19,000. Recipients included Senators Walter (Dee) Huddleston (Ky.) and Claiborne Pell (R.I.) and three unsuccessful contenders—Davis of Idaho, Frank Kelley (Mich.) and Nick Galifianakis (N.C.).

Ninety-four House Democratic incumbents and challengers received $175,500 from the Democratic Study Group, according to Common Cause. Conlon, the organization's director, said 60 per cent of the contributions went to non-incumbents and 40 per cent to incumbents.

John Wagley's Committee for Twelve contributed $165,136 to a dozen liberal Democratic candidates for the House, Common Cause said.

The League of Conservation Voters, according to the Common Cause study, gave $59,501 to 13 House and Senate candidates. The league reported contributing another $11,000 to the unsuccessful gubernatorial campaigns of Gov. Russell Peterson (R Del.) and Secretary of State John D. (Jay) Rockefeller IV (D W.Va.).

A 26-Year History

Today's liberal fund-raising organizations date back to 1948, when the National Committee for an Effective Congress was established to aid liberal and internationalist congressional candidates. The committee had the field to itself through the early 1960s, when other groups began to be formed to raise money for liberal candidates for federal office.

The Council for a Livable World, an organization directed mainly at the liberal academic community, was founded in 1962 by the late Leo Szilard, a University of Chicago nuclear physicist. Interested mainly in the arms control issue, the group concentrates on Senate contests.

Set up in 1959 by Democratic liberal representatives, the Democratic Study Group made a start at fund-raising for liberal House incumbents and challengers in 1966, but it did not begin its concerted program until 1968, when Conlon became staff director. It is a quasi-party organization, unlike the other groups, which are not officially affiliated with the Democratic Party. Much of its work centers around research on legislative issues.

The Vietnam war, the subsequent split in the Democratic Party and the rise of the environmental issue spawned several new liberal fund-raising groups in the late 1960s and early 1970s. George Agree, who had headed the National Committee for an Effective Congress for 16 years, left in 1966 to establish his own money-raising operations for liberal Democrats running for the Senate. He ran the 1968, 1970, 1972 and 1974 Agree Campaign Funds.

Two smaller groups that concentrated on raising money for anti-war liberals running for the House were started in 1970 just after the invasion of Cambodia. They were the Congressional Action Fund and John R. Wagley's Committee for Ten.

A spin-off of the environmental movement, the League of Conservation Voters is not strictly a liberal fund-raising group, although it supports liberal candidates. Founded in 1969, it concentrates on helping elect candidates who take strong environmental stands and on defeating incumbents with poor environmental records.

Direct Mail

The proliferation of liberal fund-raising organizations has coincided with the rise of mass mail solicitation for political contributions in the 1960s.

The National Committee for an Effective Congress started using direct mail in 1948 "on a pretty selective basis" to raise money, according to Maurice Rosenblatt, the organization's founder. However, the group relied mainly on receptions, cocktail parties and personal solicitation of large contributors to raise money.

The major political parties and other liberal fund-raising groups did not start using direct mail until the early 1960s. The first massive political mailing was done by Sen. Barry Goldwater (R Ariz.) and the Republican Party in the 1964 presidential campaign. The 1964 Republican mailings raised about $1.1-million from 300,000 different contributors.

The Democratic Study Group made its first mailing in 1966 and started relying on large mailings for fund-raising two years later. It has also used fund-raising dinners between election years, but it broke that pattern by holding a $125-a-plate fund-raising dinner May 15 that raised about $50,000.

The Council for a Livable World started initially with a fund drive on university campuses and quickly moved into direct mail. Its staff also steers contributors to candidates it supports.

In 1968, George Agree started raising money for his Senate campaign fund via direct mail. By that time, the National Committee for an Effective Congress had developed a mailing list of 80,000 people for fund-raising; it keeps the list up to date. However, it also relies on other fund-raising approaches, because it raises only slightly more than half of its money through mass mailings, said Hemenway, its national director since 1966. The remaining money is collected directly, he said, from large contributors.

The committee also indirectly contributes money to candidates by advising its contributors on which races need money.

The League of Conservation Voters relies strictly on direct mail. It uses its mailing list of 10,000 as well as environmental mailing lists. "We stay away from the standard liberal lists. They're overused," said Marion Edey, its director.

1972 Activities of the Liberal Fund-Raising Groups

Organization	Mailing List*	Support*	1972 Contributions (number of candidates backed)**	Total 1972 Expenditures**	Percentage of Expenditures Used for Contributions**
National Committee for an Effective Congress	80,000	Bipartisan, House and Senate candidates in primary and general elections.	$393,888 to 88 candidates	$669,926	59 per cent
Council for a Livable World	30,000	Bipartisan, Senate candidates in primary and general elections	$31,250 to six candidates	$165,966	19 per cent
Congressional Action Fund	1,200	Bipartisan, House candidates in primary and general elections	$37,430 to 20 candidates	$101,919	37 per cent
1972 Campaign Fund	80,000	Democratic Senate candidates in general elections	$97,000 to 10 candidates	$210,945	46 per cent
Democratic Study Group	25,000	Democratic House candidates in general elections	$175,500 to 94 candidates	$251,718	70 per cent
Committee for Twelve	63,000	Democratic non-incumbents running for the House in general elections	$165,136 to 12 candidates	$189,913	87 per cent
League of Conservation Voters	10,000	Bipartisan, House, Senate and state-wide candidates in primary and general elections	$59,501 to 13 candidates for federal office	$ 80,833	74 per cent
Women's Campaign Fund	None	Bipartisan, women candidates for federal and statewide offices in in primary and general elections	Established in 1974		

* SOURCE: Organizations
** SOURCE: *Common Cause Study of 1972 Federal Campaign Finances: Interest Groups and Political Parties.* Study based on figures in 1972 campaign spending reports filed by the groups for the period after April 7, 1972.

The Congressional Action Fund used small receptions and cocktail parties to gather its money after it was established in 1970; but in 1974, it was using more mail solicitations.

John Wagley's biennial committees (10 in 1970, 12 in 1972 and 16 in 1974) are direct-mail operations. Wagley started with the list of contributors from the 1968 presidential bid of former Sen. Eugene J. McCarthy (D Minn. 1959-71) and has expanded the list to 63,000.

The organizations use a wide variety of mailing lists to reach contributors. The lists include magazines such as *The New Republic, Progressive, Commentary* and *Center* and civil rights and civil liberties groups.

The five large lists that reach liberal Democrats, according to several fund-raisers, have been developed by the National Committee for an Effective Congress, George E. Agree, the Democratic National Committee, the McGovern presidential campaign and Washington Information Associates, another Wagley group.

Where the Money Goes

The decisions on which candidates receive their support from the liberal fund-raisers are usually made by a single person or a small group.

John Wagley himself decides which challengers will receive his committee's money. He concentrates on liberal Democratic non-incumbents running for the House.

Wagley's fund-raising operation is different from the others in that he charges candidates for the contributions he raises. Each candidate he supported in 1974 was asked to put up $1,000 to help cover the cost of the initial mailing. That money was to be returned as soon as possible after the mailing is sent out, said Wagley, and the candidates were to be charged a fee of $500 a month while he sent out fund-raising mailings for them during the campaign.

The board of the National Committee for an Effective Congress decides on contributions. It receives recommendations from Hemenway, its national director.

George Agree relies on an allocations committee to decide where his campaign fund's contributions go.

The Congressional Action Fund lets its members make the final decision on contributions after it presents them with a list to vote on. "I picked 12 (House) races based on need, winnability, good guy versus bad guy," said Pam Fleischaker, the fund's director. "Our board winnowed the list down to five candidates, and we sent our members a ballot with the five names and asked them to vote for three."

The five Democrats on the fund's ballot were Julian Camacho (Calif.), Floyd Fithian (Ind.), Andrew Jacobs (Ind.), Dick McCormack (Pa.) and incumbent Patricia Schroeder (D Colo.). Schroeder, Camacho and Fithian won.

The League of Conservation Voters relies on a steering committee of environmentalists to select the candidates to be supported. ∎

NEW HOPE WITH THE FORD ADMINISTRATION

Conservatives might have been disenchanted with the moderate tone of President Ford's first weeks in office, but some of them found cheer in their adversity. For the President's nomination of Nelson A. Rockefeller, the long-time symbol of eastern liberal Republicanism, as Vice President gave them a new rallying cry to raise money for right-wing candidates for the 1974 congressional elections.

"Rockefeller will help us in a negative sense," predicted Wayne J. Thorburn, head of the Young America's Campaign Committee, a conservative fund-raising organization with close ties to Young Americans for Freedom. "He's the symbol of liberal Republicanism, and he's a negative pole to rally against to raise money."

Until Rockefeller's nomination, right-wing political fund-raisers were dispirited over their 1974 prospects. The last months of the Nixon presidency, as the Watergate scandal closed in, were especially gloomy for them. "Our people out there were getting a hopeless feeling when they saw Nixon hanging on and the polls showing a Democratic landslide," said Ronald B. Dear, executive director of the American Conservative Union and its Conservative Victory Fund. The feeling showed in fund-raising receipts. Thorburn reported that his group's average contribution was $9 in 1974, off from $13 in 1972.

The climate brightened somewhat when Gerald R. Ford became President Aug. 9. Conservative fund-raisers such as Thomas S. Winters, treasurer of the Conservative Victory Fund and editor of *Human Events*, a weekly right-wing newspaper, sensed that raising money would be easier with Watergate behind them. "In the brief period since Nixon's resignation, there's been an increase in optimism," he said six days after Nixon had stepped down. But Winters and other conservatives could not gauge then how Ford would affect their fortunes.

Plans for 1974

Despite their growing optimism about the post-Nixon political climate, the conservative fund-raisers' election strategy and fund-raising plans already had been shaped by the dismal political prospects brought about by the impeachment proceedings during spring and summer. The leading right-wing money-raising organizations were the Conservative Victory Fund, an arm of the American Conservative Union; the Young America's Campaign Committee; the Americans for Constitutional Action, and the Committee for Responsible Youth Politics.

At that time, it appeared that Republicans, especially conservatives, would be in serious trouble in the fall elections and that a Democratic landslide was inevitable. The organizations decided that they had to concentrate on saving incumbents such as Representatives Harold V. Froehlich (R Wis.) and Robert J. Huber (R Mich.) rather than on electing new conservatives to Congress, as they did in 1972.

The decision of the Conservative Victory Fund, the largest right-wing political fund-raising organization, was typical. "In 1972, mainly challengers got money," said Dear.

"This year, when we looked at the situation, we decided to try to save incumbents in marginal seats."

The conservatives hammered away at the "veto-proof" Congress issue to raise money before Nixon resigned. "Will big labor's challenge be met?" the Conservative Victory Fund asked in its March fund-raising mailing. In a brochure that featured on its red cover a cigar-puffing, wheeler-dealer AFL-CIO President George Meany with a "Big Labor Rubber Stamp Congress" perched on his knee, the Fund warned that "Big Labor" planned "a massive effort...to defeat conservative congressional candidates." The brochure called on conservatives to contribute to foil labor's goal. It also played on the "fed up with Watergate" theme in another mailing by asking what Congress had done about inflation, an anti-busing amendment and federal spending cuts while liberals wallowed in Watergate.

To raise money, a fund-raiser needs a "believable issue," said conservative direct-mail fund-raiser Richard A. Viguerie. The victory fund's warnings apparently were believable. Its March mailing to 50,000 names netted $36,000, according to Dear, and a high direct-mail response rate of 6 per cent.

The extent of the conservative fund-raising organizations' change in strategy from 1972 to 1974 could be seen in the political contributions they made through mid-August 1974. Thirty-seven per cent of their money went to incumbents and 63 per cent to non-incumbents and challengers in open districts, a marked shift from the 25 per cent-75 per cent pattern of two years earlier.

In 1972, the Conservative Victory Fund gave money to six incumbent members of Congress and 47 non-incumbents. The incumbents received $6,500 and the non-incumbents, $106,535. By mid-August 1974, the fund had contributed $23,000 to 13 incumbents and $38,150 to 22 non-incumbents.

The Young America's Campaign Committee also concentrated on helping incumbents in 1974. "We'll end up supporting 20 incumbent congressmen and 15 challengers this year," said Thorburn. By mid-August, his group had given money to seven incumbents and only three non-incumbents.

New Groups

Two new conservative fund-raising operations had been set up earlier in the summer to supplement the money raised by other organizations. They were the Committee for the Survival of a Free Congress, planned only for the 1974 elections, and the Gulf South Political Science Foundation.

The Washington-based Committee for the Survival of a Free Congress was basically an incumbent-saving operation established to protect conservative Republican strength on the Hill. "It appeared that we needed a new vehicle to raise funds," said Paul W. Weyrich, the prime mover behind the committee and an assistant to Sen. Carl T. Curtis (R Neb.), " since this was going to be a difficult year for conservatives because of Watergate." Conservative Republican strength in Congress was threatened, he said, both by Watergate and the retirement of incumbents. "The philosophical views of Republicans seeking those open seats are not always in line with ours," Weyrich said.

The Gulf South Political Science Foundation was established to aid conservative southern Republicans. Headed by James C. Plummer, a 27-year-old politician from New Orleans, the foundation disclosed in its registration form filed with the clerk of the House that it would aid the campaigns of five incumbents and 11 non-incumbents. "There's a much better chance for conservative candidates to be elected from the South," Plummer said. "It won't take as much money to elect candidates from the rural South as in the industrialized Northeast or West."

Fund-raising Goals

Conservative fund-raising organizations, which traditionally had raised much less money than liberal groups, hoped in 1974 to surpass their 1972 figure of more than $130,000. But several fund-raisers doubted they would exceed that by much, if at all, because of Watergate and inflation.

The Conservative Victory Fund had contributed $61,-350 to candidates by August 1974 and hoped "to top 1972" when it gave away $113,035, said Dear. The fund, he added, was preparing to start a new fund-raising push after Labor Day, using its house mailing list.

The Young America's Campaign Committee planned to contribute between $20,000 and $25,000 to candidates in 1974.

The Committee for Responsible Youth Politics, which contributed $11,000 in 1972, scaled down its effort in 1974. "We're making more limited contributions this year," reported Morton A. Blackwell, its chairman. "We're putting more money into campaign schools to train youth coordinators for conservative campaigns." Through mid-August, the committee had given $3,500 to four House campaigns—those of former Rep. George V. Hansen (R Idaho 1965-1969), Rep. John M. Ashbrook (R Ohio), State Sen. Lawrence (Pete) Naaden (R N.D.) and Republican nominee Charles E. Grassley (Iowa).

The Committee for the Survival of a Free Congress raised about $25,000 through mid-August and had set a fund-raising goal of between $50,000 and $75,000 for 1974. But Weyrich acknowledged that the response to the group's first direct mailing effort was "not overwhelming."

The newly formed Gulf South Political Science Foundation would "like to raise about $200,000 for candidates," its executive director said. Plummer, who traveled to New York in late August to meet with prospective large contributors, reported that several large right-wing donors "were stand-offish because of Watergate and because we're a new organization."

The Americans for Constitutional Action (ACA), the oldest of the existing conservative fund-raising organizations, stopped making direct contributions to candidates in 1974 because of severe money problems that almost forced the organization to fold. In 1972, it gave $6,532 to 14 House and Senate candidates. "We can't allocate large sums of money to candidates," lamented Charles A. McManus, ACA's president. "We'll be shifting completely to contributions in kind and will continue our opposition research work and our boiler room work."

Although ACA never contributed large sums of money directly to candidates, it had in the past steered contributions to them. It claimed in its 1972 annual report to have indirectly contributed $114,475 to candidates.

Conservative Who's Who

Organizations	Founded	Leaders
Americans for Constitutional Action	1959	Charles A. McManus, president
Young Americans for Freedom	1960	Ronald F. Docksai, chairman
American Conservative Union	1965	M. Stanton Evans, chairman Ronald B. Dear, executive director
Young America's Campaign Committee	1969	Wayne J. Thorburn, executive director
Conservative Victory Fund	1970	Rep. John M. Ashbrook (R Ohio), chairman Ronald B. Dear, executive director
Committee for Responsible Youth Politics	1972	Morton A. Blackwell, chairman
Committee for the Survival of a Free Congress	1974	Robert J. Casey, chairman
Gulf South Political Science Foundation	1974	James C. Plummer, executive director

McManus said he hoped to "steer" more than $75,000 to candidates in 1974. An indirect contribution is one that an organization advises a contributor to give to a candidate but does not pass through the organization's treasury.

Unlike the other conservative fund-raising organizations that concentrated on direct contributions to candidates, ACA long specialized in what McManus affectionately referred to as "boiler room work." By that he meant sponsoring luncheons, cocktail parties and dinners for candidates to which lobbyists—McManus always called them "Washington representatives"—would be invited. "Cocktail circuit fund-raising is much more difficult now because of Watergate," he complained. "Washington representatives and corporations are much less prone to participate."

In 1973, ACA helped organize Washington fund-raisers for Senators Robert Dole (R Kan.), Edward J. Gurney (R Fla.) and Peter H. Dominick (R Colo.) and Representatives Barry M. Goldwater Jr. (R Calif.) and Dan Kuykendall (R Tenn.). In 1974, ACA set up receptions for House Minority Leader John J. Rhodes (R Ariz.) and Representatives Edward J. Derwinski (R Ill.) and Albert W. Johnson (R Pa.), among others.

Fourteen candidates had been singled out for major help and had received contributions of more than $1,000 each from the Conservative Victory Fund, the Young America's Campaign Committee and the Committee for Responsible Youth Politics by mid-August 1974. They were incumbent Representatives Robert E. Bauman (R Md.), $3,200; Marjorie S. Holt (R Md.), $1,400; Ashbrook, $1,200; Dale Milford (D Texas), $2,000; Harold V. Froehlich (R Wis.), $10,000; John E. Hunt (R N.J.), $2,000, and Robert J. Huber (R Mich.), $1,500.

The non-incumbents were three House Republican candidates—former Young Americans For Freedom head J. Alan MacKay (Mass.), $5,950; former Rep. George Hansen of Idaho, $3,500, and Charles E. Grassley (Iowa), $1,500; two Republicans who lost House primary races, Gordon Knapp (Calif.), $4,000, and Michael J. Feld (Iowa),

(Continued on p. 53)

Wallace's Well-Financed List-Building Efforts

While conservative fund-raisers were trying to raise money for the 1974 congressional elections, Gov. George C. Wallace (D Ala.) was looking ahead to the 1976 presidential election and spending hundreds of thousands of dollars to add more names to his already large and successful fund-raising mailing list.

Between August 1973 and September 1974, the Wallace campaign committee in Montgomery, Ala., paid nearly $800,000 to the Richard A. Viguerie Company, Inc., a Falls Church, Va., direct mail company, to "prospect" for new names for the Wallace list. Charles S. Snider, Wallace's national campaign director, told Congressional Quarterly that the expensive effort was being undertaken with an eye on 1976. "In 1976, if the governor runs," he said, "we'll have the largest, most sophisticated mailing list in the business."

Enter Viguerie

To expand its mailing list, the Wallace operation turned to Richard A. Viguerie, a Republican who ran the most successful conservative direct mail business in the country. Until he took over the Alabama governor's account, the 40-year-old former executive secretary of the right-wing Young Americans for Freedom never had worked for a Democratic politician. "I've handled Republicans, mainly conservative Republicans, in the past," he said. "This is a new departure for us."

A 13-year veteran of direct mail fund-raising, Viguerie set up his own company in 1964. Ten years later, it had 200 employees, owned its computers and had more than four million names on tapes. It was the leading direct-mail firm for conservative causes and had handled the accounts of the American Conservative Union, the Committee for the Survival of a Free Congress and Rep. John M. Ashbrook's (R Ohio) 1972 presidential effort.

The Wallace campaign committee hired Viguerie in June 1973 to take over its direct mail camaign. "We were looking for a firm like this primarily to develop new names," Snider explained. "Since 1968, we didn't pay as much attention to capturing and keeping new names."

In the past, Wallace had maintained two lists: a smaller contributor list and a much larger favorable supporter list. Viguerie was retained to find more "salable supporters" of Wallace who could be tapped later for campaign contributions.

A large, up-to-date mailing list could give Wallace an advantage over other presidential candidates in 1976 if campaign finance reform legislation became law. At the very least, the new law would introduce partial public financing of presidential primary campaigns and would require candidates to raise a minimim of $100,000 in small contributions from at least 20 states to qualify for federal matching grants.

Wallace would have no problem raising that money, because he already would have developed his national mailing list. If the existing system of campaign financing were not changed, Wallace still could be far ahead of other contenders, because he would have laid a massive fund-raising base.

1973 Spending Reports

Wallace campaign spending reports for the first five months of 1974 filed with the General Accounting Office disclosed that Viguerie had not been hired, at least at that time, to raise money for Wallace. Between Jan. 1 and May 31, 1974, the Wallace committee reported total receipts of $758,334. However, the committee reported expenditures of $640,835, leaving it with net receipts of $117,499.

During that time, the Wallace operation paid Viguerie $396,407 for "printing, mailing fees, postage, computer processing and programming, and raw computer time" and other expenses, according to the reports. Viguerie also received $384,266 from the Alabama organization between late August and December 1973.

"We figure that any time you break even on a prospecting operation, you're in good shape," Snider said.

Viguerie started out with the old combined Wallace mailing list of one million names, which he trimmed to 750,000. He used other mailing lists owned by his firm, and outside lists of conservatives, *Saturday Evening Post* subscribers, buyers of Hank Williams books, Democrats, firemen and policemen to build the Wallace list of "salable supporters" past the two-million mark. Snider put the contributor list at about 200,000 names.

By September 1974, Viguerie had sent out three mailings for Wallace: a presidential preference poll, a general solicitation and a commemorative coin solicitation. Wallace operatives reported that their mailing lists had been computerized to isolate Wallace supporters by postal zip code, occupation and income.

A Boost from Hargis

Wallace's campaign director said he approached Viguerie to take the governor's direct mail account because "we found that Viguerie was involved with conservative individuals and organizations and involved with religious groups like Rev. Billy James Hargis' Christian Crusade. We got good references on Viguerie from Rev. Hargis," Snider added.

Viguerie, who called himself a Republican although "I consider myself a conservative," was receptive to the Wallace approach. "Recently, the Republican Party has gotten away from standing for things," he said. "What do Nixon and Ford stand for?" he asked. "Vague, general nonentities. Eighty-five per cent of what the Republican Party stood for went out the window under Nixon. Conservatives are looking to Wallace for leadership in this area. The Republican Party is no longer seen by conservatives as a vehicle of conservatism. They see the need for a third party. This is the way I feel. With Wallace, I feel philosophically comfortable."

However, he maintained that his work for Wallace was strictly a "business arrangement."

That claim did not stop some conservative observers from speculating that Viguerie's work for Wallace was more than just a business arrangement. Several sources suggested that Viguerie's work for Wallace was an indication that some conservatives were moving away from the Republican Party toward a new, right-wing party.

(Continued from p. 51)
$2,750, and two Republican Senate candidates, H. L. (Bill) Richardson (Calif.), $4,000, and Leo Thorsness (S.D.), $8,000.

Two of the House candidates supported took on moderate Republicans in primaries. Knapp was narrowly defeated by Paul N. McCloskey Jr. (R Calif.), while George V. Hansen upset Orval Hansen (R Idaho).

The Groups and Their Roles

Conservative fund-raising organizations are smaller than their liberal counterparts, raise less money, give to fewer candidates and are much more intensely motivated ideologically. Their *raison d'etre*, as *Human Events* editor Winters explained it, "is to get more conservative representation in Congress." They want to elect not just conservatives but committed, ideological conservatives who will score high on the Americans for Constitutional Action and American Conservative Union vote ratings.

1972 Spending

A look at how the conservatives distributed their money in 1972 gives a good picture of their aims, their operations and their relationship with the Republican Party.

The three conservative groups monitored by Common Cause in 1972—The Conservative Victory Fund, Americans for Constitutional Action and the Committee for Responsible Youth Politics—contributed $128,742 to 58 candidates, all Republicans except for two conservative Republicans running as independents and a single Democrat, Rep. Bill Chappell Jr. (Fla.). Incumbents received about 25 per cent of the contributions, challengers about 28 per cent and candidates in non-incumbent races about 47 per cent.

The major recipients of conservative money who were elected were Representatives David C. Treen (R La.), Robert J. Huber (R Mich.), Steven D. Symms (R Idaho), Trent Lott (R Miss.) and Harold V. Froehlich (R Wis.) and Senators Jesse Helms (R N.C.) and Pete V. Domenici (R N.M.). Major recipients who lost were House Republican candidates William Pfender and William Hunt of Pennsylvania and Bill Kidd (Wyo.), and Republican Senate candidates Henry Hibbard (Mont.), Wesley Powell (N.H.), Robert Hirsch (S.D.), Louie Nunn (Ky.) and Fletcher Thompson (Ga.).

The Conservative Victory Fund, which contributed the bulk of the money, gave to 23 House candidates, including six incumbents who were elected, 22 unsuccessful House candidates, three Senate candidates who won and five who were defeated.

In dollar amounts, these conservative groups were outspent by liberal fund-raising organizations by 7-to-1 and gave to about half as many candidates as the liberals did. Unlike the liberal groups, which gave about 8 per cent of the $1.1-million they raised to Republican candidates, the conservative organizations gave money to only one Democrat ($2,000) and did not look for any other Democrats to give money to. *(Liberal fund-raisers, p. 45)*

Who Gets The Money

While the right-wing groups gave almost exclusively to Republicans, they were selective about which Republicans received their largess. "The beauty of groups like the Conservative Victory Fund over the Republican Congressional Campaign Committee is that they can reward ideological purity," according to Edwin Feulner, executive director of the House Republican Steering Committee, a coalition of conservative Republican representatives.

"The Senate and House Republican Campaign Committees have to give across the board," complained Winters. "Some of the money goes to liberals like Sen. Charles McC. Mathias Jr. (R Md.) and Jacob K. Javits (R N.Y.). We don't have to do that."

The rewards to ideologically pure candidates can be great, especially in special congressional elections such as Bauman's race in 1973 to replace Rep. William O. Mills (R Md. 1971-73), who committed suicide. Bauman, a former executive director of the Young Americans for Freedom and an American Conservative Union activist, received $15,000, or 17 per cent of the $86,500 he raised for his campaign, from five right-wing organizations—the American Conservative Union ($2,500), the Conservative Victory Fund ($4,500), the Committee for Responsible Youth Politics ($3,500), the Young America's Campaign Committee ($500) and the Congressional Victory Fund ($4,000), an F. Clifton White operation that raised money from contributors to Sen. James L. Buckley's (Cons-R N.Y.) 1970 campaign.

Rep. Philip M. Crane (R Ill.), a member of the board of directors of the Conservative Victory Fund, called himself "a conservative before I'm a Republican," and that best summed up the conservative fund-raisers' view of themselves within the Republican Party and where they placed their loyalty.

Almost all the conservative fund-raisers and activists surveyed by Congressional Quarterly agreed that the Republican Party, especially its congressional wing, was most hospitable to their philosophy and that the House Republicans were predominantly conservative. "Our role," as Crane saw it, "is to strengthen the hand of that dominant element in the Republican Party."

Not all congressional Republicans, however, welcomed the conservatives' push for purity, and not all conservatives were as intensely motivated ideologically.

Conservative Split

Conservative fund-raisers, in fact, were split along generational lines, with younger conservatives taking a much more rigid, activist position than their elders. The flagship of the younger group was the American Conservative Union and its fund-raising arm, the Conservative Victory Fund. The officers and directors of the fund included a who's who of the conservative movement and what one observer called the Reaganite wing of the Republican Party, named after California Gov. Ronald Reagan. Members were Ashbrook, Bauman, Crane, *Human Events* editor Winters, Ronald F. Docksai, chairman of Young Americans for Freedom (YAF), J. Daniel Mahoney, chairman of the New York Conservative Party, and William A. Rusher, publisher of *The National Review*.

Other heads of conservative fund-raising organizations included Blackwell of the Committee for Responsible Youth Politics and Thorburn, a former executive director of Young Americans for Freedom, of the Young America's Campaign Committee. The groups tended to mix socially and politically. Their leaders were mostly in their early to middle 30s, and they looked to the American Conservative Union (ACU) for leadership. For example, Thorburn reported that the Young America's Campaign Committee, which had YAF Executive Director Docksai on its board, "gets recommendations from ACU and YAF on where to make contributions." Two officials of the American Conservative Union, Dear and Winters, were on the 12-member board of the Committee for Responsible Youth Politics.

The groups were a product of the aggressive conservative movement led by *National Review* editor William F. Buckley in the early 1960s and intensified by the 1964 Goldwater presidential campaign. The American Conservative Union was formed in 1965 and established the Victory Fund in 1970. Young Americans for Freedom, the oldest of the younger generation conservative organizations, was established in 1960, but the Young America's Campaign Committee was not set up until 1969. The Committee for Responsible Youth Politics did not get started until early 1972.

ACA vs. ACU

The oldest of the conservative political-ideological organizations was Americans for Constitutional Action, which was formed in 1959. Its head was McManus, a 47-year old former employee of U.S. Steel from Pennsylvania's Bucks County. ACA concentrated not only on analyzing the voting record of every representative and senator on a scale of "constitutional conservatism," but on giving direct and in-kind contributions to candidates and steering indirect contributions to them. All the candidates receiving its help were Republicans.

For a long time, ACA's chief sponsor was retired Navy Adm. Ben Moreel, organizer of the Seabees and former president of Jones and Laughlin Steel Company. But Moreel resigned as chairman of the organization's board in 1969 and retired completely in 1973, and McManus acknowledged that "we're having trouble finding a new chairman. We've been looking for a long time."

The ACA's leadership problems were symptomatic of its financial problems. Its contributions and interest on deposits dropped from $144,400 in 1972 to $102,325 in 1973, according to its annual reports. Its revenues had already been uneven before that. Its annual expenditures, the reports showed, also dropped from $106,725 in 1968 to $78,-600 in 1973.

In early 1974, ACA had a financial crisis. "We've always operated in the black," said McManus, "but we got to the position where the executive committee felt that unless there was an infusion of new blood on the board and we got a viable cash operating fund, we should terminate operations." McManus sent out a fund-raising letter to the organization's financial backers that, he said, generated "sufficient operating funds to let us do some but not all that we want to do."

Younger, American Conservative Union-oriented conservatives scoffed at ACA. "Charlie is very much a mainstream Republican. He likes to be in with the party," jibed one activist. "That's why you see him having fund-raisers for not staunchly conservative Republicans."

Thorburn said of ACA, "They're not too much plugged into the conservative movement in Washington. They don't mix with other social gatherings here. I've met McManus maybe twice in my whole life. I'd expect to have met him more."

Moderate Republicans in Congress preferred ACA to the American Conservative Union. "There's a substantial amount of rapport between ACA and Hill Republicans," said one source. One reason was ACA's vote ratings. They tended to give moderate Republicans higher "conservative" ratings than the more ideologically oriented American Conservative Union ratings. For example, Rep. John B. Anderson (R Ill.), chairman of the House Republican Conference, had an ACA rating of 72 in 1973, while his overall ACU rating was 36; Rep. Howard W. Robison (R N.Y.) got a 66 from ACA and a 50 from the ACU; Rep. Pierre S. (Pete) du Pont (R Del.) got a 58 from ACA and a 46 from the ACU.

"The ACU is looked upon by moderates as the quasi-fringe," said one Republican staff member. "They're zealots. They have a purge mentality. They're more interested in maintaining purity than in winning. They want to keep liberals out of the Republican Party."

One moderate Republican representative complained of the attacks on him by the American Conservative Union. "I was anathema to the hard right, and I knew it," he said. "With those people, there's no part way. You're either 100 per cent or they're against you."

Fund-Raising Problems

Conservative fund-raisers have wanted to raise more money in order to increase their influence in the Republican Party. But their fund-raising goals have been frustrated. One factor has been the relatively homogeneous make-up of the Republican Party. Unlike the factionalized and heterogeneous Democratic Party, which has many outside groups raising money for its candidates, the Republicans are predominantly conservative, with conservatives controlling the House and Senate Congressional Campaign Committees. Thus, much more money has gone into the party coffers than into outside, ideologically oriented groups. "A conservative could feel much more comfortable giving to the party and knowing it's going the right way," said Feulner of the House Republican Steering Committee.

But conservatives also have a common problem with liberals—the incestuousness of their mailing lists. Bruce Eberle, a 30-year old conservative in the direct-mail business, placed the conservative fund-raising constituency at "no more than one million active contributors. They range from the moral issue people to real Republicans."

Duplication among the mailing lists of the various conservative groups "runs at about 30 per cent," Eberle said. Leading conservative lists include the Young Americans for Freedom list of 256,000 names, the *Human Events* special select list of about 100,000 names, the Conservative Book and Reprint Buyers list of 150,000 names, the American Conservative Union select list of 55,000 names and the small but profitable Potomac Arts political list of 18,000 contributors to Buckley's 1970 campaign.

The problem was accentuated because the groups rent lists from each other. Several fund-raisers, such as Dear and Eberle, had tried to reach out beyond the closed circle and add new names to their mailing lists.

One approach they tried was to place newspaper advertisements opposing gun control and amnesty for Vietnam War resisters and deserters and criticizing liberals for wallowing in Watergate. The newspapers in which the ads had been placed were in predominantly conservative areas of the country, such as southern cities, Orange County, California, and small towns and suburbs.

"This is a way to add new blood to the conservative movement," Dear said. "The main aim is to get a name that hasn't been on a list before." ∎

INTEREST GROUPS: BIGGER SPENDERS ON '74 RACES

Special-interest groups spent an estimated $13-million on campaign contributions and related political activities in the first eight months of 1974, according to a study of reports filed with federal officials.

A total of 526 groups representing business, labor, agriculture, doctors, educators and other interests reported expenditures of $15.3 million by Aug. 31. About $2-million of this was simply transfers of cash between national groups and their state committees, however. In addition, the same political committees reported another $12.9-million in cash on hand ready for use before the November elections.

The reports, required by the Federal Election Campaign Act of 1971, provided the first timely, comprehensive picture available during an election year of total campaign spending. With seven weeks to go in the 1974 campaigns, spending by special-interest committees already was running about $2-million ahead of the previous record for an entire non-presidential year. Similar groups reported spending $11-million on the 1970 election campaigns, according to records then available.

Part of the increase could be attributed to the tougher reporting requirements of the 1971 law, which replaced the Federal Corrupt Practices act of 1925, often described as more loophole than law. But a larger flow of campaign dollars from some older groups and a proliferation of new committees also added to the record outpouring of funds.

The 1971 Law

The Federal Election Campaign Act of 1971 (PL 92-225), in effect since April 7, 1972, requires disclosure by all political candidates and committees of receipts and expenditures of $100 or more, including the names and addresses of contributors and recipients of funds. The law requires that financial reports, filed with the clerk of the House and the secretary of the Senate, include the total sum of receipts and expenditures during a calendar year. Reports are to be filed five times before and once after federal elections. Any contribution of more than $5,000 received after the last pre-election report (Sept. 10 for the eight months

ending Aug. 31) is to be reported within 48 hours of its receipt.

Individual contributions to candidates and committees are limited to $5,000 for each calendar year. The law also restricts the role of unions and corporations in political campaigns. *(Background p. 2, text of law p. 93)*

Biggest Spenders

The biggest spenders by category as of Aug. 31 were labor, $6.3-million; medical and health professionals, $3.9-million, and business, $2.2-million. These were gross figures, not adjusted for transfers. Actual labor spending, for instance, was closer to $5-million.

Teachers, contributing through new political action committees, joined the top spenders for the first time, disbursing $682,833 and reporting another $740,999 in cash available for the final weeks of the congressional campaigns.

The largest amounts are usually spent on campaigns in the final weeks before an election. By combining expenditures through Aug. 31 with cash on hand, it was possible to calculate the total funds available as of that date to various groups for political spending in 1974.

The special-interest committee with the largest campaign treasury was C-TAPE, the political arm of the Associated Milk Producers Inc. (AMPI) of San Antonio, Texas, with $1,876,678 in expenditures and cash on hand. Another dairy industry group, SPACE, operated by Dairymen Inc. of Louisville, Ky., ranked ninth with a total of $511,338. *(Milk producers' spending in 1972 p. 12)*

The American Medical Political Action Committee (AMPAC) of the American Medical Association (AMA) had the second largest campaign treasury, $1,759,715, and the political arm of the Marine Engineers' Beneficial Association ranked third, with $1,254,656.

National and local committees of the National Education Association (NEA) had a combined total of $1,094,849 in spending and available cash and ranked fourth. Stanley J. McFarland, NEA director of government relations, told

Interest-Group Spending

(From Reports for period ending Aug. 31, 1974)*

Category	Receipts	Expenditures	Cash on Hand
Agriculture	$1,139,599	$589,475	$2,592,312
Business	2,901,753	2,248,934	2,852,660
Education	896,307	682,833	740,999
Health	4,105,670	3,884,157	1,605,617
Ideological	1,589,820	1,585,761	300,500
Labor	6,139,997	6,318,252	4,833,950
Grand total	$16,773,146	$15,309,412	$12,957,680

Figures not adjusted for transfers among committees.

(SOURCE: National Information Center on Political Finance)

Sources of Data

This Congressional Quarterly study of reports by special-interest committees was compiled with the assistance of the National Information Center on Political Finance, Washington, D.C. The center is an election-year research facility of the Citizens' Research Foundation, Princeton, N.J.

The nonpartisan center has on file all reports made by candidates and political committees to the clerk of the House, the secretary of the Senate and the General Accounting Office. Reports used in this study cover the period Jan. 1, 1974, through Aug. 31, 1974.

Top 10 Political Campaign Committees

(Rank based on the sum of expenditures and cash on hand for each committee)

Committee	Expenditures	Cash on Hand	Total (Expenditures Plus Cash on Hand)
1. Committee for Thorough Agricultural Political Education, C-TAPE (Associated Milk Producers Inc.)	$193,969	$1,682,708	$1,876,678
2. American Medical Political Action Committee (national, American Medical Association)	1,775,531	-15,816	1,759,715
3. MEBA Retirees' Group Fund (national, Marine Engineers' Beneficial Association, AFL-CIO)	982,532	272,124	1,254,656
4. National Education Association (national and state groups)	421,863	672,986	1,094,849
5. AFL-CIO COPE Political Contributions Committee (national, AFL-CIO)	960,393	102,697	1,063,090
6. UAW-V-CAP, United Auto Workers Voluntary Community Action Program (International Union of Automobile Aerospace and Agricultural Implement Workers of America)	402,268	519,103	921,371
7. Laborers Political League (Laborers' International Union of North America, AFL-CIO)	360,451	263,628	624,079
8. United Steelworkers of America Political Action Fund (United Steelworkers of America, AFL-CIO)	146,794	366,267	513,061
9. Trust for Special Political Agricultural Community Education, SPACE (Dairymen Inc.)	161,703	349,635	511,338
10. Machinists Non-partisan Political League (national, International Association of Machinists, AFL-CIO)	334,915	171,873	506,788

SOURCE: National Information Center on Political Finance

Congressional Quarterly the organization would support about 160 candidates for the House and Senate.

Legislative Targets

"Our major push in the 94th Congress will be for collective bargaining for public employees and for general federal aid to education," McFarland said. The teacher group raised only modest sums for political purposes in 1972, but emerged in 1974 as a major source of campaign funds. Other education groups spent or had on hand an additional $328,983 as of Aug. 31.

The other well-heeled special-interest groups had their legislative interests as well. Phil Porter, an AMPI official, said his group was prepared to contribute up to $1.5-million to House and Senate candidates if necessary to attempt to restrict imports of dairy products.

Many of the recipients of AMPAC funds included congressional sponsors of Medicredit, the AMA's proposal for national health insurance. The Maritime Engineer's Beneficial Association channeled its contributions mainly to members of Congress who supported a bill requiring that a great portion of oil imports be shipped in U.S. tankers manned by U.S. crews.

Top Ten

The top 10 groups in combined contributions and cash on hand included: (1) C-TAPE, $1,876,678; (2) AMPAC, $1,759,715; (3) The Retirees' Group Fund of the Marine Engineers' Beneficial Association, AFL-CIO, $1,254,656; NEA (through national and state committees), $1,094,849; (5) the AFL-CIO's Committee on Political Education, $1,063,090.

Also (6) UAW-V-CAP (International Union of Automobile Workers), $921,371; (7) LPL (Laborer's International Union), $624,079; (8) United Steelworkers, PAF, $513,061; (9) SPACE, $511,338, and (10) MNPL (National International Association of Machinists), $506,788.

Among other groups raising substantial campaign treasuries in 1974 was the Real Estate Political Action Committee, a group representing the National Association of Realtors. The committee reported spending of $171,381 and $220,635 in cash on hand. William R. Magel, a spokesman for the committee, said its main interests were housing and the mortgage market.

The dairy groups were not the only agricultural interests raising funds, although dairy money accounted for most of the total. Cattlemen, cotton, rice and soybean growers were all represented by political committees.

Liberal and conservative groups were again prominent fund-raisers. The liberal National Committee for an Effective Congress ranked first among spenders in the ideological category. In recent non-election years, the Committee has played a lobbying role in campaign reform legislation and in efforts to restructure Congress and reform budget procedures. In election years, the committee's funds are channeled primarily to candidates, and that legislative activity tapers off. As of Aug. 31, the committee reported expenditures of $493,216 for candidates. A Common Cause study found that the committee gave $393,888 to candidates for federal office in 1972. *(Liberal fund-raisers, p. 45)*

The Conservative Victory Fund said it spent $121,697, and the Young America's Campaign Committee, another conservative group, reported expenditures of $208,968. *(Conservative fund-raisers, p. 50)* ∎

DIFFERING APPROACHES TO CAMPAIGN FINANCING

An excess of spending in political campaigns has been endemic to all free electoral systems. Even back in ancient Rome the demand for political funds was so great that at one time an election caused the doubling of the interest rates. However, the European electoral systems established early in the 19th century on the basis of the "natural" rights of the individual seemed to overlook man's inherent weakness. Each voter in England was originally viewed as an independent, freely acting man, without social or economic ties except those which originated in his self-interest. There was no kind of state interference of any kind.

However, by the 1870s it became clear that the un-regulated rise of political parties could completely undermine the original, idealistic intent of the philosophers. As Oswald Spengler was to observe in *The Decline of the West*, "Money organizes elections in the interests of those who possess it; and the elections themselves are a rigged game staged as though the people were making decisions."

The Corrupt and Illegal Practices Act of 1883 thoroughly reformed the political scene in England. Electoral bribery by gift, loan or promise of money or payment in kind, including the offer or promise of employment, was banned. More subtly, "treating," or the provision to any person of meat, drink or entertainment in order to either induce him to vote or to abstain from voting was also prohibited. And the expenses of the candidates were also strictly proscribed. Since this time, the regulations, restrictions and practices of campaign finance in Western Europe have varied markedly from country to country. In no European state, however, is television time now on sale to any political candidate or party during an election campaign. And nearly every state now provides some degree of support to the political parties.

In attempting to design a system of campaign financing as fair and as fool proof as possible, American legislators could take a careful look at how other democratic states, particularly in Western Europe, have tackled the problem. Some of the election laws in Japan, Germany and France have worked no better than in America, but most nations have been able to prevent the most obvious finance abuses. The British and the Scandinavians in particular have been widely admired for their generally honest and fair election campaigns. Americans may possibly gain new insights by examining how these democracies have fashioned a resolution to this political conundrum.

Campaign Spending in Britain

Compared to U.S. elections, British elections are run on a shoestring basis. As the *Economist* pointed out in March 1974, Britain now spends less money (in real terms, discounting inflation) than it did in 1900 per candidate for Parliament. Part of the reason that expenditures are so modest is not only that they are restricted by law, but also that election campaigns, such as the one in February 1974, are compressed into a three-week period.

The Representation of the People Act of 1974 pushed the legally permitted spending of each candidate to $2,500 plus about 2.5 cents for each voter in the constituency. As the average English electoral district holds about 65,000 voters, each candidate's election campaign was limited to a total of about $3,750 in the cities and $4,150 in the rural constituencies where the allowances are marginally higher. The legal limits imposed on the approximately 630 candidates both the Conservative and the Labor Parties managed to field was therefore about $2.5 million. By comparison, the average candidate for the United States House of Representatives spent about $52,000 to defend his seat and in the Senate close to $500,000.

To illustrate the modesty of British campaign expenditures, the Labor Party suggested to its candidates in the last election that their budgets be split as follows: $338 for an agent, $1,000 for printing, $100 for advertising, $200 for stationery, $100 for stamps and telephone, $100 for renting a hall, $85 for committee meetings, and a miscellaneous $120 for such items as messengers and speakers.

The laws covering campaign spending by the candidates are both explicit and rigorous. Should a candidate spend more than his legal limit, his campaign may be invalidated and he will face heavy fines plus court costs. The result is that the law is almost never broken. Despite the continuous depreciation in the value of money and the fivefold increase in the size of the electorate since 1900, it is remarkable that constituency campaigns have cost less in real terms in each successive election.

Of course there are big systemic differences with the United States which account for much of the discrepancy in expenditure. American constituencies are much larger, candidates have to pay for television time in America, and during an election campaign in Britain there is almost no political advertising in the press or on billboards. Any such advertising counts as constituency spending and might cause the candidate to be disqualified.

Party Spending and Fund Raising

There is no legal limit on the amount spent by the political parties in Britain as opposed to the expenditures by the local candidates. British law does not require the reporting of party contributions or expenditures. For example, total contributions to the Conservative Party during the non-election year of 1973 were said to have amounted to about $2.2-million. But any disclosures made are purely voluntary. Traditionally the Tories have been heavier spenders during election campaigns. The Conservatives spent close to $250,000 on private polls during the last election, as opposed to a quarter of that figure for the Labor Party. In the month before the election was called, both parties spent about $150,000 each on posters and press advertising.

Annual income may vary, but it was reported that for the year 1972-73 the Conservatives spent $535,000 on research and $636,000 on publicity. The election itself, according to a February 1974 issue of *The Guardian*, probably cost the Central Office of the Conservatives an extra $720,-000 on top of its usual spending. Apart from its business contributions, Conservative finance depends primarily on local fund raising, which averages about $1,000 per year for each constituency, as well as in dues and affiliation fees. The Conservative Party has 2 million individual members, each of whom should pay about $2.50 a year in fees.

Traditionally the Tories relied on appeals to a "few hundred people," the aristocratic rich, the businessman or the wealthy who would pay for a political career or who hoped for a title. Those days have gone. The largest contributor in 1973 was thought to be the Rank-Xerox Organization, which donated $84,000. The British United Industrialists, an anonymous businessman's group, raised $600,000.

The Labor Party raises most of its funds by charging each of the 5½ million members of the Trade Union movement affiliated with Labor 36 cents a year. This adds up to a total income of about $2-million. Some unions also contribute by sponsoring candidates and paying the regular bills of the member of Parliament. The Amalgamated Union of Engineering Workers and the National Union of Mineworkers each sponsored 19 candidates in 1974. However, Labor will probably have to increase its affiliation fees again if it is going to keep up with inflation. The average member now contributes less than half an hour of his earnings per year to the party.

The present structure of British politics involves a disparity of resources available to smaller parties, such as the Liberals. The Liberals, who refuse to accept company donations unless voted by the shareholders, have attacked the ways in which the main parties raise their money. When Tory funds come from the rich and from industry and when the Labor Party is primarily dependent on the sponsorship of the unions, the case could be made for public subsidies. However, in addition to lack of tradition of a governmental responsibility for politics, there is a persistent belief in Britain that both elections and politicians can be had inexpensively.[1] *(Footnotes p. 72)*

Control of Abuses through Paid Agents

One of the unique features of the British system is the use of party agents at the constituency level. It is obligatory for every candidate to appoint an official election agent. Halsbury's *Laws of England* points out that a candidate's electoral liability for the acts of his agent is well defined. For example, a court decided back in 1870 that bribes by an agent would annul an election even though the candidate was not implicated. It is therefore the duty of each candidate to select a trustworthy agent.

The agent is responsible for almost all the financial transactions during an election campaign. It is the agent who hires all the paid campaign workers, and he is the only one permitted to receive donations or loans for use during the campaign. In addition, he is the only person, apart from the candidate, who is allowed to incur election expenses. He may, however, give written authorization for a campaign assistant to cover specific expenditures. All expenses must be precisely accounted for by the agent. He must submit a special form detailing the costs of the campaign within 35 days after the election. All bills and receipts for expenses must be included in his submission and the names of contributors must be listed.

Both the candidate and his agent must sign a declaration as to the validity of these returns and false declarations are punishable by imprisonment. Failure to submit a return also constitutes an illegal practice. Publication of these returns is then assured because ten days after receiving the information, the local officials must publish a summary of the return in at least two newspapers in the constituency. All the relevant information must then be kept available for a period of two years. These laws are so restrictive that there have been no members of Parliament of either major party who have been debarred in more than 40 years for campaign finance violations.

Public Funding in Scandinavia

Several of the democracies in Scandinavia—Finland, Norway and Sweden—have been introducing novel and often radical innovations in their systems of campaign financing. All three states now practice federal subsidy of political parties.[2] In Norway, the parties entering candidates in at least half of the districts in the previous election receive subsidies in direct proportion to the vote they received. In 1974 the Norwegian government distributed a little more than $2-million among the 13 parties which took part in the last parliamentary elections. However, the government makes no conditions on the parties and in no way controls the use of these subsidies.

In Sweden parties have received state subsidies proportional to their voting strength since 1965. To be eligible a party must receive at least two per cent of the total vote. The amount of the grants is calculated mechanically and distributed according to fixed rules which do not admit any arbitrary discretion. In fact, no state control of any kind exists over the use of the grants. These subsidies now amount to about $23,000 for each seat in Parliament. The parties have used these funds mainly to subsidize their publications and professional organizations.

There is no direct subsidy by the Swedish state to cover party campaign expenses. The parties generally have to collect their dues from their members at the local level. In certain constituencies a sliding scale, based on the income of the members, is used to determine the amount of dues to be paid. Thus state subsidy has eased the burden of campaign costs but has not eliminated the need for a broad base of private political financing.

In Finland the Parliament decided in 1966 to support the activities of the political parties. The appropriation has been renewed annually since then and it was increased to $4.3-million in 1973. The idea of giving state support to political parties was highly controversial when introduced in Finland and remains unpopular. Nevertheless, because the parties found themselves in an unsatisfactory financial position in the mid 1960s, it was felt that only state subsidies could reduce the advantage that certain groups or individuals might derive from their command of superior financial resources. State support in Finland now accounts for approximately a third of all party expenditures.[3]

In none of the Scandinavian countries are there any rules to limit the amount of money to be spent by a candidate or party towards financing elections. When it comes to the control of income or expenditure, most of the parties have been reluctant to reveal their sources of income. Thus far there has been no legislation forcing the parties to reveal their financial status. Consequently, little has been done to limit the ever rising costs of running elections and until now even voluntary agreements have not proven a satisfactory substitute for statutory regulation.

Free Allocation of TV Time

In every world democracy except the United States both radio broadcasting time and television are free to all political parties and are allocated according to their electoral strength. It is unthinkable in any European country that a politician could sell himself through spot advertisements on television. During the election campaign in Britain, for example, the Labor and Conservative parties each get five broadcasts of 10 minutes apiece on television and the Liberals receive three broadcasts of 10 minutes. All these "party political broadcasts" are aired during prime viewing time.

Much to the irritation of some British viewers, each of the three channels broadcasts these political messages simultaneously, forcing viewers either to watch or to turn the set off. According to a number of polls taken this spring, a substantial majority of British viewers felt that the 1974 general election coverage by the BBC was excessive. Only one per cent of the viewers, according to *The Guardian*, felt that there had been insufficient election news.

Broadcasting in Sweden is the monopoly of the Swedish Radio Joint Stock Company. In 1962 rules were adopted which stated that the company should broadcast information and different views on political problems while at all times maintaining a position of neutrality and objectivity. All parties in Sweden are therefore able to explain their platforms and to reply to questions raised by the opposition. All parties participate in panel discussions on current social, economic and political problems. A provision is made that on the final discussion on the day before the elections, the party in power is given 50 per cent more time than the opposition on the grounds that those in power need more time to counter the attacks being made against them.

In parliamentary elections the major parties in Belgium, Holland, Denmark, Germany and Italy all receive free time according to their relative parliamentary strength. In France, which has a presidential system in addition to a parliament, each candidate has two hours of free television and broadcast time for each of the two successive rounds of ballots. This free time is intended for the personal use of the candidate, although he might request that associates appear with him. A commission is given the option, however, of reducing this allocation of time if it is thought there are too many presidential contenders in the first round.

Drawbacks of State Subsidies

European democracies have, in many instances, had to tackle the same problems of escalating political campaign costs as in the United States. In many instances, such as in Germany, the spending limits have never been effective and seem at best to have had only a minor inhibiting influence. In France the Federal Constitutional Court declared in Paris in 1966 that the general subsidizing of political parties was unconstitutional as it endangered the freedom of the parties to be responsible to the popular will. The finances of the Gaullists, the Socialists and the Independent Republicans have remained secret and there have been no real checks on the money received or spent by the candidates in the two-round presidential elections in April and May 1974.

In Finland there is still considerable opposition to state support even after eight years of relatively successful practice. The reasons given include the general feeling that such federal subsidies endanger democracy. The argument runs that support paid to national party organizations concentrates power in party headquarters, thus creating strong oligarchies which are incompatible with the democratic process. The Finns argue that such support has aggravated internal party tensions to the point of promoting splits. Such an interpretation was given to the split of the Rural Party in 1972 when a constitutional amendment was being debated.

The Finns further contend that state support for political parties exerts a reactionary force on the political system because it aids existing groups, strengthens the status quo, and makes it difficult for new ideas and new organizations to rise in competition with the state-subsidized groups. Moreover, the extension of state support has not served to make the financial position of the parties more open; other financial resources of the parties are not revealed. And finally, during the years of state subsidy, the political parties have found it far more difficult to collect contributions from their private supporters.

Public Finance in Italy, Germany

When Italy adopted a law in April 1974, to provide government subsidies for the eight major parties on a proportional basis, three principal motives were given. The first, and most important, was to try to limit corruption. The second was to impede certain groups and individuals from using their superior financial resources to gain political advantage. The third reason was the hope to control, limit or even possibly reduce the soaring cost of politics.

Germany is one of the few countries which now has had prolonged experience with subsidies. When the Germans drew up their new electoral system after the war, they adopted the idea of paying each party's election expenses out of government funds. Parties receiving at least five per cent of the national vote in parliamentary elections became eligible for subsidies for the "necessary costs of an appropriate campaign." A substantial proportion of the subsidy is in advance and adjustments are made after the campaign. The accounting reports must list receipts separately for membership fees, regular contributions by members of the party, and any other income received. Although party dues and contributions are tax deductible, contributions of over $7,000 a year must be specifically identified. Detailed provisions concerning bookkeeping and auditing are included in the German law and party members may not be the auditors of these statements.

The West German parties have voluntarily attempted to reduce or limit their progressively mounting campaign costs during the past elections. In 1965 the Christian Democrats and the Socialists made an agreement to limit campaign costs to 15 million marks. However, the terms of the accord were violated because the parties felt that they needed more money than was allowed to run the campaign effectively. The politicians of both parties agreed that if such ceilings were to be effective, they had to be accompanied by some provisions for public disclosure as well as specific penalties for violations.

Prospects for Using European Models in America

The question of whether the United States can profit from the European experience is focused on three general

(Continued on p. 72)

PRESIDENTIAL, SENATE COSTS DROPPED IN 1972 CAMPAIGNS

Candidates in 1972's presidential election spent only half as much on political broadcasts as their counterparts in 1968, according to a report prepared by the Federal Communications Commission. The 350-page document, based on a nationwide survey of television and radio station receipts, shows that presidential candidates spent a total of $14.3-million on radio, television and cable television advertising in 1972, compared with $28.5-million in the previous presidential election.

The most dramatic drop in broadcast media expenditures appeared on the Republican side, where President Nixon, and candidates in Republican presidential primaries, spent only $4.4-million, down from $15.6-million in 1968. Nixon spent $4.3-million on broadcasting during the general election, about one-third of his $12.6-million total in the 1968 general election. *(Chart p. 61)*

Democratic presidential candidates bought $9.6-million worth of air time in 1972, $6.2-million of which was spent in the general election by Sen. George McGovern. In 1968 they spent $10.9-million on broadcasting, $6.1-million of it in the general election.

The total amount spent on radio and television by all candidates for public office in 1972 was $59.6-million, an increase of one per cent over the 1968 total of $58.9-million. *(Broadcast spending in 1970 campaigns, Dollar Politics Vol. I, p. 19)*

Under the federal campaign law that took effect April 7, 1972, stations are required to sell time to candidates at their lowest unit rate, so that more time may have been bought for less money in the 1972 campaign. Total time comparisons are not possible using the FCC study.

Spending Limitations

The limits on media spending imposed by the new campaign law had nothing to do with Nixon's comparatively meager outlay in 1972, said DeVan L. Shumway, a spokesman for the Nixon re-election committee. "Television is basically an exposure medium," Shumway explained, "and the President already had a clear record of accomplishment...no serious thought was given to spending up to the limit."

Presidential candidates in the 1972 general election were limited to $8.5-million for radio and television, and $14.3-million for all communications media.

Shumway added that instead of spending large sums on air time, the Nixon campaign concentrated on "an extensive people to people program" of political organizing. Some of the most effective Nixon television spots, he said, were paid for by "Democrats for Nixon," a group headed by John Connally.

Senate Campaigns. The FCC report shows that broadcast spending in the 1972 senatorial races was also down from 1970 and 1968 totals. Senatorial candidates

Media Spending Limit

The Federal Election Campaign Act of 1971 limits the amount candidates for federal office may spend on media advertising to a total equal to ten cents multiplied by the voting age population of the area in which the election is held, or $50,000, whichever is greater. No more than 60 per cent of that money may be spent on broadcast media.

The media limit for 1972 was set at $52,150 to account for increases in the consumer price index since 1970, the base year.

The Act defines media as radio, television, cable television, magazines, newspapers, bill-boards and telephones used for voter convassing. Broadcast media includes only radio, television and cable television.

Candidates for presidential nomination are limited to the amounts prescribed for senatorial spending in the various states, while presidential candidates in the general election are limited to a figure based on the total U.S. population.

U.S. Comptroller General Elmer B. Staats released April 14, a list of final media spending limits for 1972 campaigns. The over-all limit for presidential media spending in the general election is $14.3-million, and the comparable limit for broadcast spending is $8.5-million.

The 1972 broadcast spending limits for senatorial races ranged from $850,212 for California to $31,290 (the lowest legal amount—60 per cent of $52,150) for Alaska, Delaware, Idaho, Montana, Nevada, North Dakota, South Dakota, Vermont and Wyoming. The broadcast spending limit for all 1972 House races except the District of Columbia and Puerto Rico was $31,290. *(Senate limits, table p. 62)*

spent $6.4-million last year, compared with $16.0-million in 1970 and $10.4-million in 1968. Democrats outspent Republicans over-all in 1972, $3.3-million to $3.0-million.

Buehl Berentson, director of the Republican Senatorial Campaign Committee, said he believed the media spending limit had a "psychological" effect on many candidates' 1972 campaign strategies. "The limits on broadcast and print media advertising directed their attention toward other things...they put more money into direct mail and ads in print media other than newspapers," he said.

The legal restrictions had less impact on presidential campaign planning, Berentson noted, because it was a "once in a century situation...they had planned on heavy media spending and then when they lucked out with their opposition, they spent more on organizational effort and that sort of thing instead."

Presidential Radio and TV Spending in General Elections

IN MILLIONS OF DOLLARS

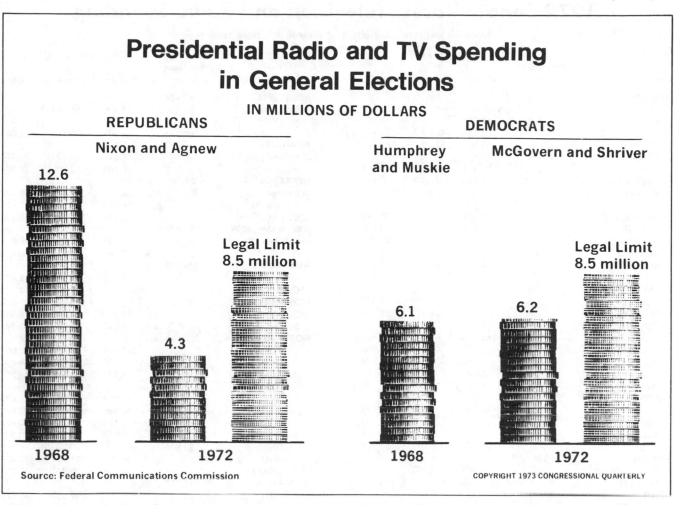

REPUBLICANS — Nixon and Agnew: 1968: 12.6; 1972: 4.3 (Legal Limit 8.5 million)

DEMOCRATS — Humphrey and Muskie / McGovern and Shriver: 1968: 6.1; 1972: 6.2 (Legal Limit 8.5 million)

Source: Federal Communications Commission

COPYRIGHT 1973 CONGRESSIONAL QUARTERLY

Republican senatorial candidates spent $2.5-million on broadcasting in the general election, compared with the Democrat's $1.9-million. As in the presidential campaign, Democratic Senate races were more heavily contested in the primaries. Frank N. Hoffman, director of the Democratic Senatorial Campaign Committee, declined comment on the FCC findings until he had studied them.

House Spending. Broadcast spending in House races increased from $6.1-million in 1970, when the FCC first computed it, to $7.4-million in 1972. Democrats spent $4.3-million, about evenly divided between primaries and the general election. Republicans spent $3.1-million with $2.4-million of their total going into general election campaigns. The two parties spent nearly equal amounts in their 1968 House campaigns.

Governor's Races. Candidates for Governor and Lieutenant Governor, who are not regulated by the new federal campaign law, spent $9.7-million on broadcasting in 1972, compared with $6.2-million in 1968. In 1970, with more big-state gubernatorial elections taking place, the total reached $16.4-million. *(Table, p. 63)*

Democratic statehouse candidates spent $5.9-million last year to the Republicans' $3.7-million, but Republicans outspent Democrats in the general election $3.0-million to $2.5-million. Broadcast spending by candidates for other state and local offices totaled $21.7-million.

Exceeding Spending Limits. Most 1972 House and Senate candidates spent considerably less on broadcasting than they were allowed under the Federal Election Campaign Act of 1971, according to the FCC study. But the figures show several possible violations of the spending guidelines set out by the General Accounting Office in accordance with the law. *(Senate limits by State, table p. 62)*

In a close Senate race, Sen. Walter (Dee) Huddleston (D Ky.) and his opponent Louie B. Nunn (R) both exceeded the state limit of $135,611 Huddleston spent $152,937 in the general election and Nunn spent $136,634.

In another sharply contested Senate campaign, John H. Chafee (R) apparently overshot the Rhode Island limit in his unsuccessful challenge to Sen. Claiborne Pell (D). Chafee spent $49,026 on broadcasting in the general election—$1,723 over the limit. Sen. James Abourezk (D S.D.) narrowly exceeded his state's limit of $31,290, spending $31,517 in the general campaign. Chuck Lien (R) over-spent the limit by $220 in that state's Republican senatorial primary.

Four House candidates apparently exceeded the congressional broadcast spending limit of $31,290 in primary or general elections. Of those, two were winners. David C. Treen (R La.-3) spent $41,246 and James

(Continued on p. 63)

1972 Senate Races: Television and Radio Spending

(Asterisk indicates incumbent.   Winner is in **bold face** type.)

Candidate [1]	Broadcast Limit [2]	Primary	General	Total
ALABAMA	$141,368			
Allen (D)		$ 26,009		$ 26,009
Mims (D)		17,208		17,208
*Sparkman (D)		68,944	$124,275	193,219
Blount (R)		63,822	125,839	189,661
ALASKA	31,290			
Guess (D)		6,419	2,149	8,568
*Stevens (R)		11,178	21,426	32,604
ARKANSAS	81,104			
Boswell (D)		13,108		13,108
*McClellan (D)		96,374	5,419	101,793
Pryor (D)		73,674		73,674
Babbitt (R)		0	20,873	20,873
COLORADO	93,370			
Haskell (D)		9,677	39,903	49,580
*Allott (R)		201	43,225	43,426
DELAWARE	31,290			
Biden (D)		0	18,627	18,627
*Boggs (R)		222	28,536	28,758
GEORGIA	188,992			
*Gambrell (D)		155,623		155,623
Nunn (D)		72,392	86,314	158,706
Russell (D)		10,548		10,548
Vandiver (D)		65,091		65,091
Thompson (R)		1,547	56,609	58,156
IDAHO	31,290			
Davis (D)		4,348	22,707	27,055
Johnson (D)		14,199		14,199
McClure (R)		12,394	21,591	33,985
Wegner (R)		23,368		23,368
ILLINOIS	463,906			
Pucinski (D)		15,494	101,528	117,022
*Percy (R)		0	284,771	284,771
IOWA	117,901			
Clark (D)		0	66,657	66,657
*Miller (R)		0	74,796	74,796
KANSAS	95,309			
Tetzlaff (D)		0	1,784	1,784
*Pearson (R)		0	43,318	43,318
KENTUCKY	135,611			
Huddleston (D)		15,205	152,937	168,142
Gable (R)		73,996		73,996
Nunn (R)		7,425	136,634	144,059
LOUISIANA	144,059			
Johnston (D)		4,575	86,864	91,439
Toledano (R)		700	24,590	25,290
McKeithen (Ind.)			103,150	103,150
MAINE	41,365			
Hathaway (D)		0	39,002	39,002
Monks (R)		15,895		15,895
*Smith (R)		0	15	15
MASSACHUSETTS	242,998			
Droney (D)		20	21,783	21,803
*Brooke (R)		1,057	33,208	34,265
MICHIGAN	359,835			
Kelley (D)		0	170,664	170,664
*Griffin (R)		0	191,086	191,086
MINNESOTA	156,012			
*Mondale (D)		617	100,829	101,446
Hansen (R)		501	119,990	120,491
MISSISSIPPI	87,424			
*Eastland (D)		53,226	66,104	119,330
Webb (D)		17,337		17,337
Carmichael (R)		427	26,636	27,063
MONTANA	31,290			
*Metcalf (D)		2,547	28,824	31,371
Hibbard (R)		5,603	22,200	27,803
NEBRASKA	62,768			
Carpenter (D)		12,023	16,121	28,144
Ziebarth (D)		18,618		18,618
*Curtis (R)		3,534	34,586	38,120
NEW HAMPSHIRE	31,478			
*McIntyre (D)		221	15,396	15,617
Powell (R)		3,261	7,231	10,492
NEW JERSEY	306,580			
Krebs (D)		2,009	6,042	8,051
*Case (R)		0	43,438	43,438
NEW MEXICO	39,238			
Daniels (D)		35,800	38,593	74,393
Domenici (R)		6,288	34,459	40,747
NORTH CAROLINA	212,584			
Galifianakis (D)		57,896	72,191	130,087
*Jordan (D)		78,606		78,606
Helms (R)		17,533	156,672	174,205
OKLAHOMA	110,767			
Edmondson (D)		42,257	59,415	101,672
Nesbitt (D)		43,800		43,800
Terrill (D)		10,674		10,674
Bartlett (R)		9,607	91,301	100,908
OREGON	90,866			
Morse (D)		10,494	21,921	32,415
*Hatfield (R)		6,548	29,011	35,559
RHODE ISLAND	41,303			
*Pell (D)		0	39,650	39,650
Chafee (R)		0	49,026	49,026
SOUTH CAROLINA	105,260			
Ziegler (D)		0	46,555	46,555
*Thurmond (R)		177	70,667	70,844
SOUTH DAKOTA	31,290			
Abourezk (D)		5,718	31,517	37,235
Hirsch (R)		10,575	29,591	40,166
Lien (R)		31,510		31,510
Reardon (R)		25,966		25,966
TENNESSEE	166,963			
Blanton (D)		20,853	51,279	72,132
*Baker (R)		79,510	163,484	242,994
TEXAS	465,220			
Sanders (D)		71,103	195,358	266,461
Yarborough (D)		112,999		112,999
*Tower (R)		33,539	358,240	391,779
VERMONT [3]	31,290			
Major (D)			259	259
*Stafford (R)			455	455
VIRGINIA	195,625			
*Spong (D)		0	83,301	83,301
Scott (R)		0	151,754	151,754
WEST VIRGINIA	74,220			
*Randolph (D)		12,134	34,655	46,789
Leonard (R)		455	1,611	2,066
WYOMING	31,290			
Vinich (D)		0	397	397
*Hansen (R)		424	12,257	12,681

1 Candidates who spent less than $10,000 are not included unless they were major party nominees.

2 The Federal Election Campaign Act of 1971 placed limits on the amount Senate candidates could spend for radio and television advertising. The U.S. General Accounting Office released the limit figures for each state on April 14, 1972. The figures in this column apply to only the 1972 elections. A candidate could spend this amount in the primary election and in the general election.

3 Special election held Jan. 7, 1972.

1972 Governors' Races: TV and Radio Spending

(Asterisk indicates incumbent.   Winner in **bold face** type.)

Candidate [1]	Reported to FCC Primary	General	Total	Candidate [1]	Reported to FCC Primary	General	Total
ARKANSAS				Hobby (D)	36,143		36,143
*Bumpers (D)	$ 24,733	$ 9,841	$ 34,574	Taylor (D)	327,245		327,245
Blaylock (R)	0	9,066	9,066	Gardner (R)	73,613		73,613
DELAWARE				**Holshouser (R)**	56,290	67,723	124,013
Tribbitt (D)	237	6,067	6,304	**NORTH DAKOTA**			
*Peterson (R)	13,377	30,182	43,559	**Link (D)**	47	28,311	28,358
ILLINOIS				Larsen (R)	17,284	26,055	43,339
Simon (D)	104,866		104,866	McCarney (R)	10,993		10,993
Walker (D)	208,843	319,790	528,633	**RHODE ISLAND**			
*Ogilvie (R)	18,250	684,043	702,293	**Noel (D)**	0	96,576	96,576
INDIANA				DeSimone (R)	0	109,725	109,725
Welsh (D)	520	267,925	268,445	**SOUTH DAKOTA**			
Bowen (R)	1,308	341,478	342,786	*Kneip (D)	144	18,213	18,357
IOWA				Thompson (R)	4,100	22,468	26,568
Franzenberg (D)	333	24,404	24,737	**TEXAS**			
*Ray (R)	40	58,052	58,092	Barnes (D)	165,712		165,712
KANSAS				**Briscoe (D)**	485,662	201,097	686,759
*Docking (D)	1,150	192,471	193,621	Farenthold (D)	215,488		215,488
Anderson (R)	18,889		18,889	*Smith (D)	225,102		225,102
Frisbie (R)	30,794		30,794	Fay (R)	35,401		35,401
Kay (R)	81,677	196,024	277,701	Grover (R)	59,273	214,975	274,248
LOUISIANA [2]				McElroy (R)	48,733		48,733
Edwards (D)	1,654	94,908	96,562	**UTAH**			
Treen (R)	2,728	144,669	147,397	*Rampton (D)	285	34,711	34,996
MISSOURI				Strike (R)	6,999	32,421	39,420
Blackwell (D)	18,705		18,705	**VERMONT**			
Dowd (D)	127,272	205,173	412,445	**Salmon (D)**	254	14,914	15,168
Morris (D)	150,189		150,189	Hackett (R)	6,063	9,482	15,545
Teasdale (D)	17,388		17,388	**WASHINGTON**			
Bond (R)	46,787	238,929	285,716	Durkan (D)	47,041		47,041
McNary (R)	17,675		17,675	Rosellini (D)	45,918	78,520	124,430
MONTANA				*Evans (R)	13,287	55,723	69,010
Judge (D)	19,300	51,644	70,944	Woodall (R)	10,205		10,205
Smith (R)	6,832	24,721	31,553	**WEST VIRGINIA**			
NEW HAMPSHIRE				Rockefeller (D)	44,069	168,162	212,231
Crowley (D)	2,623	14,803	17,426	*Moore (R)	0	120,493	120,493
Thomson (R)	7,060	10,415	17,475				
NORTH CAROLINA							
Bowles (D)	307,121	190,312	497,433				

1 Candidates who spent less than $10,000 are not included unless they were major party nominees.
2 Election held May 1, 1972.

(Continued from p. 61)

R. Jones (D Okla-1) spent $33,808—both in the general election.

A Justice Department spokesman said a number of "apparent violations" of the spending limits are being investigated. Data in addition to the FCC figures will be reviewed to determine violations.

Interpretations. Herbert E. Alexander, head of Citizens' Research Foundation in Princeton, New Jersey, and a recognized expert on campaign finance, said that the media spending limits may have helped check broadcast spending in last year's federal elections. "I'm not surprised at the FCC findings," he said, "because the limitations set by the law were meaningful." The requirement that stations sell at their lowest going unit rates probably affected the totals also, Alexander noted.

Alexander made several other observations on broadcast spending and the FCC survey:

• Over-all spending in the 1972 presidential campaign was higher than in 1968, so Nixon and McGovern must have spent a smaller percentage of their campaign funds on broadcasting last year than was spent on it in 1968. Alexander puts Nixon's 1971-72 campaign outlay at about $48-million (although he thinks at least $52-million was raised) and McGovern's at $35-million. Final candidate reports on 1972 presidential campaign expenditures were released by the GAO in March 1974. *(p. 68)*

• The lower Senate figures may reflect "some retraction from the orgy of spending that took place in the 1970 campaigns." ∎

NIXON, McGOVERN RACE COST OVER $100-MILLION

The 1972 presidential campaign was the most expensive in American history. Precise figures on total spending are hard to come by; illegal contributions by individuals and corporations, and the money that flowed into secret funds may never be fully toted up.

In July 1974, the Senate Select Committee on Presidential Campaign Activities (Watergate committee) reported that: "President Nixon's and Senator McGovern's campaigns compiled total expenditures of over $100-million. The unsuccessful campaigns of others seeking nomination spent millions of dollars more."

No direct comparison to fund-raising in previous presidential campaigns is possible, because of sketchy reporting of contributions. Prior to 1972, no federal law required detailed disclosure of campaign financing. But Herbert E. Alexander, a political finance expert, has estimated that about $44.2-million was spent in the 1968 presidential election.

New Reporting Requirements

The 1972 campaign was, in effect, split into two periods: before April 7, and after April 7, 1972. The Federal Election Campaign Act required that all campaign committees for presidential, Senate and House candidates report loans and gifts of $100 or more. But because the disclosure requirement became law on April 7, 1972, contributions prior to that date were exempt from the reporting mandate. (Campaign act, p. 2; provisions p. 93)

Figures compiled by the General Accounting Office (GAO) under terms of the new law, and released by GAO on March 24, 1974, show that the Nixon-Agnew campaign received $43,287,435 and spent $49,072,062 in the period between April 7 and Dec. 31, 1972. The McGovern-Shriver-Eagleton campaign received $48,931,783 and spent $45,002,-742 in the same period. Lesser amounts were spent by the unsuccessful candidates for the Democratic presidential nomination. Sen. Hubert H. Humphrey (Minn.) reported receipts of $4.3-million and expenditures of $4.8-million. Gov. George C. Wallace (Ala.) received and spent $1.6-million.

The Director of GAO's Office of Federal Elections, L. Fred Thompson, emphasized at the time the report was released that the totals were incomplete.

"There are various reasons why the figures cannot be considered complete for the 1972 campaign," he said. "For example, the 'party' and 'non-party' committees usually supported candidates for other federal offices, and, in some cases, state and local candidates. These party and non-party committees were required to report total receipts and expenditures for all purposes. This means that the precise amounts properly attributable to presidential campaigns cannot be determined."

Nixon Campaign Funds

The picture before April 7 is even murkier. According to records made public by the Finance Committee to Re-elect the President on Sept. 28, 1973, fund-raisers for the 1972 Nixon campaign collected $19.9-million before the April 7, 1972, reporting deadline.

The committee released the records as part of an out-of-court settlement with the citizens' lobby Common Cause, which had brought suit to force disclosure of all early contributions.

Subsequently, however, on June 28, 1974, the court unsealed documents connected with the suit. These showed that the purportedly complete list of pre-April 7 contributors, filed by the committee on Sept. 28 of the previous year, excluded contributions estimated by Common Cause lawyers at $1,825,000. The expenditures listed in the Sept. 28 report omitted pre-April 7 spending of $1,175,000.

The GAO reports, together with the documents unsealed by the court, indicate that the Nixon camp took in more than $62-million during the 1972 campaign. A substantial amount was received in cash. The Finance Committee to Re-elect the President admitted in its Sept. 28 disclosure that $1.47-million of the pre-April 7 donations were in cash. The committee said that it had returned almost one-third of this amount by Sept. 11, after the threat of the new disclosure prompted business executives to admit that some large cash contributions had been made illegally from corporate funds.

Disclosure Issues

The McGovern campaign was notable for its early and detailed disclosure of contributions. On Feb. 28, 1972—in the heat of the primary elections—McGovern released a list of 42,020 persons who had contributed a total of $1,236,420 since January 1971. Included were the names of 86 persons who had given more than $1,000 apiece. In releasing the list, McGovern claimed his action was a "unique and unprecedented step in American presidential politics." McGovern staffers, interviewed by CQ, indicated that a number of contributors who had hoped to remain anonymous were disturbed by the release of their names.

In his Feb. 28 statement, McGovern also challenged other presidential contenders to follow his example, but few did. The Finance Committee to Re-elect the President kept its pre-April 7 lists confidential until the Common Cause law suit forced them into the open. Democratic contenders also balked at releasing the names of their pre-April 7 contributors. Sen. Henry M. Jackson (D Wash.), for example, did not reveal his backers until the names were requested by the Senate Watergate committee. That information was made public by the committee in August 1974.

Such reticence is partly explained by the existence of questionable contributions: the $200,000 in Robert Vesco's attache case, the $100,000 secret donation to the Nixon campaign from Howard Hughes which Nixon confidant Bebe Rebozo purportedly kept locked in a safe deposit box, the $2-million pledged to Nixon by the dairy industry.

But equally important is the fact that many major contributors hedged their electoral bets by giving to two or more candidates during the same campaign. The report given to the Senate Watergate committee by Sen. Jackson, for example, showed that oil executive Leon Hess, chairman of Amerada Hess Corp., had funneled $225,000 to the Jackson campaign before the April 7, 1972, deadline. In the same period, Hess had given $135,000 in secret funds to President Nixon's re-election drive. The same report showed a $25,000 contribution to Jackson from Dwayne O. Andreas, a Minneapolis soybean trader. Andreas was also a contributor to the Humphrey campaign. In addition, a $25,-000 check from Andreas was part of the $89,000 that was laundered through a Mexican bank and transferred to the Miami account of convicted Watergate burglar Bernard Barker.

Another multiple contributor was Meshulam Riklis, head of the conglomerate Rapid-American Corp. Before the April 7 deadline, Riklis gave $100,000 to Jackson, and the same amount to Humphrey. In the same period, he contributed $50,000 to the Nixon campaign, and eventually gave a total of $200,000 to re-elect the President.

Corporate Contributions

Secrecy was also motivated by the existence of a substantial number of illegal corporate donations to the presidential campaigns, especially to President Nixon's re-election effort. In a report issued in July 1974, the Senate Select Committee on Presidential Campaign Activities charged that "during the 1972 presidential campaign, it appears that at least 13 corporations made contributions totaling over $780,000 in corporate funds.... Of these, 12 gave approximately $749,000 to the President's re-election campaign, which constituted the bulk of the illegal corporate contributions."

The primary source of such corporate money, according to the Senate committee, was "foreign subsidiaries." Other sources included corporate reserves and expense accounts. The committee added that "although the bulk of the contributions preceded April 7, 1972, the date the new reporting law (Federal Elections Campaign Act of 1971) went into effect, there was no disclosure of any of the contributions until July 6, 1973—or 15 months after almost all of them were made."

Nixon's Corporate Contributors

An even more extensive list of corporate contributors was contained in a secret document kept by Rose Mary Woods, Nixon's private secretary. The Woods list, made public March 19, 1973, at the trial of John N. Mitchell and Maurice H. Stans, contained the names of executives whose individual contributions were grouped together for total corporate donations. The list follows:

Amerada Hess Corporation, New York, oil—$250,000.
Anheuser-Busch Inc., St. Louis, brewers—$56,353.
Bethlehem Steel Corporation, Bethlehem, Pa.—$49,002.
Bristol Myers Company, New York, drugs—$50,000.
Chrysler Corporation, Detroit, automobiles—$133,844.
Dart Industries, Los Angeles, retail drug sales—$50,826.
Disney Productions, Inc., Burbank, Calif., motion pictures—$34,475.
E. I. du Pont de Nemours and Company, Wilmington, Del., chemicals—$60,000.
Ernst and Ernst, Cleveland, accountants—$88,000.
General Dynamics Corporation, St. Louis, defense contractors—$83,717.
General Motors Corporation, Detroit, automobiles—$51,012.
Lehman Brothers Corporation, New York, stock brokers—$86,289.
Ling-Temco-Vought Corporation, Dallas, defense and aerospace contractor—$95,250.

Litton Industries, Los Angeles, defense contractor—$86,095.
Marathon Oil Company, Findlay, Ohio-$40,000.
McDonnell-Douglas Corporation, St. Louis, defense and aerospace contractor—$34,528.
Minnesota Mining and Manufacturing Company, St. Paul, Minn.—$142,741.
Mutual of Omaha, Omaha, Neb., insurance—$34,325.
National Homes Corporation, Lafayette, Ind., prefabricated structures—$50,000.
North American Rockwell Corporation, El Segundo, Calif., aerospace and defense contractor—$98,270.
Northrop Coproration, Los Angeles, aerospace and defense contractor—$100,000.
Price-Waterhouse Company, New York, accountants—$102,000.
St. Regis Paper Company, New York—$19,000.
Salomon Brothers, New York, brokers—$100,000.
Charles E. Smith and Company, Washington, real estate—$55,000.
Texas Eastern Transmission Company, Houston, gas pipeline—$30,000.
Texas Instruments Company, Dallas, electronics—$111,949.
Westingouse Electric Company, Pittsburgh—$35,460.

Of the 13 corporations cited by the Senate Committee on Presidential Campaign Activities, in 12 cases the corporation or one of its officers has pleaded guilty to violating federal campaign statutes. It is frequently difficult, however, to separate corporate gifts from those made by individual corporate executives.

The leading giver in the 1972 campaign was Chicago insurance executive W. Clement Stone, chairman of the Combined Insurance Company of America. In the April 7-Dec. 31, 1972, reporting period monitored by the GAO, Stone was listed as giving $73,054 to re-elect Nixon. But even before the Sept. 28 revelations forced by Common Cause, Stone had admitted to pre-April giving of $2-million. Second highest giver was Richard Scaife, heir to the Mellon banking and oil fortune, who contributed $1-million before April 7.

Kalmbach Role

The corporate gifts campaign was headed by presidential lawyer Herbert Kalmbach, who, on June 17, 1974, was sentenced to six to 18 months in jail and fined $10,000 after pleading guilty to illegal campaign operations. Kalmbach collected a total of more than $10-million from U.S. corporations, the bulk of it prior to April 7, 1972.

According to staff reports of the Senate Select Watergate Committee, Kalmbach and other fund-raisers sought donations on an industry-by-industry basis, using an influential corporate executive to raise money among other executives in his industry. One staff report shows the following breakdown, industry by industry:

● Pharmaceuticals—$885,000
● Petroleum Products—$809,000
● Investment Banking—$690,000
● Trucking—$674,000
● Textiles—$600,000
● Carpets—$375,000
● Auto Manufacturers—$354,000
● Home Builders—$334,000
● Insurance—$319,000

The staff report does not take into account an estimated $5-million collected from executives of oil firms, nor such individual contributions as those made by Stone and Scaife. Nor does it touch on funds supplied by organizations such as the Associated Milk Producers Inc.

Funding Before the Deadline

Fund-raisers for the 1972 Nixon campaign raised $19.9-million before the strict financial reporting requirements took effect. This amount was collected mainly from contributors who believed their names would never be made public.

In a collection drive in the month before the Federal Election Campaign Act of 1971 took effect April 7, 1972, the Nixon fund-raisers took in $11.4-million. They added about $5-million to Nixon campaign coffers on April 5 and 6 alone.

Nixon Contributors

The following individuals contributed $40,000 or more to the 1972 Nixon election campaign before April 7, 1972, according to an analysis made by Common Cause:

Contributor	Amount
Robert Allen, president, Gulf Resources and Chemical Corporation	$100,000 [c*]
Walter Annenberg, ambassador to England	250,000
Employees of American Airlines	75,000 [c*]
Theodore Ashley, chairman and president, Warner Brothers	137,056
Orin Atkins, chairman, Ashland Oil	100,000 [c*]
Loren Berry, chairman of an Ohio telephone directory advertising company	102,000
Elmer Bobst, honorary chairman, Warner-Lambert Pharmaceutical Company	100,000
Employees of Braniff Airlines	50,000
E. W. Brown Jr., chairman of Texas lumber and shipbuilding companies	150,000
William Burden, New York investment banker	97,895
Citizens for Good Government, LTV Corporation Employees (aerospace)	60,000
Henry Crown, chairman of a Chicago building materials company	50,819 (25,000) [c*]
Nathan Cummings, chairman of a New York manufacturing and wholesale food company	44,356
Theodore Cummings	46,407
Brownlee Currey Jr., New York investment banker	74,195
Shelby Davis, ambassador to Switzerland	100,000
Christian de Guigne, chairman of an industrial chemicals and fertilizer company	107,830
Vincent de Roulet, ambassador to Jamaica	50,000 (22,000) [c*]
Frederick L. Ehrman, New York investment banker	69,357
Harvey Firestone Jr., retired chairman, Firestone Tire and Rubber Company	48,712
Leonard Firestone, chairman, Firestone Tire and Rubber Company of California	100,000
Raymond Firestone, chairman, Firestone Tire and Rubber Company	63,441
Max M. Fisher, chairman of a Detroit real estate firm	125,000
Mrs. Edsel B. Ford	50,000
Henry Ford II, chairman, Ford Motor Company	49,776
Thomas Ford, self-employed New York investment counselor	50,000
J. Paul Getty, president, Getty Oil	75,000
Employees of Goodyear Tire and Rubber	40,000 [c*]
Albert F. Gordon, New York stockbroker	99,873

Contributor	Amount
Kingdon Gould Jr., ambassador to the Netherlands	100,000
Raymond R. Guest, Virginia horse breeder	200,000
Employees of Gulf Oil Corporation	100,000
Walter A. Haas, honorary chairman, Levi Strauss and Company	48,557
Armand Hammer, chairman, Occidental Petroleum	46,000 [c]
Bob Hope	50,000
Howard Hughes	50,000
John P. Humes, ambassador to Ireland	100,000
John N. Irwin II, ambassador to France	50,000
Marion W. Isbell, chairman, Ramada Inns	41,241
Thomas V. Jones, chairman, Northrop Corporation (aerospace)	40,000
Willard W. Keith, Los Angeles insurance broker	56,606
Peter Kiewit, president of a Nebraska construction company	100,912
Robert Kleberg, president, King Ranch (ranch, petroleum, gas), Texas	100,000
Lester B. Knight, chairman of a Chicago construction and engineering company	50,000
William S. Lasdon, chairman, Warner-Lambert Pharmaceutical Company	40,000
Gustave Levy, investment banker	70,442
Lawrence Lewis Jr., chairman of a hotel chain	90,000
Nathan Lipson, president of a carpet manufacturing company	98,120
J. Willard Marriott Sr., chairman, Marriott Corporation	67,069
Anthony D. Marshall, ambassador to Trinidad	48,505
Jack Massey, chairman of a hospital ownership and operation company	250,000
Abby Rockefeller Mauze	50,000
Lewis Maytag, chairman, National Airlines	50,000
H. W. McCullum, executive officer, Amerada Hess Corporation (crude oil and gas)	42,000
William McKnight, honorary chairman, Minnesota Mining and Manufacturing Company	100,191
Andre Meyer, New York investments company executive	90,000
Joseph Meyerhoff, chairman of a Baltimore real estate development company	104,848
Otto N. Miller, chairman, Standard Oil of California	50,000
Seymour Milstein, New York building materials manufacturing executive	65,000
Roger Milliken, president of a South Carolina textile company	84,000
John Moran, chairman of a Texas company manufacturing medical chemicals and laboratory equipment	101,008
John A. Mulcahy, president of a steel furnace subsidiary of a pharmaceutical company	573,559
Clint and John Murchison, oil producers and owners of the Dallas Cowboys football team	50,000
John M. Olin, honorary chairman, Olin Corporation (chemicals)	100,000
Spencer T. Olin, director, Olin Industries (chemicals)	94,513
Florenz Ourisman, Washington, D.C., real estate developer	150,000
David Packard, chairman, Hewlett-Packard Company (electronics defense contractor)	51,000
Thomas Pappas, head of a food and liquor importing company and a Greek oil refinery	100,673

Mrs. Charles S. Payson, owner, New York Mets baseball team	80,000
George Pfleger, director of a California electric company	47,088
Employees of Phillips Petroleum Company	100,000 c*
Lillian Phipps (widow of an investment banker)	51,000
Louis F. Polk Jr., former vice president, General Mills Inc.	49,211
Valere Blaire Potter (family ties to oil industry)	50,000
Meshulam Riklis, chairman of a company manufacturing men's clothing	50,000
John D. Rockefeller, honorary chairman, Rockefeller Foundation	50,000
Laurence Rockefeller, chairman, Rockefeller Brothers Fund	50,000
Nelson A. Rockefeller, governor of New York	50,000
John W. Rollins, president of a Delaware conglomerate in TV broadcasting, trucking	245,024
John H. Safer, Maryland real estate developer	250,000
Henry Salvatori, chairman of a company manufacturing oil drilling specialty tools	99,415
Richard Scaife, heir to Mellon oil and banking fortune	1,000,000
Taft Schreiber, vice president, Music Corporation of America	66,102
C Arnholt Smith, chairman of a California food, transportation, real estate and insurance company and of a San Diego Bank	200,000*
Kent H. Smith, retired chairman of a chemicals and fuel additives firm	244,000
Howard Stamper, chairman, Banquet Foods Corporation	46,807
Jules Stein, chairman, Music Corporation of America	117,822
Saul Steinberg, chairman of a New York computer services company	250,000
George M. Steinbrenner III, chairman, American Ship Building Company	75,000
James E. Stewart, chairman, Lone Star Industries (cement and construction materials)	50,000 c
W. Clement Stone, chairman, Combined Insurance Company of America	2,000,000
J. Fife Symington	50,000
Trust for Agricultural Political Education (TAPE—Associated Milk Producers Inc.)	187,500
Daniel J. Terra, chairman of a printing and synthetic resins company	250,000
Charles Thornton, chairman, Litton Industries	48,116
Robert L. Vesco, chairman, International Controls Corporation	200,000 c*
Elisha Walker Jr., investment company heir	100,000
DeWitt Wallace, founder of Readers' Digest	100,000
J. L. Warner, motion picture executive	100,000
Gene M. Washburn	50,000
Arthur K. Watson, former ambassador to France, former chairman of IBM World Trade Corporation	300,000
Ray A. Watt, chairman of a California real estate development firm	86,568
Cornelius V. Whitney, chairman, Whitney Industries (communications)	300,000*
Jack Wrather, chairman of a diversified company developing entertainment and tourist attractions	84,060
Toddie Wynne, president, American Liberty Oil Company	50,000

c Contributions made in cash
* All or part of contribution subsequently returned

McGovern Contributors

Senator McGovern's early and systematic release of the names of contributors to his campaign, together with the sums donated, may have impeded his fund-raising efforts, particularly in the pre-April 7 period. It is doubtful, however, that McGovern could have matched the Nixon solicitation record, even under conditions of absolute secrecy.

The publication of the names of 42,040 McGovern contributors on Feb. 28, 1972, was followed by the periodic release of additional names during the campaign. The Feb. 28 list, however, is the most extensive, and contains the names of 86 contributors of more than $1,000, between Jan. 1, 1971, and Feb. 1, 1972, to national McGovern campaign committees:

Contributor	Amount
Anderson, John, Los Angeles, Calif.	$ 2,500
Ascoli, Mrs. Lucy, Smithfield, Utah	1,000
Barish, Keith, New York, N.Y. founder Gramco Management Ltd.	15,000
Beck, Louis, New York, N.Y.	1,000
Becker, Alan, San Francisco, Calif.	5,000
Berdy, William, New York, N.Y.	3,290
Bernard, Dr. Viola, New York, N.Y.	1,000
Blau, Louis, Beverly Hills, Calif.	1,000
Boukas, Constantin, Dunnigan, Calif.	1,000
Briscoe, John D., Lakeville, Conn.	1,000
Brockelsby, Earl, Rapid City, S.D.	4,000
Bronfman, Edgar, New York, N.Y.	5,000
Buck, Joyce, Pipersville, Pa.	2,500
Burkett, William, Pebble Beach, Calif.	1,000
Chingos, Ellis, Boca Raton, Fla.	1,000
Concannon, Mr. and Mrs. Shawn, Chicago, Ill.	1,500
Dann, Robert Roy, New York, N.Y.	1,000
DeAngulo, Lucy, Berkeley, Calif.	1,000
Dees, Morris, Montgomery, Ala.	4,989
Degnan, Mrs. June Oppen, Ross, Calif.	1,000
Douglas, John, Chevy Chase, Md.	1,000
Eig, Dr. Blaine, Silver Spring, Md.	1,000
Emerson, Richards, Lakeville, Conn.	1,000
Epstein, Fred, Coral Gables, Fla.	6,000
Fairchild, Wiley, Hattiesburg, Miss.	7,500
Fishman, Elliot, St. Thomas, V.I.	1,000
Floyd, Joe, Sioux Falls, S.D.	7,000
Forbes, J. Malcolm, Cambridge, Mass.	5,125
Geocaris, Daniel, Winnetka, Ill.	2,500
Geocaris, James, Winnetka, Ill.	2,500
Goodspeed, Elinor, Washington, D.C.	5,000
Goodwin, Neil, Cambridge, Mass.	1,000
Graham, John, Santa Barbara, Calif.	1,000
Greene, Leonard, Chappaqua, N.Y.	1,000
Grumman, G. Sterling, Boston, Mass.	2,000
Hamill, Hugh, Philadelphia, Pa.	1,000
Haussamen, Carol, New York, N.Y.	5,000
Holzman, Jac, New York, N.Y.	5,000
Horowitz, Robert, Boston, Mass.	1,000
Hunt, Ann Marie, New York, N.Y.	7,000
Ingersoll, Ralph, Cornwall Bridge, Conn.	1,000
Johnson, Ester, Oldwick, N.J.	3,000
Karelson, Frank E., New York, N.Y.	3,569
Kessler, Sidney, St. Thomas, V.I.	1,000
Kimelman, Henry L., St. Thomas, V.I. Virgin Islands real estate developer	24,307
Kislak, Jay, Miami, Fla.	1,500
Kriegel, Norbert, St. Thomas, V.I.	10,000
Lautenberg, Frank, Montclair, N.J.	10,000
Levine, Abner, Lawrence, N.Y.	4,881
Lewis, Salim, New York, N.Y.	1,000
McVitty, E. V., New York, N.Y.	2,000
Martindell, Mrs. Anne, Princeton, N.J.	1,000

Merrill, Charles, Boston, Mass.	1,000
Mertens, Mrs. R. E., Woodstock, Vt.	2,000
Meyerhoff, Jane, Baltimore, Md.	2,500
Meyerhoff, Robert, Baltimore, Md.	2,500
Mott, Stewart R., New York, N.Y.	5,000
Mudd, Harvey S., III, Arroyo Hondo, N.M.	5,000
Munson, Dr. H. B., Rapid City, S.D.	1,000
Palevsky, Max, Los Angeles, Calif.	
former chairman, Xerox Data Systems	25,000
Parten, J. R., Houston, Texas	2,000
Perkins, Charles, Manhattan, Kan.	1,000
Preston, Mrs. William, Lincoln, Mass.	1,050
Rapoport, Bernard, Waco, Texas	1,000
Rauh, Joseph, Washington, D.C.	1,000
Rodin, Bernard, Wantagh, N.Y.	5,500
Rodin, Mrs. Bernard, Wantagh, N.Y.	4,500
Rosensweig, Stanley, Washington, D.C.	1,500
Rubin, Miles, Los Angeles, Calif.	
chairman, Optical Systems Corp.	12,500
Saalfield, Mrs. Albrecht, Shaker Heights, Ohio	15,000
Saalfield, Albrecht, Shaker Heights, Ohio	15,000
Salomon, Richard, New York, N.Y.	2,500
Sarnoff, Dr. Stanley, Bethesda, Md.	1,000
Small, Albert, Bethesda, Md.	2,000
Smith, Charles E., Washington, D.C.	2,100
Smith, Frances, Washington, D.C.	1,000
Starr, Mrs. Donald, Boston, Mass.	1,000
Stein, Judith, Rockville, Md.	1,500
Swibel, Charles, Chicago, Ill.	
president, Mark & Co. estate management	12,500
Towbin, Belmont, New York, N.Y.	2,500
Vernet, Sergius, Yellow Springs, Ohio	1,000
Wheatland, Miss Barbara, Topsfield, Mass.	1,000
Weiss, Neil, St. Thomas, V.I.	1,000
Weissbourd, Bernard, Chicago, Ill.	7,000
Willets, Mr. and Mrs. Robin, Durham, N.H.	1,000
Zaffaroni, A., Atherton, Calif.	1,000

An appendix to the list noted that the McGovern campaign had received loans totaling $85,000 from Henry L. Kimelman ($15,000), Stewart R. Mott ($40,000) and Max Palevsky ($30,000). Of the total, $47,200 had been repaid, but loans of $7,800 from Kimelman and $30,000 from Palevsky remained outstanding. The appendix also listed an additional $53,150 in transfers from McGovern state committees.

Funding After the Deadline

On Aug. 23, 1973, the General Accounting Office released a list of some 70,000 persons who had contributed $100 or more to the 1972 presidential candidates.

Included among the names were such diverse personalities as entertainer Frank Sinatra, artist Andy Warhol, United Auto Workers President Leonard Woodcock, former Teamsters President James R. Hoffa, recluse industrialist Howard Hughes and Jacqueline Kennedy Onassis.

The GAO list indicated that these persons donated $79.1-million to all presidential candidates between April 7 and Dec. 31, 1972. According to the GAO, President Nixon received $37.6-million in gifts and $1.6-million in loans. George McGovern, the Democratic nominee, received $13-million in gifts and $8.2-million in loans.

The GAO list was prepared in compliance with the Federal Election Campaign Act of 1971. It did not contain the names of donors prior to the April 7 deadline for recording and reporting donations. Nor did it contain figures on campaign contributions of less than $100.

1972 Campaign Financing

The following table shows receipts and expenditures for Republican and Democratic presidential and vice presidential candidates from April 7 through Dec. 31, 1972, as reported to the General Accounting Office under the Federal Election Campaign Act of 1971:

	Receipts (excluding transfers)	Expenditures (excluding transfers)
Democratic Party		
McGovern-Shriver-Eagleton*	$48,931,783	$45,002,742
Stanley Arnold	11,249	147,998
Sen. Birch Bayh	7,737	22,368
Rep. Shirley Chisholm	95,346	114,163
Sen. Mike Gravel	65,652	68,138
Sen. Vance Hartke	34,777	27,375
Rep. Wayne L. Hays	1,100	930
Sen. Hubert H. Humphrey	4,267,777	4,838,794
Sen. Henry M. Jackson	209,725	364,961
Gov. Patrick J. Lucey	4,054	4,349
Eugene McCarthy	30,085	40,774
Rep. Wilbur D. Mills	398,506	469,580
Rep. Patsy T. Mink	4,813	9,345
Sen. Edmund S. Muskie	722,991	1,053,398
Endicott Peabody	59,178	74,063
Terry Sanford	407,348	1,086,629
Gov. George C. Wallace	1,600,303	1,603,465
Sam Yorty	124,523	117,846
Republican Party		
Nixon-Agnew*	43,287,435	49,072,062
Rep. John M. Ashbrook	204,575	215,683
Rep. Paul N. McCloskey Jr.	0	270

* GAO did not compute separate totals for these candidates.

SOURCE: General Accounting Office

Final GAO Figures

On March 24, 1974, the GAO issued a supplementary report giving total receipts and expenditures of all the 1972 candidates. The later report included donations of under $100, but did not include amounts collected prior to April 7, 1972. (Summary, box above)

The final GAO figures put Nixon-Agnew campaign receipts at $43,287,435, and spending at $49,072,062. The McGovern-Shriver-Eagleton campaign, said the GAO, took in $48,931,783 and spent $45,002,742. The figures for unsuccessful Democratic and Republican candidates were also reported. The largest amounts listed were for Hubert Humphrey (receipts: $4,267,777; expenditures: $4,838,794) and George Wallace (receipts: $1,600,303; expenditures: $1,603,465).

As previously noted, the GAO reports by no means give a full or complete picture of 1972 campaign financing. W. Clement Stone, the $2-million Nixon contributor, is listed as giving only $73,054. John Mulcahy, a former executive of the Quigley Co., a subsidiary of Pfizer Inc., gave $600,000 before the April deadline, but does not appear at all in the GAO list of top Nixon contributors. In addition, the campaign financing of GOP candidate Rep. Paul N. McCloskey Jr. (R Calif.) is not reported since he withdrew from the race in March 1972.

Nonetheless, a Congressional Quarterly review of the donor list and committee quarterly reports yielded these findings:

- Many big donors gave in several states other than their own, and some smaller states had few or no in-state donors of more than $100 in the November-December period.
- Many committees recorded contributions of more than $100 on fewer than 10 days out of a two-month period.
- Various executives in large firms gave to the same committees on the same day.
- Some families went all out for candidates, donating in six-figure amounts.
- Celebrities not only endorsed candidates verbally but also with money.

Filing: Quirks and Complications

The state finance committees and other committees—with titles such as Democrats for Nixon or Writers for McGovern—were created to prevent big contributors from being inhibited by gift taxes. An individual can give up to $3,000, tax-free, to an independent campaign committee. Records show that the Nixon campaign included 220 of these finance committees. McGovern had 785 such committees, according to his national campaign treasurer, Marian Pearlman, "created for Stewart Mott." Mott, an investor who donated a net of about $350,000, even declared himself a campaign committee. (Box, this page)

The Internal Revenue Service interprets campaign committees as being independent if one out of three officers is different from officers for other committees, if the candidates supported by the committees are different or if the committee's purposes are different. As a result, campaign finance committees proliferated in 1972, and contributors were hardly deterred from giving large sums to one candidate. In April 1974, the Senate passed a bill that would limit individual contributions to $3,000 and committee contributions to $6,000 to a single candidate. Individuals and committees were limited to $25,000 in contributions to all candidates in all federal elections in a calendar year. The House bill, passed in August, limited individual contributions to $1,000 per candidate and committee contributions to $5,000. As in the Senate bill, the House placed a $25,000 limit on individual and committee contributions to all candidates.

Confused Names, Numbers

Meanwhile, even with the mounds of paperwork available, it is impossible to tell much about the contributors at a glance. Names are not always spelled accurately, as the GAO report lists contributors just as their names appeared on individual finance and campaign committee reports. The GAO is trying to correct some of the clerical errors. "We're preparing an edited version," said Robert Higgins of the GAO, "but to clarify each case we'd have to go to the original source. If the errors are ours, they will be corrected, but if they are committee errors, we won't change them."

So discrepancies remain on the GAO list. For instance, George and Ruth Farkas of New York appear occasionally as Faikas or Furkas. Henry J. Heinz II of Pittsburgh, Pa., chairman of the H. J. Heinz Company, is listed also as Henry J. Henry and Henry J. Huing. These are alphabetized accordingly. Identification of donors is further confused by the use of initials instead of first names, listings of two or three residences and, in some areas, omission of the donor's city.

The Major Contributors

Listed below are the contributors of more than $50,000 to the 1972 presidential campaigns of Richard M. Nixon and George McGovern. The period covered, in reports filed with the General Accounting Office, was April 7-Dec. 31, 1972. Large contributions before and after that period are omitted.

NIXON DONORS

W. T. Duncan, Bryan, Texas	$300,000
Roy L. Carver, Muscatine, Iowa	$279,634
Samuel Schulman, Beverly Hills, Calif.	$253,500
Roy A. Kroc, Chicago	$237,000
F. L. Cappaert, Vicksburg, Miss.	$234,000
Jack Dreyfus, New York City	$150,000
Evan P. Helfaer, Milwaukee, Wis.	$160,900
Meshulam Riklis, New York City	$141,000
John duPont, Newtown Square, Pa.	$141,126
John C. Newington, Greenwich, Conn.	$144,553
George and Ruth Farkas, New York City	$138,000
Neil A. McConnell, New York City	$113,977
Edward J. Daly, Oakland, Calif.	$105,800
Garrick Stephenson, Southampton, N.Y.	$104,192
Eugene Dixon, Lafayette Hills, Pa.	$102,000
Edward J. Frey, Grand Rapids, Mich.	$102,000
Eugene Barwick, Chamblee, Ga.	$100,000
Howard Hughes, Houston, Texas	$100,000
Henry F. McNeil, Plymouth Meeting, Pa.	$ 99,900
Robert B. Evans, Detroit, Mich.	$ 95,000
Arthur E. Johnson, Denver, Colo.	$ 92,000
John H. Perry Jr., Riviera Beach, Fla.	$ 90,603
William J. Levitt, Lake Success, N.Y.	$ 94,712
Frank McMahon, Riviera Beach, Fla.	$ 96,000
Del E. Webb, Hollywood, Calif.	$ 88,065
W. S. Farish III, Houston, Texas	$ 82,720
Milledge A. Hart III, Dallas, Texas	$ 76,323
W. Clement Stone, Chicago, Ill.	$ 73,054
Ralph W. Parsons, Los Angeles, Calif.	$ 71,500
Potter Palmer, Lake Forest, Ill.	$ 67,564
H. F. Johnson, Racine, Wis.	$ 72,900
Sam Wyly, Dallas, Texas	$ 65,554
Elmer Bobst, New York City	$ 54,000
Henry J. Heinz II, Pittsburgh, Pa.	$ 72,517
Abe Plough, Memphis, Tenn.	$ 57,002
Frank Sinatra, Cathedral City, Calif.	$ 53,000
Delbert Coleman, Chicago, Ill.	$ 50,000

McGOVERN DONORS

Stewart Mott, New York City	$724,430
Max Palevsky, Los Angeles, Calif.	$308,919
Alejandro Zaffaroni, Atherton, Calif.	$210,765
Nicholas Noyes, Bloomington, Ind.	$203,000
Daniel Noyes, Bloomington, Ind.	$196,747
Richard Salomon, New York City	$137,000
Leonard Davis, New York City	$132,000
Alan S. Davis, New York City	$124,773
Bruce Allen, Chicago, Ill.	$102,000
Stanley Scheinbaum, Beverly Hills, Calif.	$ 77,263
Howard Metzenbaum, Cleveland, Ohio	$ 64,740
Miles Rubin, Malibu, Calif.	$ 61,600
Cornelius Dutcher, La Jolla, Calif.	$ 60,000

Numbers as well as names are fallible. For example, the GAO list shows that Edsko Hekman of Grand Rapids, Mich., contributed $100,000 to the Republican campaign. Actually, according to the report filed with the GAO by the Kent County, Michigan, Republican Finance Committee, Hekman donated only $1,000.

Occupational Hazards

The GAO decided not to include donors' occupations on the computerized list. McCoy explained the problem this way: "How are you going to list Mrs. John Rockefeller? As a 'housewife'?" Ruth Farkas, the sociologist wife of the head of Alexander's department store, and Jean du Pont McConnell, former wife of the president of the Bank of Delaware, are indeed listed as "housewives" in the quarterly reports turned in by various Nixon state finance committees. But Joan Palevsky, former wife of Xerox Corporation executive Max Palevsky and one of McGovern's donors, is described as "unemployed."

Occupational ambiguity is not limited to women. McGovern's biggest contributor, Stewart R. Mott of Stewart R. Mott & Associates, a New York City investment firm, is listed on McGovern committee reports as "Stewart Mott, philanthropist." (He is an heir to the General Motors fortune.)

In several of the quarterly reports, the donor's occupation has been omitted altogether. In some cases, a cryptic job description fails to shed much light on a donor's corporate status. For instance, one of Nixon's biggest donors, F. L. Cappaert of Vicksburg, Miss., is an oil explorer, landowner and chairman of Guerdon Industries, a mobile home manufacturing firm. Cappaert is also a director of City Investing, which owns Guerdon, and he acquired Diamond Reo, a heavy truck manufacturing firm. He is described by the state finance committee quarterly reports as a "farmer."

Another understated trio gave in the six-figure range to the McGovern campaign. Nicholas Noyes, a "student," and his brother, Daniel, a "congressional intern," are heirs to the Eli Lilly pharmaceuticals fortune. Alan S. Davis, a New York University law student, is the son of another six-figure donor, Leonard Davis, chairman of Colonial Pennsylvania Insurance Group.

Gross Sums

The amounts listed beside the name of each donor are gross sums, without explanation of subsequent events that may have altered them. There is W. T. Duncan, for instance, a land speculator and entrepreneur from Bryan, Texas, who, according to the GAO list, donated $300,000 to the Nixon campaign in August and September 1972. What the GAO records do not add is that Duncan never paid the money.

Back in May 1972, Duncan wanted to give $300,000 to the campaign of Democratic aspirant Hubert H. Humphrey. Duncan did not have the money in cash, so he borrowed it—through intermediaries—from two Washington, D.C., banks. He defaulted on both loans, and one loan for $200,000 was paid off by Dwayne Andreas, a Minnesota Humphrey supporter later to become a Nixon contributor. The $100,000 owed the other bank was renewed three times, and five Humphrey backers were obliged to pay off $20,000 of it.

After Humphrey failed to get the Democratic presidential nomination, Duncan switched to Nixon, bringing with him a $300,000 IOU. The Nixon re-election finance committee discounted the IOU at a Washington bank, but when land owned by Duncan was sold at a Texas foreclosure auction, Nixon finance director Maurice H. Stans ordered that Duncan's loan be forgiven, and the re-election committee repaid the bank.

The GAO lists Stewart Mott as contributing $724,430. But McGovern treasurer Pearlman said that amount is not accurate. "It showed the value of the stocks that Mott turned over (to McGovern). All he donated was the appreciated value of the stock," she said. Pearlman put the true amount of Mott's donation at about $350,000.

Garbled Times

The dates of the contributions are the hardest element to pin down. Although each date is supposed to reflect the date the contribution was made, several factors intervene. The date may reflect when a check was cashed or when shares of stock were sold. The committee may have been notified by telephone of a contribution and recorded it, or it may have waited for written confirmation. A brokerage house may have allowed money from sales of stock to accumulate, forwarding it all at once.

The GAO reports do not specify if gifts are in cash or stock, but round sums indicate cash contributions and figures with pennies are likely to represent money received from the sale of stock. Therefore, it is puzzling to comprehend the timing of a donor's 56 contributions of $1,824.85, made to committees over a period of almost four weeks on about 10 different days, coinciding with other major contributions.

The shortage of dates listed on state finance committee reports also raises questions. If one is to accept these dates at face value, during the period Oct. 27-Dec. 31, 1972, the District of Columbia Finance Committee to Re-elect the President took in $84,750.90, but on only six days. In Arkansas, the amount was $41,759.83 on four days. In Colorado, it was $76,871.48 taken in on seven days. This occurs frequently in medium-sized and smaller states, where much of the money received came from out-of-state donors who gave consistently, such as F. L. Cappaert, Meshulam Riklis, Roy Carver and others, and it suggests that the money might have come from the sale of stock.

Nixon Money Transfers

The smaller and medium-sized states also provide a look at how money was transferred to the national Finance Committee to Re-elect the President. In large states such as New York and California, expenses ran high to cover personnel, television advertising, canvassing and so on. The finance committee provided money to keep these state committees operating. In the smaller states, costs were lower, and a much larger amount, proportionately, was transferred to the finance committee in Washington.

For instance, the Utah committee had $12,383 in cash at the beginning of the Oct. 27-Dec. 31 reporting period. Contributions totaled $29,444.86, and expenses were $12,466.99. The state committee transferred $26,500 to the Washington finance committee and had $3,795.12 left over.

In a few states, the amount of money transferred to the Finance Committee to Re-elect the President was close to the total contributions from out-of-state donors.

● During the Oct. 27-Dec. 31 period, the Kansas committee took in $58,017.70, of which $48,709.42 came from out-of-state donors. It transferred $47,000 to the national finance committee.

● Georgia took in $65,514.97, with out-of-state donors accounting for $53,770.71. Georgia transferred $53,815 to the finance committee.

● North Carolina took in $132,755.56, with $87,176.65 from out-of-state donors. Its transfer to the finance committee was $84,975.

● Tennessee received $87,867.01 from out-of-state donors out of a total of $96,917.97. It sent $87,000 to the finance committee.

Giving at the Office

Much attention has been paid to illegal cash political donations by corporations. American Airlines' July 6, 1973, admission of an illegal $75,000 gift to the Nixon campaign led to several similar disclosures by other companies. A more subtle—and more difficult to prove—method of "home laundering" involves individual contributions by corporate executives to political campaigns. Later, the firm reimburses them in the form of appropriate Christmas bonuses or temporary wage increases.

A common practice is for companies to designate a person to collect and forward employees' donation checks. The contributions, each in a sealed envelope, are bunched together according to beneficiary and delivered the same day. In another packaging approach, a top executive may match other executives' gifts with money of his own.

Individual donations made through such packaging plans are not designated as such in the GAO reports, but the quarterly reports filed by campaign committees provide clues. Some addresses in large cities are certain to be business addresses.

A group of executives from one company, all giving on the same day, also indicates a company package. For instance, in the New York Nixon finance committee report alone:

● Five partners of Kuhn, Loeb & Company donated a total of $9,500 on Nov. 8.
● Seven executives of Ralph M. Parsons Company donated a total of $7,000 on that same day.
● On Nov. 11, eight more Kuhn, Loeb partners chipped in another $8,000.
● Three Georgia Pacific officers gave $991.57, $970.01 and $956.15 on Dec. 11.

In the North Carolina report, 18 executives of the J. A. Jones Construction Company Nov. 6 contributed a total of $5,300, most of it in $200 to $500 denominations.

The scenario worked the same way for McGovern. The name Salomon meant money. Richard Salomon, group vice president of the Squibb Corporation, donated $137,000. William Salomon of Salomon Brothers led six executives of that firm in giving $3,000 each to Businessmen for McGovern on Aug. 30.

The Family Plan

In some instances, contributing to political campaigns seems to be a family affair. The GAO donors list of post-April 7, 1972, contributions includes several husband-wife combinations. But other relationships enter the picture.

Davis

Take the case of Leonard Davis, a regular contributor to Democratic candidates and the chairman of Colonial Pennsylvania Insurance Group, in New York. Davis donated $132,000 over several months ending in October 1972. But his son, Alan, a law student at New York University, was not far behind. With his wife, Shane, Alan Davis gave McGovern fund-raisers $124,773.25 in the summer of 1972.

Noyes

The Noyes brothers, heirs to the Eli Lilly pharmaceutical fortune, were also very close in their support of McGovern. From September through Nov. 6, 1972, Nicholas S. Noyes, listed as a Bloomington, Ind., student, gave $203,000. His brother, Daniel, who described himself as a

Patterns of Giving

In November and December 1972, according to reports filed with the General Accounting Office (GAO) by state finance committees for the Nixon campaign, four of the President's top donors contributed a total of nearly $732,000.

The dates of the contributions followed a definite pattern in all but three states, with more than one of the four donors, and sometimes all four, contributing to one or more state committees on the same days. The four, and their contributions (rounded off to the nearest dollar) as reported to the GAO:

● Neil A. McConnell, $113,977.
● F. L. Cappaert, $234,000.
● Garrick Stephenson, $104,191.
● Roy J. Carver, $279,634. *(Major contributors' list, box, p. 69)*

Nobody questioned by Congressional Quarterly could explain the patterns. Stephenson, an antique dealer from Southampton, N.Y., was the only one of the four contributors who was available for comment. He had no explanation for the choice of state committees to which his donation, in stocks, went. He said he actually made the donation in September 1972, when he was approached by Maurice H. Stans, finance director of the Nixon campaign. The re-election finance committee handled the sale of the stock and the distribution of the proceeds, Stephenson said. He was not acquainted with any of the other three men, he said.

The personal secretary to Carver, a business executive from Muscatine, Iowa, told Congressional Quarterly that Carver's gift had been in stocks and the committee took care of its distribution. An attorney for McConnell, an investor from New York City, said he had no idea how the Nixon finance committee handled his client's contribution in cash and stocks. A secretary to Cappaert, a Vicksburg, Miss., mobile home company executive, said she did not know where he was or when he would return.

The explanation given by Paul Barrick, treasurer of the President's re-election finance committee, differed from that of Stephenson and of Carver's secretary. The Washington-based committee, he said, provided contributors with a list of state committees, from which the contributors could make their choices to receive cash or shares of stock. The main committee did not guide donors in choosing state committees, Barrick said.

Why did Cappaert, Carver, McConnell and Stephenson give so frequently on the same days to the same committees? Contributors are given an alphabetical list, said Barrick, and "they normally start down and some give to certain states and want to skip others." Among their favorite choices are New York, Florida and Michigan, he added.

Why did all four contributors skip Utah but not Wisconsin or Wyoming? "It's meaningless to skip a state," said Barrick. "It's based on (the donor's) budget."

congressional intern, donated $196,747.50 recorded on Dec. 26. Much of Nicholas Noyes' largess was in the form of forgiven loans. Relatively less generous was the brothers' grandfather, Nicholas H. Noyes, who is recorded by the GAO as contributing $7,000 to the Nixon campaign.

Du Pont

Some donors are united by both family and corporate ties. The du Ponts of Delaware, Nixon contributors, are a case in point. John du Pont, a Greenville, Del., naturalist who lives in Pennsylvania, leads the du Ponts with the sum of $141,125.86, given in December. The Delaware finance committee report for Oct. 27-Dec. 31 reads like a du Pont family roster: Reynolds du Pont, not employed, $3,000; Pierre S. du Pont, a self-employed investor, $3,000; Hugh R. Sharp Jr., director of E. I. du Pont de Nemours & Company, $3,000; William K. du Pont, self-employed investor, $2,000; Richard C. du Pont Jr., president of Summit Aviation, $500; Lammot du Pont Copeland, a director and past chairman of the du Pont Company, $3,000; Daniela C. Copeland, housewife, $2,500; C. B. McCoy Jr., chairman of the du Pont Company, $200; Jean du Pont McConnell, housewife, $1,000.

The Washington Post reported in May 1973 that 90 persons associated with E. I. du Pont de Nemours & Company—directors, executives and family members—had donated a total of $235,742.

Rockefeller

Another famous family, the Rockefellers, spent slightly less money but spread it over more candidates. Their choices indicate a generation gap, with the elders lining up on the Nixon side. David Rockefeller, chairman of Chase Manhattan Bank, donated $55,500. New York Gov. Nelson A. Rockefeller gave $50,000. Laurence Rockefeller, president of the Rockefeller Brothers Fund, gave $11,000, and the late former Arkansas Gov. Winthrop Rockefeller contributed $44,200.

The younger Rockefellers, however, supported Democratic aspirants. David Rockefeller's son, Richard, came up with $2,000 for McGovern, while his daughter, Abby, gave Shirley Chisholm $1,000. John D. Rockefeller IV, the unsuccessful candidate for governor of West Virginia in 1972, and his wife, Sharon, jointly contributed $8,626 to the Democrats. His sister, Alida Rockefeller, contributed $1,-000 to the McGovern campaign.

The 'Sparklies'

Celebrities, particularly entertainers and actors, have been a fixture of American political campaigns for years. The "sparklies," as campaign workers have dubbed them, donate time and talent to fund-raising concerts and personal appearances.

And they often give money. The biggest entertainer-contributor of 1972 was Frank Sinatra. In October and November, he donated $53,000 to various Nixon finance committees. It was the first time Sinatra supported a Nixon campaign—he gave $1,000 to Humphrey in 1968.

But it was not the first time the Republicans benefitted from Sinatra's largess. In 1970, he gave $35,000, divided among Democratic and Republican candidates in state elec-

tions. The lion's share went to Republican Gov. Ronald Reagan of California.

A large contributor to the McGovern campaign was film-maker and artist Andy Warhol. He donated a total of $35,623 from September through November.

Among show-business celebrities who contributed between $1,000 and $3,000 to one of the presidential nominees were ventriloquist Edgar Bergen ($2,000 to Nixon), actor Cliff Robertson ($1,000 to Nixon) and singer Polly Bergen ($2,800 to McGovern).

Jacqueline Kennedy Onassis, wife of Greek shipping magnate Aristotle Onassis and widow of John F. Kennedy—and sister-in-law of Sargent Shriver, the Democratic vice presidential candidate—gave only $2,500 in her name to the McGovern-Shriver committee.

Feminist leader Gloria Steinem gave $415 to McGovern. Donations from two labor leaders reflected the divisions in their ranks in 1972: Leonard Woodcock of the UAW gave $526 to McGovern, and Teamster James R. Hoffa contributed $400 to Nixon.

Conclusion

The details of the financing of the 1972 presidential race may never be sorted out. But the impact of the financing procedures used in the campaign will continue to be felt for years. Part of the difficulties that forced President Nixon's resignation from office can be traced to the irregularities of his re-election effort, and to the practices used by the Finance Committee to Re-elect the President.

The total amount spent by all presidential candidates is certainly in excess of $100-million. The Nixon effort cost at least $62-million and may have surpassed $70-million. The McGovern campaign probably approached $50-million. Millions more were spent by unsuccessful candidates in primary races, and by lesser parties in the national elections.▪

(European Finance continued from p. 59)

areas of reform: the extent of public financing of campaigns, the ways of enforcing controls, and whether limits should be set on spending. While Britain, which has not used an election petition to punish a false statement of expenses since 1929, stands out as an enviable example, the self-policing aspects of British campaigns may not—particularly in the light of the finance abuses of Watergate—appear to be relevant to the American situation. And critics have cautioned that the fact that public financing has been adopted to some degree by several of the European democracies is no guarantee that it would be a panacea to cleanse American election campaigns.   ▪

1. Philip Rawstorne, "The British Way of Democracy," *The Financial Times*, February 8, 1974.
2. Nils Andren, "Partisan Motivation and Concern for System Legitimacy in the Scandinavian Deliberations on Public Subsidies," *Comparative Political Finance*, 1970, p. 50.
3. Pertti Pesonen, "Impact of Public Financing on Political Parties: the Finnish Experience," Citizens Research Foundation, 1974, p. 23.

THE POWER OF INCUMBENCY: MONEY FLOWS TO THE WINNERS

Incumbent members of Congress, Democrats and Republicans alike, have a powerful advantage over their challengers when it comes to raising money for re-election. But when neither major-party candidate is an incumbent, the ability to raise funds evens out.

These were two of the findings of a study on campaign spending conducted by Common Cause, the "citizens' lobby." The results, based on analysis of reports filed by congressional candidates and their campaign committees, were announced on Sept. 13, 1973.

Further data collected by Common Cause on the 1972 House and Senate Campaigns was released on Nov. 30, 1973. At that time Fred Werthmeir, Common Cause legislative director, commented, "In Congress today we have neither a Democratic nor a Republican Party. Rather we have an incumbency party which operates a monopoly." Common Cause Chairman John Gardner stated in Sept. 19 testimony before a Senate subcommittee that the advantage of imcumbency "raises grave doubts as to whether we presently have a competitive system of representation."

The Common Cause finance monitoring project pored over the reports of 1,896 congressional candidates and their committees. The period covered by the study was April 7-Dec. 31, 1972. April 7 was the date the 1971 federal disclosure law took effect. Some of the principal findings and conclusions of the study:

● Total spending reported by all congressional candidates was about $77-million.

● Subtracting the expenditures of 780 Senate and House primary losers, the total reported spent by candidates who survived to run in the November elections was $66.4-million. *(Box below)*

● The total raised for the candidates who ran in November was $69.7-million.

● These general election candidates reported $7.4-million cash on hand on April 6, 1972—the day before the new law took effect—and raised the other $62.3-million between April 7 and the end of the year. About $5.9-million of the cash on hand was in the treasuries of incumbents.

● Of the total raised after April 7, 35 per cent came from 41,600 individuals who contributed more than $100 each. More than half of this amount was in donations of $500 or more.

● Twenty-six per cent of the contributions over $100 was given by political and special-interest committees.

● Thirty-two per cent was in contributions of $100 or less.

● Seven per cent represented net loans of more than $100. Of $5.9-million borrowed by candidates to meet their expenses, $1.5-million had been paid back by Dec. 31.

Intake and Output for 1972 Congressional Campaigns *

	Total	Senate	House
Cash on hand (April 7)	$ 7,358,393	$ 3,573,787	$ 3,784,606
Total receipts (April 7—Dec. 31)	$62,285,985	$23,767,291	$38,518,694
Individual contributions	$21,723,868	$ 9,696,320	$12,027,548
Out-of-state—$101 and over	$ 4,169,954	$ 2,413,029	$ 1,756,925
In-state—$500 and over	$12,222,431	$ 5,298,171	$ 6,924,260
In-state—$101 to $499	$ 5,331,483	$ 1,985,120	$ 3,346,363
Committee contributions—$101 and over	$16,547,108	$ 6,016,390	$10,530,718
Political parties—$101 and over	$ 7,654,097	$ 3,263,480	$ 4,390,617
Other committees—$101 and over	$ 8,893,011	$ 2,752,910	$ 6,140,101
Net loans of $101 and over	$ 4,390,682	$ 1,432,612	$ 2,958,070
Loans of $101 and over	$ 5,886,270	$ 1,967,324	$ 3,918,946
Loans repaid	$ 1,495,588	$ 534,712	$ 960,876
Other receipts ($100 and less)	$19,624,327	$ 6,621,969	$13,002,358
Total contributions	$69,644,378	$27,341,078	$42,303,300
Total expenditures	$66,405,769	$26,446,393	$39,959,376
Number of candidates	1,116	106	1,010

* *Not including primary losers.*

SOURCE: Common Cause

Contributions, Expenditures for 1972 Senate Races

Listed below are the amounts contributed to and spent by the major candidates for the Senate in 1972.

Figures for losers in party primaries are not included. Winners are listed first. Asterisk (*) denotes incumbent.

Candidates	Contributions	Expenditures
ALABAMA		
John Sparkman* (D)	$ 703,342	$ 702,109
Winton Blount (R)	774,039	764,961
ALASKA		
Ted Stevens* (R)	259,856	195,123
Gene Guess (D)	46,348	47,131
ARKANSAS		
John L. McClellan* (D)	516,666	516,573
Wayne Babbitt (R)	72,643	72,643
COLORADO		
Floyd H. Haskell (D)	178,024	176,243
Gordon Allott* (R)	344,457	308,305
DELAWARE		
Joe Biden (D)	238,762	262,699
Caleb Boggs* (R)	167,657	167,657
GEORGIA		
Sam Nunn (D)	629,570	567,968
Fletcher Thompson (R)	454,586	444,635
IDAHO		
James A. McClure (R)	446,382	405,788
William E. Davis (D)	222,963	204,878
ILLINOIS		
Charles H. Percy* (R)	1,399,374	1,408,822
Roman Pucinski (D)	339,402	335,482
IOWA		
Dick Clark (D)	244,714	241,803
Jack Miller* (R)	335,276	328,263
KANSAS		
James B. Pearson* (R)	202,145	105,651
Arch Tetzlaff (D)	5,226	6,742
KENTUCKY		
Walter (Dee) Huddleston (D)	653,412	658,590
Louie Nunn (R)	611,013	603,649
LOUISIANA		
J. Bennett Johnston Jr. (D)	556,912	511,616
John McKeithen (I)	394,510	394,510
Ben Toledano (R)	118,906	156,347
MAINE		
William D. Hathaway (D)	202,798	202,208
Margaret Chase Smith* (R)	13,461	14,950
MASSACHUSETTS		
Edward W. Brooke* (R)	672,334	368,038
John Droney (D)	82,888	82,888
MICHIGAN		
Robert P. Griffin* (R)	1,443,304	1,394,927
Frank Kelley (D)	544,009	547,819
MINNESOTA		
Walter F. Mondale * (D)	497,851	538,532
Philip Hansen (R)	305,131	304,750

Candidates	Contributions	Expenditures
MISSISSIPPI		
James O. Eastland* (D)	$ 416,900	$ 410,221
Gil Carmichael (R)	153,307	152,531
MONTANA		
Lee Metcalf* (D)	194,557	136,551
Henry Hibbard (R)	284,164	286,748
NEBRASKA		
Carl T. Curtis* (R)	280,753	250,392
Terry Carpenter (D)	16,500	38,629
NEW HAMPSHIRE		
Thomas J. McIntyre* (D)	90,162	82,800
Wesley Powell (R)	104,907	104,779
NEW JERSEY		
Clifford P. Case* (R)	170,584	145,275
Paul Krebs (D)	46,242	46,160
NEW MEXICO		
Pete V. Domenici (R)	489,380	517,310
Jack Daniels (D)	463,735	496,980
NORTH CAROLINA		
Jesse A. Helms (R)	659,895	654,246
Nick Galifianakis (D)	496,667	470,093
OKLAHOMA		
Dewey F. Bartlett (R)	625,639	625,095
Ed Edmondson (D)	525,900	512,058
OREGON		
Mark O. Hatfield * (R)	286,849	299,626
Wayne Morse (D)	231,682	251,904
RHODE ISLAND		
Claiborne Pell* (D)	515,685	528,347
John Chafee (R)	472,984	457,409
SOUTH CAROLINA		
Strom Thurmond* (R)	666,263	666,329
Eugene Zeigler (D)	156,473	167,755
SOUTH DAKOTA		
James Abourezk (D)	421,215	427,063
Robert Hirsch (R)	316,313	300,800
TENNESSEE		
Howard H. Baker Jr.* (R)	887,817	830,769
Ray Blanton (D)	239,699	244,653
TEXAS		
John G. Tower* (R)	2,303,355	2,301,870
Barefoot Sanders (D)	630,440	629,008
VIRGINIA		
William Lloyd Scott (R)	648,138	619,908
William Spong* (D)	384,804	380,921
WEST VIRGINIA		
Jennings Randolph* (D)	129,859	133,670
Louise Leonard (R)	47,861	45,513
WYOMING		
Clifford P. Hansen* (R)	261,923	169,878
Mike Vinich (D)	10,388	10,411

SOURCE: Common Cause

• One of every three dollars reported spent by general election candidates went into communications media—radio, television, newspapers, magazines, billboards and telephone banks. Total: $22.5-million.

• Incumbents of either party could raise funds twice as easily as could their challengers. In races without incumbents, sufficient money was available to candidates of both major parties.

• Large amounts of money were required in order to finance closely contested races or to defeat incumbents. "Winners consistently outspent losers," the Common Cause report said, although there were well-financed exceptions.

Senate Races. The 106 candidates who ran for the Senate in the November 1972 elections raised about $27.3-million and spent about $26.4-million, according to Common Cause. Winners of the 33 elections outspent their major-party opponents by about two to one. And incumbents outspent challengers by about the same ratio. The study found that:

• In 19 of 25 races, incumbents outspent challengers.
• In 28 of 33 races, winners outspent losers.
• In all eight races in which there was no incumbent, winners outspent losers.

The four biggest spenders in Senate contests were Republican incumbents, and all four won re-election. They were John G. Tower (Texas), $2.3-million; Charles H. Percy (Ill.), $1.4-million; Robert P. Griffin (Mich.), $1.4-million, and Howard H. Baker (Tenn.), $831,000.

Losers outspent winners in Alabama, Colorado, Iowa, Montana and New Hampshire. The incumbents were considered vulnerable in all five states, and in two—Colorado and Iowa—incumbent Republicans were unexpectedly unseated.

House Races. Similar patterns prevailed in the contests for House seats. The 318 incumbents who had major-party challengers out-collected and out-spent their opponents by wide margins, but not so wide as in the Senate. Democratic incumbents spent an average of $50,009 and Republican incumbents an average of $51,947. Democratic challengers, on the other hand, spent an average of $5, and Republican challengers $33,587.

The 17 challengers who turned out incumbents spent, on the average, far more than the incumbents. Among the 10 biggest spenders in House races, not one was a winning challenger who outspent an incumbent. Seven of the top 10 spenders lost. (Box, this page)

Races without incumbents not only featured a more equal distribution of spending, but a lot more spending in general. Democrats in these House districts spent an average of $90,074, Republicans a nearly identical $90,030.

In 52 House districts, incumbents had no major-party challengers in 1972.

Cost and Close. Common Cause reported finding a connection between plurality and cost—the closer a race was, the more expensive it was likely to be. House candidates who won with more than 60 per cent of the vote spent an average of less than $55,000. Elections won with less than 55 per cent cost more than $100,000, on the average, not only for the winner but for the loser as well.

Only 10 incumbents were unseated by challengers in the general election in 1972, but here, too, money played its role. The incumbents who lost were significantly outspent. They averaged expenditures of $86,075, compared to $125,521 for their successful opponents.

The 10 House incumbents defeated represented less than 5 per cent of all the incumbents who ran for re-election. It marked the third straight time that the re-election rate for House incumbents was over 95 per cent.

Biggest House Spenders in 1972

Listed below are the 10 candidates whose records indicated that they spent more than any others for House campaigns in 1972. Asterisk (*) denotes incumbents. Losers are in italics.

Candidates	States, Districts		Expenditures
Paul N. McCloskey Jr. (R)*	Calif.	17	$321,558
Jack Brown (D)	Ariz.	4	$318,254
Allard K. Lowenstein (Lib.)	N.Y.	14	$285,475
John Kerry (D)	Mass.	5	$279,746
William Weeks (R)	Mass.	12	$269,046
Roger Boas (D)	Calif.	6	$266,760
Fortney H. (Pete) Stark (D)	Calif.	8	$266,684
Louis Watkins (D)	La.	3	$229,767
Abner Mikva (D)*	Ill.	10	$218,543
Manuel Lujan Jr. (R)*	N.M.	1	$212,093

SOURCE: Common Cause

The re-election rate for Senate incumbents was significantly lower—80 per cent. Four of the six incumbent senators who lost were outspent. One of them, Margaret Chase Smith (R Maine 1949-73) was outspent $202,208 to $14,950 by her challenger, William D. Hathaway (D).

Most Expensive. The most expensive Senate race of 1972—and quite possibly of all time, some observers think —occurred in Texas, where Republican John G. Tower defended his seat against the challenge of Democrat Bare foot Sanders. Tower spent $2,301,870 to only $629,008 for Sanders, and beat him 53 per cent to 44.

Two other Republican senators went over the million mark in spending, and both won. It cost Robert P. Griffin $1,394,927 to defeat Democrat Frank J. Kelley, who spent $547,819. In Illinois, Charles H. Percy spent $1,-408,822 in his campaign against Democratic Rep. Roman C. Pucinski (1959-73). The $335,482 that Pucinski spent made him the most heavily outspent Senate candidate in any of the 10 costliest races, with a ratio of better than four-to-one against him.

Spending in House races was small by comparison, but far higher than most observers think it had ever gone before. In each of two races, the total cost was more than $500,000.

One of these was in the 5th District of Massachusetts, where activist Vietnam veteran John F. Kerry (D) opposed Paul J. Cronin (R) for the seat of the resigned Rep. F. Bradford Morse (R 1961-72). Kerry spent $279,746 to $171,414 for Cronin, who won. An independent candidate spent $62,952, bringing the total to $514,112.

In California, Rep. Paul N. McCloskey Jr. (R) spent $321,558 to win a third full term in the House. Spending by a Democrat and by a conservative write-in challenger brought the total for McCloskey's 17th District to $506,946. McCloskey's personal total was the highest recorded for any 1972 House candidate in the Common Cause study.

The only House race in which both candidates went over $200,000 was in Illinois' 10th District, where Rep. Abner J. Mikva (D 1969-73) spent $218,543 but still lost to Republican Samuel H. Young, who spent $206,166. Mikva had moved to the area after his own 2nd District was eliminated by redistricting.   ∎

CONTRIBUTIONS, EXPENDITURES FOR 1972 HOUSE RACES

SOURCE: Common Cause

State and District	General Election Candidates	Per cent of Primary Vote	Per cent of General Election Vote	Contributions	Expenditures
ALABAMA					
1	Edwards* (R)	—	76.5	$ 42,862	$ 27,612
	McCrory (D)	69.3	17.8	525	1,063
2	Dickinson* (R)	—	54.8	61,432	50,193
	Reeves (D)	52.8**	41.5	122,603	122,067
3	Nichols* (D)	—	75.6	44,377	34,984
	Kerr (R)	—	20.6	7,019	6,718
4	Bevill* (D)	91.3	69.6	49,265	38,918
	Nelson (R)	49.7	30.0	12,550	12,550
5	Jones* (D)	78.1	74.2	33,596	30,786
	Schrader (R)	—	24.4	11,175	11,175
6	Buchanan* (R)	—	59.8	35,898	33,976
	Erdreich (D)	81.3	35.6	18,947	18,947
7	Flowers* (D)	64.8	84.8†	18,277	16,303
ALASKA					
1	Begich* (D)	—	56.2	77,565	64,893
	Young (R)	84.5	43.8	47,781	46,300
ARIZONA					
1	Rhodes* (R)	88.1	57.3	73,267	48,315
	Pollock (D)	62.7	42.7	27,755	28,646
2	Udall* (D)	—	63.5	38,174	38,174
	Savoie (R)	—	36.5	32,791	31,694
3	Steiger* (R)	—	63.0	55,446	37,691
	Wyckoff (D)	—	37.0	24,629	24,648
4	Conlan (R)	41.5	53.0	150,341	154,662
	Brown (D)	37.1	47.0	303,719	318,254
ARKANSAS					
1	Alexander* (D)	—	—	1,040	none
2	Mills* (D)	—	—	none	none
3	Hammerschmidt* (R)	—	77.3	34,683	27,588
	Hatfield (D)	53.0**	22.7	4,138	4,243
4	Thornton (D)	51.3	—	51,854	51,854
CALIFORNIA					
1	Clausen* (R)	—	62.3	70,526	49,450
	Nighswonger (D)	44.4	34.2	6,632	6,601
2	Johnson* (D)	—	68.4	60,906	37,981
	Callahan (R)	53.1	28.7	28,966	28,985
3	Moss* (D)	—	69.9	50,799	39,314
	Rakus (R)	57.4	30.1	8,049	8,042
4	Leggett* (D)	—	67.4	18,971	19,128
	Chang (R)	53.8	32.6	24,957	24,957
5	Burton* (D)	66.7	81.8	53,606	46,899
	Powell (R)	—	18.2	19,076	18,715
6	Mailliard* (R)	—	52.1	165,636	148,550
	Boas (D)	77.7	47.9	265,272	266,760
7	Dellums* (D)	73.1	55.9	91,259	100,853
	Hannaford (R)	39.3	38.1	104,530	100,286
	Cortese (Am. Ind.)	—	6.0	48,980	48,980
8	Stark (D)	55.7	52.9	217,248	266,684
	Warden (R)	64.5	47.1	39,748	44,499
9	Edwards* (D)	87.4	72.3	27,592	25,398
	Smith (R)	—	25.1	5,386	4,792
10	Gubser* (R)	—	64.6	63,136	48,529
	Gillette (D),	51.4	35.4	26,848	26,433
11	Ryan (D)	—	60.5	53,033	52,127
	Chase (R)	53.6	36.9	52,622	52,441
12	Talcott* (R)	—	54.0	71,760	61,828
	Camacho (D)	58.1	43.1	57,870	57,865
13	Teague* (R)	—	73.8	47,791	39,546
	Cleveland (D)	—	26.1	8,998	10,143
14	Waldie* (D)	—	77.6	48,272	47,160
	Sims (R)	—	22.4	4,604	4,524
15	McFall* (D)	—	—	35,776	22,647
16	Sisk* (D)	—	79.1	90,472	54,890
	Harner (R)	—	20.9	17,728	19,219
17	McCloskey* (R)	43.7	54.6	313,856	321,558
	Stewart (D)	36.8	35.9	103,905	109,418
	Knapp (I)	—	9.5	76,068	75,970
18	Mathias* (R)	—	66.4	66,570	47,737
	Lavery (D)	—	33.6	9,624	10,072
19	Holifield* (D)	51.9	67.2	50,311	26,110
	Fisher (R)	66.6	27.9	5,754	5,202
20	Moorhead (R)	51.2	57.4	104,140	97,617
	Binkley (D)	—	42.6	52,793	56,380
21	Hawkins* (D)	—	82.9	14,112	10,459
	Lundy (R)	—	17.1	325	325
22	Corman* (D)	85.5	67.6	58,895	58,544
	Wolfe (R)	65.8	29.3	17,992	19,169
23	Clawson* (R)	—	61.4	73,016	65,007
	Tuohey (D)	54.1	38.6	39,039	45,844
24	Rousselot* (R)	—	70.1	67,970	61,473
	Mandell (D)	66.0	29.9	4,660	4,660
25	Wiggins* (R)	—	64.9	53,107	34,643
	Craven (D)	64.5	31.9	5,926	5,925
26	Rees* (D)	86.1	68.6	70,820	45,963
	Rutta (R)	78.1	27.9	229	193
27	Goldwater* (R)	—	57.4	134,263	134,263
	Novak (D)	37.0	42.6	44,292	42,840
28	Bell* (R)	—	60.7	50,604	48,719
	Shapiro (D)	68.7	37.5	56,437	60,424
29	Danielson* (D)	—	62.7	50,186	30,832
	Ferraro (R)	—	33.5	14,533	14,526
30	Roybal* (D)	85.7	68.4	26,224	24,574
	Brophy (R)	83.0	28.6	27,681	31,143
31	Wilson* (D)	50.7	52.3	67,942	67,713
	Valentine (R)	—	42.5	63,432	62,875
32	Hosmer* (R)	—	65.9	47,529	23,572
	Murray (D)	55.0	31.9	25,252	23,072
33	Pettis* (R)	—	75.0	80,029	36,833
	Thompson (D)	48.7	25.0	5,151	5,311
34	Hanna* (D)	—	67.1	74,530	40,785
	Ratterree (R)	55.4	29.0	13,850	13,181
35	Anderson* (D)	—	74.8	61,574	38,077
	Brown (R)	—	25.2	214	3,051
36	Ketchum (R)	80.9	52.7	111,303	106,576
	Lemucchi (D)	28.5	43.5	57,013	58,066
	Armour (AI)	—	3.8	16,938	16,913
37	Burke (D)	53.6	73.2	131,756	138,024
	Tria (R)	59.7	24.6	24,112	24,112
38	Brown, Jr. (D)	28.2	55.9	154,932	154,743
	Snider (R)	45.4	43.4	109,509	108,537
39	Hinshaw (R)	45.6	65.7	162,293	161,814
	Black (D)	47.0	34.3	10,549	10,515
40	Wilson* (R)	—	67.8	49,638	32,066
	Caprio (D)	—	30.3	6,718	7,349
41	Van Deerlin* (D)	—	74.0	69,936	44,931
	Kau (R)	—	26.0	16,231	15,776
42	Burgener (R)	78.7	67.5	107,395	91,664
	Lowe (D)	52.6	29.1	4,952	4,917

State and District	General Election Candidates	Per cent of Primary Vote	Per cent of General Election Vote	Contri- butions	Expendi- tures
43	Veysey* (R)	—	62.7	73,823	60,432
	Robles (D)	78.8	37.3	21,920	21,920
COLORADO					
1	Schroeder (D)	54.8	51.6	86,002	80,508
	McKevitt* (R)	—	47.5	109,535	78,436
2	Brotzman* (R)	—	66.3	81,784	60,004
	Brush (D)	—	33.4	5,419	5,509
3	Evans* (D)	—	66.3	58,426	45,734
	Brady (R)	77.9	33.7	9,435	9,435
4	Johnson (R)	60.3	51.0	59,855	51,747
	Merson (D)	52.7	49.0	88,504	104,994
5	Armstrong (R)	—	62.3	97,142	88,538
	Johnson (D)	66.7	36.5	17,291	17,273
CONNECTICUT					
1	Cotter* (D)	—	56.9	96,208	96,208
	Rittenband (R)	—	41.9	56,375	55,985
2	Steele* (R)	—	65.9	141,485	141,485
	Hilsman (D)	—	34.1	60,575	60,226
3	Giaimo* (D)	—	53.3	79,997	79,608
	Povinelli (R)	—	46.7	35,046	33,591
4	McKinney* (R)	—	63.1	96,629	112,669
	McLoughlin (D)	—	36.9	41,009	39,809
5	Sarasin (R)	—	51.2	81,067	80,251
	Monagan* (D)	—	48.8	86,661	84,436
6	Grasso* (D)	—	60.2	85,968	85,968
	Walsh (R)	—	39.8	60,217	59,956
DELAWARE					
1	DuPont" (R)	—	62.5	98,003	82,333
	Handloff (D)	—	36.9	43,795	42,831
FLORIDA					
1	Sikes* (D)	80.8	—	55,143	36,651
2	Fuqua* (D)	72.5	—	49,159	24,186
3	Bennett* (D)	—	82.0	22,301	22,301
	Bowen (R)	—	18.0	2,375	2,439
4	Chappell, Jr.* (D)	—	55.9	98,141	93,103
	Fleuchaus (R)	—	44.1	39,841	38,840
5	Gunter, Jr. (D)	82.7	55.5	139,160	107,745
	Insco (R)	50.6**	44.5	80,505	79,654
6	Young* (R)	—	76.0	38,748	31,686
	Plunkett (D)	—	24.0	3,177	2,925
7	Gibbons* (D)	—	68.0	19,050	8,194
	Carter (R)	—	32.0	14,218	14,218
8	Haley* (D)	—	57.8	36,984	36,960
	Thompson, Jr. (R)	—	42.2	37,678	38,587
9	Frey, Jr.* (R)	—	—	56,428	22,255
10	Bafalis (R)	71.6	62.0	129,393	129,393
	Sikes (D)	56.4**	38.0	56,031	55,035
11	Rogers* (D)	—	60.2	104,917	87,253
	Gustafson (R)	—	39.8	59,108	59,108
12	Burke* (R)	—	62.8	38,195	30,600
	Stephanis (D)	—	37.2	56,434	56,434
13	Lehman (D)	57.6**	61.6	123,858	122,725
	Bethel (R)	56.1	38.4	34,010	31,660
14	Pepper* (D)	64.3	67.6	95,863	95,864
	Estrella (R)	—	32.4	44,007	34,921
15	Fascell* (D)	—	56.8	63,690	61,370
	Rubin (R)	51.6	43.2	9,511	9,522
GEORGIA					
1	Ginn (D)	55.1**	—	106,000	76,835
2	Mathis* (D)	—	—	4,548	2,042
3	Brinkley* (D)	—	—	2,125	1,030
4	Blackburn* (R)	—	75.9	46,335	34,276
	Welborn (D)	58.9	24.1	3,886	3,886
5	Young (D)	60.7	52.8	170,051	159,431
	Cook (R)	—	47.2	160,391	149,616
6	Flynt* (D)	76.9	—	14,204	2,612
7	Davis* (D)	52.1	58.3	32,249	18,500
	Sherrill (R)	60.7	41.7	4,511	4,511
8	Stuckey* (D)	65.7	62.4	105,282	103,254
	Thompson (R)	—	37.6	17,061	17,448
9	Landrum* (D)	—	—	2,970	1,378
10	Stephens* (D)	85.3	—	13,421	8,520
HAWAII					
1	Matsunaga* (D)	—	54.7	177,389	127,753
	Rohlfing (R)	91.4	45.3	183,448	179,221
2	Mink* (D)	74.8	57.1	82,348	71,620
	Hansen (R)	—	42.9	44,390	39,836
IDAHO					
1	Symms (R)	45.7	55.6	92,099	89,306
	Williams (D)	—	44.4	59,819	59,585
2	Hansen* (R)	—	69.2	26,516	11,457
	Ludlow (D)	—	27.0	14,360	13,632
ILLINOIS					
1	Metcalfe* (D)	—	91.4	21,036	9,861
	Coggs (R)	—	8.6	none	1,235
2	Murphy* (D)	—	75.0	30,109	22,510
	Doyle (R)	—	25.0	4,250	3,044
3	Hanrahan (R)	72.3	62.3	36,229	34,839
	Coman (D)	—	37.7	40,853	40,712
4	Derwinski* (R)	—	70.5	22,862	17,896
	Dore (D)	51.4	29.5	12,155	11,342
5	Kluczynski* (D)	86.5	72.8	20,566	12,936
	Jarzab (R)	—	27.2	none	1,694
6	Collier" (R)	—	61.2	35,195	32,303
	Galasso (D)	—	38.8	40,050	40,050
7	Collins* (D)	83.8	82.8	5,535	1,585
	Lento (R)	—	17.2	792	792
8	Rostenkowski* (D)	—	74.0	25,943	13,737
	Stepnowski (R)	—	26.0	225	225
9	Yates* (D)	—	68.3	56,767	29,723
	Fetridge (R)	—	31.7	16,679	16,353
10	Young (R)	59.7	51.6	193,219	208,186
	Mikva* (D)	65.6	48.4	220,944	218,543
11	Annunzio* (D)	—	53.3	122,484	117,415
	Hoellen (R)	69.7	46.7	91,467	108,126
12	Crane* (R)	—	74.2	61,574	52,661
	Frank (D)	—	25.8	4,225	4,154
13	McClory* (R)	—	61.5	24,603	25,010
	Beetham (D)	—	38.5	18,607	20,120
14	Erlenborn* (R)	—	72.8	28,004	24,871
	Wall (D)	—	27.2	7,392	7,183
15	Arends* (R)	57.2	57.2	43,007	33,450
	Hall (D)	52.8	42.8	5,119	7,753
16	Anderson* (R)	—	71.9	48,050	33,544
	Devine, Jr. (D)	69.0	28.1	1,522	1,463
17	O'Brien (R)	—	55.6	59,980	55,360
	Houlihan (D)	—	44.4	32,748	32,748
18	Michel* (R)	—	64.8	22,976	20,850
	Nordvall (D)	65.3	35.2	2,667	2,901
19	Railsback* (R)	—	—	27,185	25,610
20	Findley* (R)	—	68.8	84,683	71,187
	O'Shea (D)	—	31.2	15,671	15,671
21	Madigan (R)	68.7	54.8	86,573	85,958
	Johnson (D)	—	45.2	30,577	29,802
22	Shipley* (D)	—	56.5	55,343	52,812
	Lamkin (R)	—	41.0	60,046	83,554
23	Price* (D)	—	75.1	24,435	17,134
	Mays (R)	39.7	24.9	1,691	2,734
24	Gray* (D)	—	93.7†	27,941	11,624

State and District	General Election Candidates	Per cent of Primary Vote	Per cent of General Election Vote	Contributions	Expenditures
INDIANA					
1	Madden* (D)	46.5	56.9	66,678	72,655
	Haller (R)	71.0	43.1	8,690	9,551
2	Landgrebe* (R)	54.5	54.7	70,700	55,474
	Fithian (D)	—	45.3	43,015	44,359
3	Brademas* (D)	—	55.2	140,906	133,634
	Newman (R)	74.9	43.2	45,160	45,160
4	Roush* (D)	—	51.5	63,875	63,613
	Bloom (R)	48.0	48.5	123,796	165,984
5	Hillis* (R)	85.9	64.1	71,309	64,781
	Williams (D)	37.5	35.9	6,644	9,026
6	Bray* (R)	—	64.8	36,341	32,297
	Evans (D)	—	35.2	8,296	8,253
7	Myers* (R)	—	61.6	58,855	58,186
	Henegar (D)	66.5	38.4	30,950	40,000
8	Zion* (R)	—	63.4	48,192	24,731
	Deen (D)	62.9	36.6	1,634	1,634
9	Hamilton* (D)	—	62.9	63,625	61,021
	Johnson (R)	37.9	37.1	6,555	6,389
10	Dennis* (R)	—	57.2	52,731	51,906
	Sharp (D)	67.0	42.8	69,879	69,879
11	Hudnut (R)	45.5	51.2	163,442	165,016
	Jacobs* (D)	84.7	48.8	71,166	64,422
IOWA					
1	Mezvinsky (D)	63.7	53.4	116,349	113,546
	Schwengel* (R)	—	45.7	69,514	69,615
2	Culver* (D)	—	59.2	59,910	40,794
	Ellsworth (R)	—	40.8	63,480	67,946
3	Gross* (R)	—	55.7	43,983	41,053
	Taylor (D)	62.4	44.3	26,795	26,795
4	Smith* (D)	—	59.6	57,382	56,370
	Kyl* (R)	—	40.4	108,153	112,154
5	Scherle* (R)	—	55.3	47,296	35,105
	Harkin (D)	—	44.7	25,871	24,437
6	Mayne* (R)	—	52.5	54,232	50,166
	Bedell (D)	—	47.5	87,712	87,694
KANSAS					
1	Sebelius* (R)	—	77.2	53,186	20,545
	Coover (D)	—	21.6	none	none
2	Roy* (D)	—	60.6	145,381	148,995
	McAtee (R)	63.4	37.1	116,087	115,985
3	Winn* (R)	—	71.0	46,191	37,310
	Barsotti (D)	—	25.4	5,991	5,991
4	Shriver* (R)	—	73.2	47,682	34,954
	Stevens (D)	50.7	24.8	7,300	6,557
5	Skubitz* (R)	—	72.3	28,251	21,765
	Kitch (D)	—	27.7	3,785	3,676
KENTUCKY					
1	Stubblefield* (D)	73.1	64.8	30,055	30,940
	Banken (R)	—	33.7	1,655	2,558
2	Natcher* (D)	—	61.5	9,396	9,396
	Carter (R)	—	38.5	1,699	7,327
3	Mazzoli* (D)	93.9	62.1	63,140	58,410
	Kaelin, Jr. (R)	70.7	37.0	19,648	21,161
4	Snyder* (R)	—	73.8	77,274	29,411
	Rogers (D)	46.0	26.2	445	375
5	Carter* (R)	—	73.5	15,806	12,155
	Willis (D)	50.1	26.5	21	216
6	Breckinridge (D)	57.8	52.4	65,056	69,216
	Jackson (R)	44.1	46.8	82,177	82,152
7	Perkins* (D)	93.4	61.9	6,455	5,746
	Holcomb (R)	72.9	38.1	48,035	48,035
LOUISIANA					
1	Hebert* (D)	—	—	500	500
2	Boggs* (D)	83.7	—	116,434	90,380
3	Treen (R)	—	54.0	139,578	155,629
	Watkins (D)	54.2**	46.0	228,495	229,767
4	Waggonner* (D)	—	—	8,304	1,596
5	Passman* (D)	61.0	—	38,295	37,545
6	Rarick* (D)	60.8	—	53,312	42,459
7	Breaux* (D)	55.0**	—	141,924	137,420
8	Long (D)	52.9	68.5	107,919	107,919
	Strickland (R)	—	14.7	5,705	5,612
	Abramson (A)	—	16.8	21,165	20,835
MAINE					
1	Kyros* (D)	66.5	59.4	58,245	56,093
	Porteous (R)	72.4	40.6	64,303	64,104
2	Cohen (R)	60.2	54.4	126,369	165,397
	Violette (D)	78.4	45.6	81,415	94,696
MARYLAND					
1	Mills* (R)	80.2	70.5	94,806	93,945
	Hargreaves (D)	53.1	29.5	40,580	40,419
2	Long* (D)	76.1	65.8	71,593	66,425
	Bishop (R)	66.0	34.2	75,928	75,606
3	Sarbanes* (D)	53.3	69.7	61,203	1,272
	Morrow (R)	34.1	30.3	2,505	4,498
4	Holt (R)	71.1	59.4	111,488	113,513
	Fornos (D)	22.5	40.6	133,918	145,973
5	Hogan* (R)	93.5	62.9	108,488	108,282
	Conroy (D)	51.4	37.1	76,584	92,301
6	Byron* (D)	59.9	64.8	77,220	77,186
	Mason (R)	54.5	35.2	59,065	60,333
7	Mitchell* (D)	50.5	80.0	44,898	55,577
	Adair (R)	44.4	20.0	471	592
8	Gude* (R)	—	63.9	74,924	70,899
	Anastasi (D)	78.3	36.1	61,904	61,904
MASSACHUSETTS					
1	Conte* (R)	—	—	10,971	2,346
2	Boland* (D)	—	—	none	none
3	Donohue* (D)	—	—	11,415	125
4	Drinan* (D)	—	48.8	191,801	199,703
	Linsky (R)	33.5	45.8	139,576	148,285
	Collins (In-Con)	—	5.4	23,526	22,579
5	Cronin (R)	58.5	53.5	145,532	171,414
	Kerry (D)	27.5	44.7	267,815	279,746
	Durkin (I)	—	1.8	45,572	62,952
6	Harrington* (D)	74.3	64.1	115,546	114,317
	Mosely (R)	—	35.9	90,957	93,400
7	Macdonald* (D)	82.3	67.7	28,810	19,918
	Aliberti (R)	37.3	32.3	25,274	25,213
8	O'Neill* (D)	—	88.7	42,107	35,901
	Powers (SW)	—	11.3	229	229
9	Moakley (I)	—	43.2	144,867	157,560
	Hicks* (D)	37.7	41.1	32,356	29,686
	Miller (R)	51.4	14.2	58,240	58,240
10	Heckler* (R)	—	—	14,704	10,518
11	Burke* (D)	—	—	15,957	15,971
12	Studds (D)	—	50.3	200,728	195,758
12	Weeks (R)	—	49.7	269,858	269,046
MICHIGAN					
1	Conyers* (D)	—	88.4	39,663	29,661
	Girardot (R)	64.7	10.8	1,513	978
2	Esch* (R)	—	56.0	73,416	71,649
	Stempien (D)	32.1	43.3	53,141	55,292
3	Brown* (R)	—	59.2	32,012	23,116
	Brignall (D)	63.1	39.9	25,375	26,320
4	Hutchinson* (R)	61.5	67.3	40,401	40,110
	Jameson (D)	58.9	32.7	10,894	12,300

State and District	General Election Candidates	Per cent of Primary Vote	Per cent of General Election Vote	Contributions	Expenditures
5	Ford* (R)	—	61.1	98,576	87,345
	McKee (D)	43.1	37.7	10,223	8,796
6	Chamberlain* (R)	59.2	50.6	53,757	52,136
	Carr (D)	—	49.4	53,469	52,462
7	Riegle, Jr.* (R)	—	70.1	29,734	23,892
	Mattison (D)	50.2	29.9	1,200	1,200
8	Harvey* (R)	—	59.3	53,534	50,546
	Hart (D)	74.0	39.4	27,517	27,517
9	Vander Jagt* (R)	—	69.4	50,983	23,887
	Olson (D)	—	29.5	4,635	4,636
10	Cederberg* (R)	81.7	66.7	19,410	17,684
	Graves (D)	—	30.9	5,197	4,666
11	Ruppe* (R)	—	69.4	30,854	27,045
	McNamara (D)	63.1	29.8	308	526
12	O'Hara* (D)	—	50.8	66,463	62,472
	Serotkin (R)	55.8	49.2	44,075	43,619
13	Diggs* (D)	—	85.6	3,791	2,566
	Edwards (R)	—	13.3	10	10
14	Nedzi* (D)	43.0	54.9	36,189	32,765
	McGrath (R)	71.3	45.1	16,568	16,568
15	Ford* (D)	61.9	65.8	57,399	42,352
	Fackler (R)	—	32.9	40	43
16	Dingell* (D)	85.8	68.1	33,611	26,593
	Rostron (R)	—	29.7	239	239
17	Griffiths* (D)	—	66.4	31,027	22,506
	Judd	55.0	32.5	645	527
18	Huber (R)	63.3	52.6	66,240	66,061
	Cooper (D)	37.0	47.4	84,588	83,280
19	Broomfield* (R)	57.6	70.4	66,986	41,708
	Montgomery (D)	—	28.6	9,769	9,566
MINNESOTA					
1	Quie* (R)	—	70.7	37,552	32,586
	Thompson (D)	60.6	29.3	379	438
2	Nelsen* (R)	—	57.1	72,206	68,855
	Turnbull (D)	—	42.9	26,612	28,883
3	Frenzel* (R)	93.1	62.9	119,544	97,933
	Bell (D)	—	31.3	37,338	38,775
4	Karth* (D)	—	72.4	59,862	50,094
	Thompson (R)	—	27.6	3,926	3,926
5	Fraser* (D)	—	65.8	97,654	93,628
	Davisson (R)	72.8	24.4	9,399	9,399
6	Zwach* (R)	—	51.0	110,133	87,233
	Nolan (D)	—	49.0	95,943	97,481
7	Bergland* (D)	—	59.0	135,451	92,871
	Haaven (R)	—	41.0	92,625	90,524
8	Blatnik* (D)	76.1	75.9	54,566	54,612
	Johnson (R)	—	24.1	745	395
MISSISSIPPI					
1	Whitten* (D)	86.7	—	4,100	4,100
2	Bowen (D)	57.0**	61.9	149,100	142,522
	Butler (R)	—	34.7	80,759	80,449
3	Montgomery* (D)	—	—	1,550	381
4	Cochran (R)	—	47.8	102,880	100,634
	Bodron (D)	50.8**	44.0	100,108	100,128
5	Lott (R)	70.7	55.3	119,837	119,190
	Stone (D)	52.4**	44.2**	158,844	163,976
MISSOURI					
1	Clay* (D)	75.8	64.0	31,619	17,480
	Funsch (R)	—	36.0	59,335	59,672
2	Symington* (D)	—	63.5	92,056	67,938
	Cooper (R)	55.3	36.5	35,533	30,298
3	Sullivan* (D)	93.9	69.3	34,404	29,225
	Holst (R)	66.3	30.4	5,151	5,151
4	Randall* (D)	—	57.4	33,324	24,531
	Barrows (R)	—	42.6	6,310	5,922

State and District	General Election Candidates	Per cent of Primary Vote	Per cent of General Election Vote	Contributions	Expenditures
5	Bolling* (D)	—	62.8	25,559	25,054
	Rice (R)	—	35.6	575	442
6	Litton (D)	35.7	54.6	171,635	188,642
	Sloan (R)	59.8	45.4	102,269	100,059
7	Taylor (R)	49.0	63.7	121,572	97,127
	Thomas (D)	78.1	36.3	10,995	10,864
8	Ichord* (D)	—	62.1	54,508	33,779
	Countie (R)	—	37.9	10,194	9,309
9	Hungate* (D)	—	66.5	38,197	26,147
	Prange (R)	60.3	33.5	7,719	7,719
10	Burlison* (D)	76.0	64.3	35,841	14,730
	Svendrowski (R)	—	35.7	293	3,065
MONTANA					
1	Shoup* (R)	90.0	53.7	72,742	65,224
	Olsen (D)	44.8	46.3	50,414	54,940
2	Melcher* (D)	—	76.1	51,025	49,092
	Forester (R)	—	23.9	10,475	10,475
NEBRASKA					
1	Thone* (R)	84.0	64.2	90,130	90,130
	Berg (D)	—	35.8	28,655	21,704
2	McCollister* (R)	—	63.9	81,645	74,569
	Cooney (D)	—	36.1	21,456	22,050
3	Martin* (R)	—	69.6	43,435	11,687
	Fitzgerald (D)	54.2	30.4	9,425	9,425
NEVADA					
1	Towell (R)	41.6	52.2	81,779	83,106
	Bilbray (D)	52.0	47.8	174,086	179,406
NEW HAMPSHIRE					
1	Wyman* (R)	—	72.9	33,210	32,945
	Merrow (D)	59.2	27.1	2,786	3,122
2	Cleveland* (R)	—	67.9	24,678	23,479
	Officer (D)	—	32.1	35,065	37,030
NEW JERSEY					
1	Hunt* (R)	—	52.5	22,921	23,837
	Florio (D)	79.6	47.1	36,373	36,107
2	Sandman* (R)	—	65.7	11,780	11,780
	Ruse (D)	—	34.3	5,958	5,341
3	Howard* (D)	—	53.0	70,721	62,773
	Dowd (R)	—	47.0	50,718	50,718
4	Thompson* (D)	—	58.0	51,454	48,221
	Garibaldi (R)	—	42.0	8,083	7,983
5	Frelinghuysen* (R)	—	62.0	20,765	20,765
	Bohen (D)	63.5	38.0	55,641	54,888
6	Forsythe* (R)	—	62.8	40,228	38,604
	Brennan (D)	34.2	36.1	9,815	9,811
7	Widnall* (R)	—	58.0	33,938	30,567
	Lesemann (D)	—	39.9	31,020	30,102
8	Roe* (D)	—	63.1	66,101	66,706
	Johnson (R)	—	36.9	756	776
9	Helstoski* (D)	—	55.8	44,643	55,244
	Schiaffo (R)	74.8	44.2	59,790	60,812
10	Rodino* (D)	57.4	79.7	113,169	90,115
	Miller (R)	—	20.3	1,122	770
11	Minish* (D)	—	57.5	85,554	68,709
	Waldor (R)	—	39.7	48,326	55,185
12	Rinaldo (R)	—	63.5	130,232	131,790
	English (D)	68.1	36.1	36,335	32,839
13	Maraziti (R)	49.7	55.7	63,872	83,972
	Meyner (D)	—	42.9	67,746	65,573
14	Daniels* (D)	55.6	61.2	53,286	53,286
	Bozzone (R)	70.9	34.3	2,871	6,320
	Zampella (CAC)	—	3.1	7,923	7,923
15	Patten* (D)	—	52.3	27,605	27,605
	Brooks (R)	—	47.7	51,333	51,081

State and District	General Election Candidates	Per cent of Primary Vote	Per cent of General Election Vote	Contributions	Expenditures
NEW MEXICO					
1	Lujan* (R)	90.5	55.7	210,173	212,093
	Gallegos (D)	35.1	44.3	127,386	126,219
2	Runnels* (D)	—	72.2	99,198	91,784
	Presson (R)	55.2	27.6	14,491	14,810
NEW YORK					
1	Pike* (D)	—	52.5	54,327	51,842
	Boyd (R)	—	36.9	78,887	90,302
	Gardiner (CON)	—	9.5	37,717	37,877
2	Grover* (R)	—	65.8	9,967	4,054
	Dennison (D)	—	32.7	6,864	6,325
3	Roncallo (R)	—	53.1	89,313	109,652
	Bales (D)	51.4	37.6	109,219	112,455
4	Lent* (R)	—	62.4	52,825	45,306
	Horowitz (D)	—	35.9	20,150	27,178
5	Wydler* (R)	—	62.4	50,105	44,644
	Steckler (D)	—	31.7	28,369	25,333
6	Wolff* (D)	—	51.5	64,072	64,069
	Gallagher (R)	—	48.5	36,398	45,449
7	Addabbo* (D)	64.2	75.0	24,128	22,487
	Hall (R)	—	20.6	1,201	1,540
8	Rosenthal* (D)	—	64.7	18,892	18,739
	La Pina (R)	—	35.3	6,279	6,279
9	Delaney* (D)	55.4	93.4†	56,173	56,396
10	Biaggi* (D)		93.9†	13,066	12,719
11	Brasco* (D)	73.0	63.9	43,723	38,943
	Solomon (R)	52.6	31.3	none	none
12	Chisholm* (D)	—	87.9	5,800	4,796
	Coleman (R)	—	9.7	none	none
13	Podell* (D)	68.0	65.1	84,107	71,852
	Marcucci (R)	56.2	25.5	350	1,842
	Simon (LIB)	—	5.3	51,846	52,235
14	Rooney* (D)	54.2	53.9	117,855	110,054
	Lowenstein (LIB)	45.8	28.1	281,028	285,475
	Voyticky (R)	51.4	17.5	270	270
15	Carey* (D)	—	52.1	90,294	122,905
	Gangemi (R)	—	43.0	49,519	49,296
16	Holtzman (D)	44.5	65.6	84,724	104,318
	Macchio (R)	62.4	22.9	none	none
17	Murphy* (D)	—	60.3	82,585	105,581
	Belardino (R)	—	39.7	88,180	87,559
18	Koch* (D)	—	69.9	69,295	69,295
	Langley (R)	—	29.3	107,812	120,351
19	Rangel* (D)	75.6	96.0†	33,834	31,390
20	Abzug* (D)	31.2	55.7	169,731	164,245
	Ryan (LIB)	—	28.0	52,713	51,412
	Levy (R)	—	11.8	2,360	2,360
	Michelman (CON)	—	4.1	5,274	5,261
21	Badillo* (D)	77.8	86.9	52,487	52,558
	Ramos (R)	22.2	11.4	26,950	26,950
22	Bingham* (D)	55.5	76.5	127,376	126,138
	Avarello (R)	—	23.5	16,460	16,416
23	Peyser* (R)	—	50.4	173,528	154,567
	Ottinger (D)	—	49.6	198,914	195,784
24	Reid* (D)	—	52.2	164,224	209,007
	Vergari (R)	71.5	47.8	190,890	190,890
25	Fish* (R)	—	71.7	27,072	23,208
	Burns (D)	—	26.9	19,347	18,431
26	Gilman (R)	57.9	47.8	100,623	112,729
	Dow* (D)	—	39.3	68,184	52,197
	Rapkin (I)	42.1	12.9	94,193	80,595
27	Robison* (R)	—	62.2	14,998	14,853
	Blazer (D)	—	29.8	1,746	2,585
28	Stratton* (D)	—	80.0	51,712	27,297
	Ryan (R)	—	20.0	1,299	1,308
29	King* (R)	—	69.9	24,555	17,567
	Gordon (D)	—	30.1	2,849	2,849
30	McEwen* (R)	85.4	66.0	12,261	9,861
	La Baff (D)	—	34.0	9,938	10,019
31	Mitchell (R)	33.3	51.0	82,811	81,740
	Buckley (LIB)	—	3.7	39,643	39,643
	Castle (D)	—	39.1	91,885	91,869
	Nichols (Amer.)	—	6.2	18,358	18,358
32	Hanley* (D)	—	57.2	76,134	63,011
	Koldin (R)	—	42.8	66,937	75,175
33	Walsh (R)	—	71.4	22,516	34,795
	Kadys (D)	—	28.6	19,283	19,283
34	Horton* (R)	—	72.1	37,909	32,326
	Rubens (D)	—	23.5	5,412	5,411
35	Conable* (R)	—	67.9	21,239	18,907
	Spencer (D)	—	28.4	7,473	6,753
36	Smith* (R)	—	57.3	72,547	72,678
	McCarthy (D)	—	42.7	61,774	61,774
37	Dulski* (D)	—	72.2	13,206	8,018
	McLaughlin (R)	—	27.8	3,316	3,316
38	Kemp* (R)	—	73.2	93,717	89,617
	LaRusso (D)	—	26.8	15,200	20,342
39	Hastings* (R)	—	71.9	24,668	17,794
	White (D)	—	28.1	450	1,663
NORTH CAROLINA					
1	Jones* (D)	—	68.8	19,959	8,727
	Bonner (R)	53.0	31.2	4,394	17,057
2	Fountain* (D)	58.8	71.6	44,177	40,630
	Little (R)	—	28.4	19,002	19,002
3	Henderson* (D)	79.3	—	7,590	4,258
4	Andrews (D)	52.1**	50.4	121,326	110,947
	Hawke (R)	—	49.6	77,678	77,573
5	Mizell* (R)	—	64.8	49,114	37,264
	Hays (D)	—	35.2	34,570	34,358
6	Preyer* (D)	—	93.9†	9,642	8,657
7	Rose (D)	55.6	60.4	91,298	86,933
	Scott (R)	50.2	38.7	11,177	12,402
8	Ruth* (R)	—	60.2	41,016	29,110
	Clark (D)	—	39.8	51,809	51,809
9	Martin (R)	80.4	58.9	135,874	149,508
	Beatty (D)	84.1	41.1	71,856	63,107
10	Broyhill* (R)	—	72.5	40,568	34,251
	Beck (D)	—	27.5	360	357
11	Taylor* (D)	—	59.6	22,174	21,721
	Ledbetter (R)	—	40.4	11,085	12,066
NORTH DAKOTA					
1	Andrews* (R)	—	72.7	58,227	58,196
	Ista (D)	—	27.1	18,935	18,935
OHIO					
1	Keating* (R)	—	70.3	76,450	71,848
	Heiser (D)	—	29.7	12,594	13,453
2	Clancy* (R)	88.8	62.8	45,923	27,034
	Manes (D)	—	37.2	8,859	8,859
3	Whalen* (R)	—	76.2	22,178	17,973
	Lelak (D)	—	23.8	3,285	3,930
4	Guyer (R)	72.3	62.7	40,462	40,014
	Nicholas (D)	32.1	37.3	38,412	38,412
5	Latta* (R)	—	72.7	31,796	24,016
	Edwards (D)	—	27.3	4,132	3,645
6	Harsha* (R)	—	—	2,500	1,665
7	Brown* (R)	—	73.3	51,111	31,534
	Franke (D)	—	26.7	2,652	2,838
8	Powell* (R)	67.0	52.2	67,814	66,098
	Ruppert (D)	81.0	47.8	70,813	73,706
9	Ashley* (D)	89.0	69.1	27,781	17,416
	Richards (R)	46.9	30.9	20,019	20,019
10	Miller* (R)	86.9	73.2	40,542	26,983
	Whealey (D)	59.2	26.8	4,251	5,452

State and District	General Election Candidates	Per cent of Primary Vote	Per cent of General Election Vote	Contributions	Expenditures
11	Stanton* (R)	—	68.2	21,743	19,853
	Callahan (D)	50.5	31.8	23,256	22,822
12	Devine* (R)	—	56.1	67,862	51,930
	Goodrich (D)	—	43.9	105,987	125,145
13	Mosher* (R)	80.6	68.1	19,502	13,218
	Ryan (D)	—	31.9	5,593	5,593
14	Seiberling* (D)	82.3	74.4	27,649	26,325
	Holt (R)	77.5	25.6	4,779	6,391
15	Wylie* (R)	—	65.8	65,945	53,091
	McGee (D)	50.1	31.5	20,475	23,398
16	Regula (R)	85.7	57.3	81,468	81,383
	Musser (D)	57.6	42.7	24,800	23,328
17	Ashbrook* (R)	74.1	57.4	58,173	58,173
	Beck (D)	45.8	38.7	13,062	13,062
18	Hays* (D)	84.4	70.2	34,318	20,009
	Stewart (R)	—	29.8	4,221	3,300
19	Carney* (D)	57.1	64.0	69,148	54,037
	Parr (R)	—	36.0	21,306	21,307
20	Stanton* (D)	76.0	84.3	44,792	44,272
	Vilt (R)	—	11.9	8,157	8,157
21	Stokes* (D)	82.5	81.1	17,718	17,718
	Johnson (R)	—	11.3	6,992	7,531
22	Vanik* (D)	—	63.9	36,067	36,067
	Gropp (R)	—	32.6	114,646	120,430
23	Minshall* (R)	87.1	49.4	133,233	127,212
	Kucinich (D)	51.0	47.3	28,096	28,096

OKLAHOMA

1	Jones (D)	80.4	54.5	63,405	64,850
	Hewgley (R)	50.8**	43.7	179,986	179,986
2	McSpadden (D)	62.3	71.1	93,654	93,103
	Toliver (R)	—	28.9	7,787	7,787
3	Albert* (D)	84.7	93.4†	39,170	7,275
4	Steed* (D)	87.5	71.3	17,141	6,609
	Crozier (R)	—	28.7	3,310	3,622
5	Jarman* (D)	65.0	60.4	66,351	27,534
	Keller (R)	51.0	39.6	8,751	7,798
6	Camp* (R)	—	72.7	33,492	33,492
	Schmitt (D)	—	27.3	5,310	5,310

OREGON

1	Wyatt* (R)	—	68.6	75,093	75,093
	Bunch (D)	66.9	31.4	6,871	6,810
2	Ullman* (D)	—	—	61,106	13,307
3	Green* (D)	—	62.4	41,726	41,031
	Walsh (R)	—	37.5	58,080	58,403
4	Dellenback* (R)	78.7	62.5	54,659	49,711
	Porter (D)	33.1	37.4	19,406	20,635

PENNSYLVANIA

1	Barrett* (D)	—	66.1	16,261	16,261
	Pedicone (R)	—	33.2	44,574	43,547
2	Nix* (D)	47.0	70.1	7,837	4,073
	Bryant (R)	71.4	29.9	5,865	4,936
3	Green* (D)	57.2	63.3	66,088	65,107
	Marroletti (P)	—	36.2	17,813	16,938
	Monteiro (Com)	—	0.5	13,106	12,861
4	Eilberg* (D)	—	55.9	70,028	61,471
	Pfender (R)	—	44.1	101,820	102,923
5	Ware* (R)	49.5	64.7	29,506	26,200
	Yerger (D)	52.3	35.3	6,230	6,841
6	Yatron* (D)	—	64.5	60,979	56,237
	Hubler (R)	63.8	34.6	17,277	16,623
7	Williams* (R)	—	60.6	81,955	73,023
	Bowie (D)	—	39.4	13,881	11,879
8	Biester* (R)	80.3	64.4	17,862	17,345
	Williams (D)	45.3	35.6	25,236	24,219

State and District	General Election Candidates	Per cent of Primary Vote	Per cent of General Election Vote	Contributions	Expenditures
9	Shuster (R)	61.3	61.8	64,231	73,852
	Collins (D)	—	38.2	17,461	17,815
10	McDade* (R)	—	73.6	26,943	24,934
	Coveleskie (D)	67.3	26.4	4,049	6,281
11	Flood* (D)	88.0	68.3	28,688	26,393
	Ayers (R)	55.6	31.7	10,115	10,113
12	Saylor* (R)	72.1	68.1	38,839	34,992
	Murphy (D)	—	31.9	20	95
13	Coughlin* (R)	—	66.6	36,941	36,423
	Camp (D)	59.9	33.4	35,301	34,263
14	Moorhead* (D)	85.7	59.3	38,313	36,205
	Catarinella (R)	—	40.4	82.409	78,400
15	Rooney* (D)	86.0	60.8	34,858	29,315
	Steigerwalt (R)	—	39.2	2,170	2,170
16	Eshleman* (R)	—	73.5	15,433	14,041
	Garrett (D)	—	26.5	1,305	2,242
17	Schneebeli* (R)	—	72.2	59,376	19,311
	Rippon (D)	—	26.5	2,230	2,386
18	Heinz* (R)	—	72.8	109,700	103,542
	Walgren (D)	—	27.2	3,320	3,123
19	Goodling* (R)	60.0	57.5	43,862	37,168
	Noll (D)	—	41.2	13,159	13,159
20	Gaydos* (D)	—	61.5	42,522	44,379
	Hunt (R)	—	38.5	64,701	63,843
21	Dent* (D)	64.5	62.0	46,093	32,024
	Young (R)	—	38.0	325	325
22	Morgan* (D)	72.5	60.8	44,340	32,157
	Montgomery (R)	55.6	39.2	807	807
23	Johnson* (R)	61.4	56.5	28,907	31,582
	Kassab (D)	56.9	43.5	53,656	66,948
24	Vigorito* (D)	86.2	68.8	13,692	13,504
	Levenhagen (R)	—	31.2	11,856	10,479
25	Clark* (D)	—	55.8	20,350	26,444
	Myers (R)	64.9	44.2	6,963	8,910

RHODE ISLAND

1	St Germain* (D)	—	62.3	51,186	48,071
	John Feeley (R)	—	34.7	20,371	20,371
2	Tiernan* (D)	—	63.1	42,034	47,418
	Ryan (R)	—	36.9	6,000	5,012

SOUTH CAROLINA

1	Davis* (D)	72.5	54.5	86,009	84,377
	Limehouse (R)	—	45.5	101,225	100,902
2	Spence* (R)	—	—	20,676	5,936
3	Dorn* (D)	—	75.2	25,649	24,797
	Ethridge (R)	—	24.8	5,780	5,849
4	Mann* (D)	—	66.1	35,515	35,475
	Whatley (R)	—	33.9	13,913	14,322
5	Gettys* (D)	—	60.9	26,655	22,640
	Phillips (R)	—	39.1	14,468	14,349
6	Young (R)	—	54.4	90,257	93,590
	Jenrette (D)	50.6**	45.6	94,019	94,019

SOUTH DAKOTA

1	Denholm* (D)	—	60.5	41,062	40,445
	Vickerman (R)	—	39.5	53,017	52,588
2	Abdnor (R)	64.4	54.9	96,252	96,252
	McKeever (D)	—	45.1	62,271	62,235

TENNESSEE

1	Quillen* (R)	—	79.4	17,065	3,799
	Cantor (D)	—	20.6	5,807	5,807
2	Duncan* (R)	—	—	8,928	9,585
3	Baker* (R)	—	55.2	78,502	77,199
	Sompayrac (D)	—	41.9	40,856	39,974
4	Evins* (D)	—	81.1	12,455	11,520
	Finney (R)	—	18.9	500	1,738

State and District	General Election Candidates	Per cent of Primary Vote	Per cent of General Election Vote	Contributions	Expenditures
5	Fulton* (D)	73.2	62.6	80,219	83,697
	Adams Jr. (R)	72.9	36.8	99,493	97,482
6	Beard (R)	76.8	55.3	149,697	151,605
	Anderson* (D)	60.7	43.1	98,087	105,022
7	Jones* (D)	—	70.5	48,600	81,789
	Adkins (R)	—	29.5	20,307	20,136
8	Kuykendall* (R)	—	55.4	127,913	119,023
	Patterson Jr. (D)	74.9	44.1	83,433	67,444

TEXAS

State and District	General Election Candidates	Per cent of Primary Vote	Per cent of General Election Vote	Contributions	Expenditures
1	Patman* (D)	57.5	—	22,025	26,423
2	Wilson (D)	63.0	73.8	87,836	93,579
	Brightwell (R)	65.2	26.2	2,772	2,784
3	Collins* (R)	67.7	73.3	155,304	147,487
	Hughes (D)	59.9	26.7	2,566	2,775
4	Roberts* (D)	—	70.2	6,383	6,383
	Russell (R)	—	29.8	502	685
5	Steelman (R)	63.2**	55.7	69,551	69,581
	Cabell* (D)	76.2	44.3	72,352	67,800
6	Teague* (D)	—	72.6	12,976	3,668
	Nigliazzo (R)	—	27.4	2,511	2,287
7	Archer* (R)	—	82.3	82,512	72,173
	Brady (D)	75.8	17.7	17,890	18,500
8	Eckhardt* (D)	79.6	64.6	17,763	15,463
	Emerich (R)	—	34.7	9,634	9,392
9	Brooks* (D)	—	66.2	76,473	33,565
	Reed (R)	—	33.8	6,565	6,527
10	Pickle* (D)	—	91.2	none	none
	Singler (SW)	—	8.8	none	none
11	Poage* (D)	61.2	—	49,915	36,549
12	Wright* (D)	—	—	6,713	2,765
13	Price* (D)	—	54.8	206,774	206,171
	Purcell* (D)	—	45.2	156,179	149,453
14	Young* (D)	63.7	—	29,993	17,706
15	de la Garza* (D)	84.7	—	7,365	4,456
16	White* (D)	—	—	5,197	2,009
17	Burleson* (D)	—	—	17,062	5,341
18	Jordan (D)	80.4	80.6	61,886	57,065
	Merritt (R)	79.0	18.2	3,875	3,257
19	Mahon* (D)	—	—	3,288	4,358
20	Gonzalez* (D)	—	96.9	1,612	1,012
	Wattenmaker (SW)	—	3.1	none	none
21	Fisher* (D)	—	56.8	26,198	18,463
	Harlan (R)	60.3	43.2	34.422	32,810
22	Casey* (D)	69.5	70.2	97,311	93,322
	Griffin (R)	73.0	29.0	3,122	3,108
23	Kazen Jr.* (D)	75.0	—	17,678	8,354
24	Milford (D)	54.2**	65.1	94,410	92,963
	Roberts (R)	72.3**	34.9	33,247	33,247

UTAH

State and District	General Election Candidates	Per cent of Primary Vote	Per cent of General Election Vote	Contributions	Expenditures
1	McKay* (D)	—	55.4	52.647	52,320
	Wolthuis (R)	53.0	42.0	61,669	62,472
2	Owens (D)	—	54.5	127,686	118,252
	Lloyd* (R)	68.2	44.0	109,571	90,591

VERMONT

State and District	General Election Candidates	Per cent of Primary Vote	Per cent of General Election Vote	Contributions	Expenditures
1	Mallary* (R)	—	65.0	11,289	4,085
	Meyer (D)	—	35.0	5,122	5,193

VIRGINIA

State and District	General Election Candidates	Per cent of Primary Vote	Per cent of General Election Vote	Contributions	Expenditures
1	Downing* (D)	—	78.1	47,601	48,469
	Wells (R)	—	21.9	34,376	35,264
2	Whitehurst* (R)	—	73.4	52,102	45,864
	Burlage (D)	—	26.6	42,790	42,790
3	Satterfield* (D)	—	—	3,476	none
4	Daniel Jr. (R)	—	47.1	59,237	59,140
	Gibson (D)	—	37.5	33,902	40,546
5	Daniel Jr.* (D)	—	—	3,892	3,429
6	Butler (R)	—	54.6	104,127	116,363
	Anderson (D)	—	39.2	49,578	49,078
7	Robinson* (R)	—	66.2	108,336	73,777
	Williams (D)	—	33.8	44,735	44,972
8	Parris (R)	63.3	44.4	111,817	109,271
	Horan (D)	42.2	37.8	53,670	53,129
	Durland (I)	—	13.7	35,777	41,176
	Harris (I)		4.1	18,855	18,956
9	Wampler* (R)	—	71.9	35,304	23,937
	Christian (D)	—	26.4	15,708	29,534
10	Broyhill* (R)	—	56.3	185,237	141,290
	Miller (D)	—	43.7	93,087	91,501

WASHINGTON

State and District	General Election Candidates	Per cent of Primary Vote	Per cent of General Election Vote	Contributions	Expenditures
1	Pritchard (R)	75.8	50.3	112,631	112,933
	Hempelmann (D)	71.2	49.1	84,644	84,136
2	Meeds*(D)	—	60.5	53,655	42,062
	Reams (R)	63.3	39.5	54,717	54,717
3	Hansen* (D)	63.5	66.3	61,016	43,351
	McConkey (R)	61.8	33.7	4,318	4,309
4	McCormack* (D)	—	52.1	70,543	66,130
	Bledsoe (R)	56.6	47.9	141,560	141,560
5	Foley* (D)	—	81.3	42,890	27,476
	Privette (R)	—	18.7	500	500
6	Hicks* (D)	—	72.1	33,854	7,770
	Lowry (R)	—	27.9	23,995	23,888
7	Adams* (D)	—	85.4	77,640	36,058
	Freeman (R)	—	12.1	512	512

WEST VIRGINIA

State and District	General Election Candidates	Per cent of Primary Vote	Per cent of General Election Vote	Contributions	Expenditures
1	Mollohan* (D)	—	69.4	30,836	29,619
	Kapnicky (R)	—	30.6	2,387	2,392
2	Staggers* (D)	73.0	70.0	29,520	29,520
	Dix (R)	—	30.0	3,847	3,897
3	Slack* (D)	—	63.7	26,018	12,019
	Higgins (R)	—	36.3	4,356	4,358
4	Hechler* (D)	52.2	61.0	21,976	20,249
	Neal (R)	—	39.0	36,398	36,362

WISCONSIN

State and District	General Election Candidates	Per cent of Primary Vote	Per cent of General Election Vote	Contributions	Expenditures
1	Aspin* (D)	91.4	64.4	82,852	70,326
	Stalbaum (R)	43.1	34.9	12,062	12,062
2	Kastenmeier* (D)	—	68.2	38,861	24,997
	Kelly (R)	58.5	31.4	23,080	23,080
3	Thomson* (R)	79.6	54.7	76,866	76,853
	Thoresen (D)	39.0	44.6	49,202	49,328
4	Zablocki* (D)	83.2	75.7	16,782	15,871
	Mrozinski (R)	—	22.8	375	375
5	Reuss* (D)	—	77.3	14,829	12,613
	Van Hecke (R)	—	20.4	4,730	4,743
6	Steiger* (R)	—	65.8	34,708	33,599
	Adams (D)	—	32.0	6,548	6,528
7	Obey* (D)	—	62.8	74,427	64,054
	O'Konski* (R)	55.0	37.2	42,480	42,772
8	Froehlich (R)	38.1	50.4	85,759	78,640
	Cornell (D)	72.9	48.5	34.413	28,680
9	Davis* (R)	58.6	61.4	72,879	59,737
	Fine (D)	—	36.7	6,579	6,579

WYOMING

State and District	General Election Candidates	Per cent of Primary Vote	Per cent of General Election Vote	Contributions	Expenditures
1	Roncalio* (D)	—	51.7	65,646	50,548
	Kidd (R)	51.1	48.3	122,712	122,580

* Incumbent.
** Percentage is for runoff primary.
— Unopposed.
† No major party opposition; minor party candidates not included in Common Cause tabulation.

OFFICIALS GAVE MORE TO NIXON CAMPAIGN IN 1972

Executives of the largest defense-related contractors gave eight times more money in 1972 to the campaigns of President Nixon and other Republican candidates than to their Democratic counterparts.

Officers and directors of these companies gave $2,555,740 to Republicans and $319,983 to Democrats, according to data compiled by the Citizens' Research Foundation of Princeton, N.J. *(Box, p. 86)*

The amounts, as well as the margin by which Republicans were favored, were up sharply from 1968. A similar Citizens' Research survey for that presidential election year showed Republicans favored 6 to 1 in donations. They received $1,235,402, compared with $180,550 for Democrats. *(CQ paperback, Dollar Politics, p. 36)*

Both surveys covered campaign gifts reported by officials of the companies ranking among the top 25 contractors to the Defense Department (DOD), Atomic Energy Commission (AEC) and National Aeronautics and Space Administration (NASA).

The three agencies are the federal government's largest buyers of military and other hardware. DOD spends more than $20-billion a year on weapons systems and equipment. The AEC supplies nuclear warheads for bombs and missiles. And NASA rocketry aids in the development of intercontinental ballistic missiles.

Added Disclosures

The 1972 survey was even more revealing than that for 1968, which was one of the first and most comprehensive of its kind.

For example, billionaire recluse Howard Hughes, president of Hughes Aircraft Corp., emerged in the 1972 survey as the largest single contributor, with gifts of $247,500 to Republicans and $4,000 to Democrats. The 1968 survey showed no gifts by Hughes or other executives of his company.

One reason for the clearer picture of campaign contributions is that a 1972 law, the Federal Election Campaign Act (S 382—PL 92-225), closed loopholes that allowed many previous donations to go unreported. It required reporting of all gifts of more than $100 to candidates for federal office, whether before or after nomination.

The old Federal Corrupt Practices Act of 1925 required no reporting of campaign gifts made before the nominating primary or convention. This loophole ceased as of April 7, 1972, the effective date of the new law.

The change did not affect the long-standing prohibition on campaign contributions by corporations. Executives of corporations may make campaign contributions as individuals.

Most, if not all, pre-April 7 campaign gifts of corporate executives and other donors were disclosed as a result of lawsuits brought by the citizens' organization, Common Cause. One such list showed only corporation totals, but a breakdown by individuals was provided by Rose Mary Woods, then President Nixon's personal secretary, at the March 1974 trial of Maurice H. Stans, former director of the

Finance Committee for the Re-election of the President, and John N. Mitchell, former director of the Committee for the Re-election of the President. Stans and Mitchell were acquitted of soliciting $200,000 in cash from financier Robert L. Vesco for Nixon's campaign, in exchange for stopping a Securities and Exchange Commission investigation of Vesco's operations. *(Stans-Mitchell trial p. 11; Woods list p. 65)*

Other sources used by the Citizens' Research Foundation for its survey included the Office of Federal Elections, the General Accounting Office, reports filed with the secretary of the Senate and the clerk of the House, and information filed in selected states.

Scope of Survey

Because of overlapping on the DOD, AEC and NASA lists, the survey covered 52 separate companies rather than a total of 75. Forty-six of the 52 companies had officials who gave to political campaigns. Not all the officers and directors of these 46 companies made campaign contributions. But the 483 who did gave an average of $5,953, compared with an average of $4,202 in 1968.

The compilation showed that 54 individuals contributed $10,000 or more. *(List p. 88)*

In 1968, only 43 corporate executives had given $5,500 or more.

All 25 companies on the DOD list had officers or directors who contributed to 1972 campaigns.

Sixteen of the companies on the AEC list also had officials who gave, including the four companies that were duplicated on the DOD or NASA lists.

All companies except one on the NASA list had officials who contributed. The exception was Computing Software Inc. All but six of the top 25 NASA contractors also were among the largest DOD and AEC contractors. *(Box, p. 85)*

Watergate Relationship

The survey showed that officials of the top DOD, AEC and NASA contractors donated a significant portion of the $19.9-million in then-secret contributions that Stans raised for Nixon's re-election before April 7, 1972. Officials of 28 such companies contributed $1,239,316 before the April 7 mandatory disclosure deadline. Of this amount, $1,231,816 went to the Nixon campaign and $7,500 went to the unsuccessful effort of Sen. Edmund S. Muskie (D Maine) to win the 1972 presidential nomination. *(Box, p. 84)*

Throughout the Watergate controversy, the existence of a large secret cash fund frequently was blamed as the means and incentive for illegal and unscrupulous acts on Nixon's behalf that eventually forced him from office.

Leverage

Stans, who secretly had lobbied against the 1972 campaign reform act, readily conceded at the Senate Watergate hearings that he had used it to extract pre-April 7 contributions from businessmen by reminding them that gifts made after that date would have to be disclosed publicly.

But Stans insisted that this procedure was completely ethical and legal.

"Under the old law, the fact that contributions need not be reported gave the committee and its contributors a right of confidentiality," Stans testified.

Convictions

Two of the pre-April 7 Nixon campaign contributions, purported to be from individuals, proved to be corporate funds and this led to the conviction of the donors and the corporation, the Northrop Corp. Northrop president Thomas V. Jones and his assistant, James Allen, pleaded guilty May 1, 1974, to making an illegal contribution of $150,000 in corporate funds to the Nixon campaign. Jones and the corporation were fined $5,000 each and Allen was fined $1,000.

The illegal $150,000 gift was made up of $130,000 from Jones (out of a total of $133,000 he gave to Republican candidates) and $20,000 from Allen.

Northrop in fiscal 1973 ranked 15th on DOD's list of largest contractors, and 21st on NASA's list. The company's total contracts from the two agencies rose from $374.4-million in fiscal 1972 to $462.9-million in fiscal 1973.

Counting the illegal $150,000, Northrop ranked fourth highest in 1972 political contributions from officials of defense firms. *(Top 10 list below)*

Northrop and Jones were the first contributors charged under a 1948 law that prohibits donations by companies doing a substantial portion of their business with the federal government, according to the Senate Watergate committee.

Russell DeYoung, chairman of both Goodyear Tire and Rubber Co. and Goodyear Atomic Corp., AEC's fourth largest contractor, pleaded guilty Oct. 17, 1973, to illegally giving $40,000 of Goodyear funds to the Nixon campaign. DeYoung was fined $1,000 and Goodyear Tire and Rubber was fined $5,000. The $40,000, including $5,000 attributed to DeYoung, subsequently was returned by the Stans committee.

Pre-April 7 Donations

Besides Northrop and Goodyear Atomic Corp., several other defense companies had officials whose donations were made almost entirely before the April 7 mandatory disclosure date. Among them were General Dynamics Corp., 79.6 per cent of officials' gifts made before April 7; Litton Industries Inc., 73 per cent; Boeing Co., 73.6 per cent; Martin Marietta Corp., 64.6 per cent; Hughes Aircraft Co., 59.4 per cent; Westinghouse Corp., 58.8 per cent; and LTV Corp., 54.2 per cent.

Top-Ranking Companies

There was no direct correlation between the amount of business a company got from the defense agencies and the size of campaign contributions from the company's officials.

For example, executives of Litton Industries Inc. gave the largest amount ($278,209) to political campaigns but Litton ranked only 15th in the value ($622-million) of DOD-NASA contracts it received for fiscal 1973, which began July 1, 1972.

On the other hand, Lockheed Aircraft Corp., by far the largest defense contractor ($1.7-billion for fiscal 1973), ranked almost at the bottom among the 46 companies on the lists whose officials reported at least some political contributions in 1972.

(Continued on p. 87)

'Secret' Gifts By Contractors

Many executives of the top 25 DOD, AEC and NASA contractors unsuccessfully sought anonymity in their 1972 campaign contributions. Almost half of their money was given before April 7, 1972, when a federal law took effect requiring disclosure of such gifts.

Twenty-eight of the companies on the three lists had officers or directors who made contributions before the April 7 deadline. Their pre-April 7 contributions totaled $1,239,316 or 48.1 per cent of the $2,691,775 contributed by officials of these 28 companies, after allowance is made for duplications where contributors were officials of more than one company on the lists.

Virtually all of the pre-April 7 money went to President Nixon's re-election campaign. He received $1,231,816 while $7,500 went to the presidential campaign of Sen. Edmund S. Muskie (D Maine). The man ultimately chosen as the Democratic presidential nominee, Sen. George S. McGovern (D S.D.), received none of the pre-April 7 money contributed by the officials of these companies.

Company	Officials' total donations	Officials' pre-April 7 donations	Pre-April 7 per cent of total
American Telephone & Telegraph Co.	$236,551	$46,913	19.8
Atlantic Richfield Co.	33,150	3,000	9.1
Bendix Corp.	34,847	2,000	5.7
Boeing Co.	40,750	30,000	73.6
Brown and Root Inc.	65,117	14,717	22.6
Chrysler Corp.	58,312	21,350	36.6
E. I. duPont de Nemours & Co.	129,025	47,000	36.4
Ford Motor Co.	148,796	52,776	35.5
General Dynamics Corp.	150,656	119,975	79.6
General Electric Co.	49,862	12,750	25.6
General Motors Corp.	133,835	56,187	42.0
Goodyear Atomic Corp.	5,000	5,000	100.0
Hughes Aircraft Co.	254,200	151,000	59.4
International Business Machines Corp.	102,176	2,000	2.0
International Telephone and Telegraph Corp.	81,658	9,958	12.2
LTV Corp.	155,392	84,242	54.2
Litton Industries Inc.	278,209	203,151	73.0
Lockheed Corp.	3,800	1,000	26.3
McDonnell Douglas Corp.	73,027	33,498	45.9
Martin-Marietta Corp.	19,350	12,500	64.6
Northrop Corp.	200,500	176,500	88.0
RCA Corp.	199,500	47,807	24.0
Sperry Rand Corp.	7,000	2,000	28.6
TRW Inc.	10,954	500	4.6
Tenneco Inc.	39,475	7,000	17.7
Textron Inc.	3,364	1,000	29.7
United Aircraft Corp.	7,500	2,550	34.0
Westinghouse Corp.	187,650	110,400	58.8
	$2,709,656	$1,256,774	
Adjustment for duplications	−58,920	−17,458	
Totals	**$2,650,736**	**$1,239,316**	**48.1**

Breakdown of pre-April 7 contributions:

Richard M. Nixon	$1,231.816
Edmund S. Muskie	7,500
	$1,239,316

Top Defense, AEC and NASA Contractors

The following shows the ranking in fiscal 1973 of the top 25 contractors for the Defense Department, Atomic Energy Commission (AEC) and National Aeronautics and Space Administration (NASA). Numbers in parentheses indicate the company's rank in fiscal 1972.

Dollar amounts shown represent the total net value of contracts the companies received from each of the three agencies for fiscal 1972 and fiscal 1973.

(Contract amounts in thousands of dollars.)

Defense

Company	Fiscal 1972	Fiscal 1973
1. Lockheed Aircraft Corp. (1)	$ 1,705,434	$ 1,658,859
2. General Electric Co. (4)	1,258,673	1,416,238
3. Boeing Co. (5)	1,170,878	1,229,193
4. McDonnell Douglas Corp. (2)	1,700,217	1,143,286
5. Grumman Corp. (7)	1,119,760	909,014
6. American Telephone & Telegraph Co. (6)	1,121,512	774,696
7. Textron Inc. (24)	241,469	746,601
8. United Aircraft Corp. (8)	995,619	741,290
9. General Dynamics Corp. (3)	1,289,167	707,152
10. Rockwell International Corp. (9)	702,862	703,967
11. Raytheon Co. (12)	506,762	679,684
12. Hughes Aircraft Co. (10)	688,132	546,659
13. Westinghouse Electric Corp. (16)	387,386	504,720
14. Sperry Rand Corp. (15)	414,427	447,023
15. Northrop Corp. (17)	369,562	446,424
16. Litton Industries Inc. (11)	616,299	423,947
17. LTV Corp. (14)	449,343	347,078
18. International Business Machines Corp. (20)	259,654	301,779
19. Honeywell Inc. (18)	334,382	272,425
20. RCA Corp. (19)	274,554	250,020
21. International Telephone and Telegraph Corp. (21)	257,754	249,171
22. General Motors Corp. (23)	255,714	249,115
23. Exxon Corp. (25)	209,112	237,010
24. Martin Marietta Corp. (22)	255,942	224,870
25. Tenneco Inc. (13)	504,874	214,043
Totals	$17,089,488	$15,428,673

AEC

Company	Fiscal 1972	Fiscal 1973
1. Union Carbide Corp. (1)	$ 280,385	$ 318,723
2. E. I. du Pont de Nemours & Co. (2)	111,160	124,866
3. Bendix Corp. (3)	94,903	115,119
4. Goodyear Atomic Corp. (6)	65,258	75,853
5. Dow Chemical Co. (5)	69,335	66,796
6. Reynolds Electric and Engineering Corp. (4)	73,190	65,991
7. Atlantic Richfield Co. (7)	41,455	45,248
8. General Electric Co. (8)	36,455	44,552
9. Mason & Hanger-Silas Mason Co. (9)	35,956	36,587
10. EG&G Inc. (10	31,340	29,833
11. Rockwell International Corp. (13)	21,608	23,916
12. United Nuclear Industries Inc. (12)	23,194	22,323
13. Holmes and Narver Inc. (subsidiary of Resource Sciences Corp.) (11)	23,357	12,897
14. NL Industries Inc. (14)	11,688	12,606
15. Westinghouse Electric Corp. (16)	8,092	11,331
16. Gulf Energy and Environmental Systems (17)	6,948	8,077
17. Wackenhut Services Inc. (19)	4,466	4,348
18. Teledyne Inc. (20)	3,535	3,221
19. Babcock and Wilcox Co.*	—	2,794
20. Duquesne Light Co. (22)	1,921	2,329
21. Rural Co-op Power Association (24)	1,883	1,904
22. Lucius Pitkin Inc. (23)	1,890	1,856
23. Combustion Engineering Inc.*	—	1,545
24. Dairyland Power Cooperative (26)	1,182	1,496
25. Aerojet-General Corp. (subsidiary of General Tire and Rubber Co.) (15)	10,651	1,419
Totals	$ 959,852	$ 1,035,630

* Not listed among top AEC contractors in fiscal 1972.

NASA

Company	Fiscal 1972	Fiscal 1973
1. Rockwell International Corp. (3)	$ 175,146	$ 317,756
2. McDonnell Douglas Corp. (1)	343,131	272,064
3. Martin Marietta Corp. (2)	208,361	191,987
4. General Electric Co. (4)	114,944	86,856
5. General Dynamics Corp. (8)	66,627	80,422
6. Bendix Corp. (6)	87,956	79,054
7. Boeing Co. (5)	94,186	75,535
8. International Business Machines Corp. (7)	72,019	61,307
9. Lockheed Aircraft Corp. (10)	46,600	50,808
10. Fairchild Industries Inc. (11)	42,025	43,724
11. RCA Corp. (9)	57,210	38,227
12. Ford Motor Co. (13)	36,219	37,521
13. LTV Corp. (12)	37,398	32,824
14. International Telephone and Telegraph Corp. (17)	26,691	28,576
15. TRW Inc. (15)	33,299	28,223
16. Chrysler Corp. (19)	24,301	27,693
17. Sperry Rand Corp. (14)	33,535	26,558
18. Computer Sciences Corp. (20)	23,298	25,103
19. United Aircraft Corp. (23)	15,869	24,986
20. Hughes Aircraft Co. (21)	22,029	20,941
21. Northrop Corp. (36)	6,708	16,522
22. Honeywell Inc. (24)	12,688	13,800
23. Grumman Corp. (16)	28,478	11,998
24. Litton Industries Inc. (41)	6,031	11,235
25. Computing Software Inc. (26)	10,488	9,815
Totals	$ 1,625,237	$ 1,613,835

SOURCES: Defense Department, AEC, NASA

Contributions by Officials of Federal Contractors

Company	1972 Number Contributing	1972 Republicans	1972 Democrats	1968[1] Number Contributing	1968 Republicans	1968 Democrats	Difference, 1968-1972 Republicans	Difference, 1968-1972 Democrats
Aerojet-General Corp. (subs. The General Tire and Rubber Co.)	2	$ 500	0	2	$ 8,000	$ 15,000	− 7,500	− 15,000
American Telephone & Telegraph Co.	14	132,560	103,991	9	16,500	1,000	+116,060	+102,991
Atlantic Richfield Co.	6	32,150	1,000	12	65,000	1,000	− 32,850	0
Bendix Corp.	6	33,347	1,500	2	2,000	0	+ 31,347	+ 1,500
Boeing Co.	5	40,750	0	4	5,000	0	+ 35,750	0
Brown and Root Inc.	6	18,717	46,400	—	––	—		
Chrysler Corp.	19	57,812	500	20	30,550	5,500	+ 27,262	− 5,000
Computer Sciences Corp.	1	3,000	3,500	—	—	—		
Dow Chemical Co.	9	20,475	0	3	3,000	3,550	+ 17,475	− 3,550
Duquesne Light Co.	2	5,510	0	—	—	—		
E. G. & G. Inc.	1	700	0	—	—	—		
E. I. duPont de Nemours & Co.	18	128,525	500	11	42,800	0	+ 85,725	+ 500
Exxon Corp.	10	25,100	500	6	12,000	0	+ 13,100	+ 500
Fairchild Industries Inc.	10	11,500	25,600	—	—	—		
Fenix and Scisson Inc.	2	2,450	0	—	—	—		
Ford Motor Co.[2]	6	112,176	36,620	19	87,100	53,000	+ 25,076	− 16,380
General Dynamics Corp.	18	149,906	750	9	17,265	1,000	+132,641	− 250
General Electric Co.	60	48,037	1,825	17	27,600	1,000	+ 20,437	+ 825
General Motors Corp.	40	127,628	6,207	29	114,675	1,000	+ 12,953	+ 5,207
Goodyear Atomic Corp.	1	5,000	0	—	—	—		
Grumman Corp.	2	700	500	4	6,500	0	− 5,800	+ 500
Gulf Energy and Environmental Systems	4	7,900	10,000	—	—	—		
Honeywell Inc.	19	27,775	5,100	4	6,000	3,000	+ 21,775	+ 2,100
Hughes Aircraft Co.	3	248,500	5,700	—	—	—		
International Business Machines Corp.	15	92,388	9,788	12	104,250	32,000	− 11,862	− 22,212
International Telephone and Telegraph Corp.[3]	13	42,458	39,200	2	1,500	500	+ 40,958	+ 38,700
Litton Industries Inc.	13	277,709	500	11	151,000	0	+126,709	+ 500
Lockheed Aircraft Corp.	10	4,600	500	5	38,880	1,000	− 34,280	− 500
LTV Corp.	15	139,142	16,250	4	7,500	1,500	+131,642	+ 32,750
Martin-Marietta Corp.	4	14,350	5,000	5	3,500	4,500	+ 10,850	+ 500
Mason and Hanger—Silas Mason Co.	2	3,000	0	—	—	—		
McDonnell-Douglas Corp.	12	72,827	200	5	26,432	0	+ 46,395	+ 200
NL Industries[4]	4	16,500	500	2	6,000	0	+ 10,500	+ 500
Northrop Corp.	15	197,500	3,000	2	23,500	0	+174,000	+ 3,000
Raytheon Co.	9	21,750	1,500	3	6,000	0	+ 15,750	+ 1,500
RCA Corp.	13	191,352	8,148	6	7,000	5,500	+184,352	− 2,648
Rockwell International Corp.	17	34,337	4,340	8	20,500	2,000	+ 13,837	+ 2,340
Rural Co-op Power Association (United Power Assn.)	1	0	1,000	—	—	—		
Sperry Rand Corp.	2	7,000	0	6	7,000	0	0	0
Tenneco Inc.	29	32,975	6,500	—	—	—		
Textron Inc.	3	2,500	864	5	6,000	0	− 3,500	+ 864
TRW Inc.	11	9,454	1,500	1	1,000	0	+ 8,454	+ 1,500
Union Carbide Corp.	10	10,100	0	6	8,000	1,000	+ 2,100	− 1,000
United Aircraft Corp.	9	6,800	700	6	9,500	0	− 2,700	+ 700
United Nuclear Corp.	0	0	0	1	2,500	0	− 2,500	0
Wackenhut Corp.	1	500	0	—	—	—		
Westinghouse Electric Corp.	23	183,850	3,800	14	38,500	1,500	+145,350	+ 2,300
Totals	495	$2,601,310	$353,483					
Less duplications[5]	12	45,570	33,500					
Adjusted Totals	483	$2,555,740	$319,983					

[1] *Dashes appear for 1968 contractors where figures were not available.*
[2] *For 1972, the figures represent contributions from officials of Philco-Ford, a subsidiary of Ford Motor Co.*
[3] *1968 figures include contributions from officials of Federal Electric Corp., a subsidiary of International Telephone and Telegraph Corp.*

[4] *In 1968, the name of NL Industries was National Lead Co.*
[5] *In cases where the same persons were officers or directors of more than one company, their donations were duplicated in the amounts listed for their companies. But the duplications were subtracted to arrive at the adjusted totals.*

(Continued from p. 84)

Top 10 Contributors

Following are the companies on the DOD, AEC and NASA lists whose officers and directors were reported to have contributed the largest amounts to Democratic (D) or Republican (R) election campaigns in 1972:

1. Litton Industries Inc., $278,209 ($500 D; $277,709 R)
2. Hughes Aircraft Co. $254,200 ($5,700 D; $248,500 R)
3. American Telephone & Telegraph Co., $236,551 ($103,991 D; $132,560 R)
4. Northrop Corp., $200,500 ($3,000 D; $197,500 R)
5. RCA Corp., $199,500 ($8,148 D; $191,352 R)
6. Westinghouse Electric Corp., $187,650 ($3,800 D; $183,850 R)
7. LTV Corp., $155,392 ($16,250 D; $139,142 R)
8. General Dynamics Corp., $150,656 ($750 D; $149,906 R)
9. Ford Motor Co., $148,796 ($36,620 D; $112,176 R)
10. General Motors Corp., $133,835 ($6,207 D; $127,628 R)

Top 10 Contractors

The largest DOD, AEC and NASA contractors in fiscal 1973, based on the sums of their contracts from those agencies, were Lockheed Aircraft Corp., $1.7-billion (DOD and NASA); General Electric Corp., $1.5-billion (DOD, AEC and NASA); McDonnell Douglas Corp., $1.4-billion (DOD and NASA); Boeing Co., $1.3-billion (DOD and NASA); Rockwell International Corp., $1-billion (DOD, AEC and NASA); Grumman Corp., $921-million (DOD and NASA); General Dynamics Corp., $787-million (DOD and NASA); American Telephone & Telegraph Co., $775-million (DOD); Textron Inc., $747-million (DOD); and Raytheon Co., $680-million (DOD).

LARGEST CONTRACTORS

Of the top 10 contractors, only American Telephone & Telegraph Co. (AT&T) and General Dynamics Corp. also ranked among the 10 companies whose executives gave the largest amounts to 1972 political campaigns.

AT&T

Fourteen of AT&T's 37 officers and directors donated a total of $236,551, the third largest amount attributed to officials of any one company. Republican candidates received $132,560 and Democrats, $103,991. In 1968, AT&T officials had reported giving only $16,500 to Republicans and $1,000 to Democrats.

AT&T's DOD contracts dropped from $1.1-billion in fiscal 1972 to $775-million in fiscal 1973.

J. Irwin Miller of Columbus, Ind., an AT&T director, was one of the 10 largest individual contributors among defense contractors to 1972 campaigns. Miller gave $92,864 to Democrats and $43,100 to Republicans, for a total of $135,964.

General Dynamics

Officers and directors of General Dynamics were listed as giving $149,906 to Republicans and $750 to Democrats, for a total of $150,656. This compares with $17,265 for Republicans and $1,000 for Democrats reported from General Dynamics officials in 1968.

The company's DOD and NASA contracts dropped from $1.4-billion in fiscal 1972 to $788-million for fiscal 1973.

Lockheed

Officials of Lockheed, the largest DOD-NASA contractor, were reported as contributing only $5,100 to 1972 candidates, including $4,600 to Republicans. This compared with 1968 contributions of $38,880 for Republicans and $1,000 for Democrats from Lockheed officials.

Lockheed's contracts from the two agencies dropped slightly in fiscal 1973 from its $1.75-billion in fiscal 1972.

Lockheed was the beneficiary in 1971 of a controversial federal guarantee of $250-million in bank loans. Supporters contended that the "bail-out" legislation was needed to avoid a Lockheed bankruptcy.

Grumman

Officials of another financially troubled aircraft maker, Grumman, reported giving even less than Lockheed officials in 1972 political contributions. Two Grumman executives reported giving a total of $700 to Republicans and $500 to Democrats.

Grumman's DOD-NASA contracts dropped from $1.4-billion in fiscal 1972 to $921-million in fiscal 1973.

"Bail-out" legislation for Grumman, in the form of $100-million in advance payments on Navy contracts, was rejected by the Senate Aug. 13.

OTHER CONTRACTORS

Defense contractors whose executives gave the heaviest to 1972 political campaigns were not among the largest companies in terms of contracts.

Litton

Litton Industries Inc., which in fiscal 1973 had DOD and NASA contracts totaling $435-million, ranked highest in 1972 campaign contributions by its executives. They gave $277,709 to Republicans, $500 to Democrats. Litton officials also had been the biggest contributors in 1968, with a total of $151,000, all for Republicans.

Litton director Henry Salvatori, largest individual giver in the 1968 survey, ranked second to Howard Hughes in 1972 with contributions totaling $153,173. Of this amount, $150,173 went to Republicans, including $104,415 given before April 7 to the Nixon campaign.

Hughes Aircraft

The $247,500 reported as given by Howard Hughes to Republicans in 1972 included $150,000 given to Nixon's campaign before the April 7 disclosure date. This $150,000 included $100,000 Hughes had given in two installments in 1969 and 1970 to Nixon confidant Charles G. (Bebe) Rebozo. Rebozo has said that he kept the cash in a strongbox for three years and then returned it. *(Background, p. 18)*

In all, three Hughes executives reported campaign contributions totaling $248,500 for Republicans, $5,700 for Democrats.

Hughes Aircraft's DOD and NASA contracts dropped from $710.2-million in fiscal 1972 to $567.6-million in fiscal 1973.

duPont

Eighteen out of 28 officers and directors of E. I. duPont de Nemours & Co., the AEC's second largest contractor, donated $128,525 to Republicans, $500 to Democrats.

Five duPont executives were among the 54 in 1972 who contributed at least $10,000 to political campaigns. Their donations totaled $94,075, including pre-April 7 contributions to the Nixon campaign. The five executives and their donations (with pre-April 7 amounts in parentheses) were Lammot duPont Copeland, director, $29,500 ($5,000); Hugh R. Sharp Jr., director, $25,075 ($5,000); W. S. Carpenter Jr., honorary chairman and director, $16,500 ($3,000); Crawford H. Greenwalt, director, $13,000 ($5,000); and W. Samuel Carpenter Jr., $10,000 ($6,000).

In 1968, duPont officials reported giving $42,800, all to Republicans.

Ford Motor

Officials of Philco-Ford, a Ford Motor subsidiary that ranked 12th among NASA contractors, contributed $148,-796 to political campaigns, a slight increase from 1968.

Henry Ford II, a director, gave $54,726 to Republicans (including $49,776 before April 7 to the Nixon campaign) and $6,060 to Democrats. In 1968, he gave more money to Democrats than Republicans.

Another director, William Clay Ford, gave $30,000 to Democrats, $27,000 to Republicans. Benson Ford, also a director, contributed $28,250 to Republicans, including $3,-000 before April 7 to the Nixon campaign, and $560 to Democrats.

Sharp Increases

Several companies ranking below the 10 largest in contracts showed marked increases from 1968 to 1972 in the political contributions of their executives. Republicans got almost all the additional money.

Among these companies and their officials' total contributions, with 1968 amounts listed first, were Westinghouse Electric Corp., $40,000 to $187,650; RCA Corp., $12,500 to $199,500; Northrop Corp., $23,500 to $200,500; LTV Corp., $9,000 to $155,392; Hughes Aircraft, zero to $254,200.

An LTV director, Gustave L. Levy, with Janet Levy was the fourth largest individual contributor. Levy gave $115,442 to Republicans (including a pre-April 7 gift of $70,-442 to the Nixon campaign) and $3,000 to Democrats.

Martin B. Seretean, an RCA director, ranked fifth in contributions, with $114,845 to Republicans (all given before April 7 to the Nixon campaign) and $2,627 to Democrats.

The sixth-ranking contributor, Westinghouse director Roger S. Milliken, gave Republicans $104,000, including a pre-April 7 donation of $84,000 to the Nixon campaign.

Joined Administration

Two contributors of more than $10,000 to the Nixon campaign later joined the Nixon administration. Roy L. Ash, president and director of Litton Industries, became director of the Office of Budget and Administration. Frederick B. Dent, a General Electric director, became secretary of commerce.

Ash had given $24,500, including $20,000 to the Nixon campaign before April 7. Dent's total contribution of $10,-500 pre-dated the April 7 deadline.

Top 54 Individual Contributors

Fifty-four officers or directors of companies among the top 25 DOD, AEC and NASA contractors in fiscal 1973 gave at least $10,000 to political campaigns in 1972.

One of the largest contributors was Howard Hughes, president of Hughes Aircraft Co., who gave $247,500 to Republican candidates and $4,000 to Democrats. However, $100,000 that Hughes contributed to President Nixon's re-election campaign later was returned. *(See p. 18)*

The names of the 54 officials are listed below in alphabetical order. After each name is the amount of the 1972 contribution and the party, Democrat (D) or Republican (R) receiving the money. Nonpartisan (NP) and miscellaneous (M) contributions, such as to referendum campaigns, also are listed.

Herbert Allen, director, Tenneco Inc.: (D) 4,000; (R) 9,200.

James Allen, vice-president and assistant to the president and director, Northrop Corp.: (D) 3,000; (R) 20,000.

Robert Anderson, president and director, Rockwell International Corp.: (R) 10,544.

Robert O. Anderson, chairman and chief executive officer, Atlantic Richfield Co.: (D) 1.000; (R) 24,000.

Roy L. Ash, president and director, Litton Industries Inc.: (R) 24,500.

Stephen D. Bechtel Jr., director, General Motors Corp.: (R) 29,500.

Eugene N. Beesley, director, General Motors Corp.: (D) 500; (R) 15,679.

Karl R. Bendetsen, director, Westinghouse Electric Corp.: (D) 500; (R) 10,000.

George R. Brown, chairman and director, Brown and Root Inc., and director, International Telephone and Telegraph Corp., and **Alice Brown**: (D) 33,000; (R) 9,958.

George M. Bunker, president and director, Martin Marietta Corp.: (D) 5,000; (R) 8,500.

Walter Burke, director, Fairchild Industries Inc.: (D) 19,000.

W. S. Carpenter Jr., honorary chairman and director, E. I. du Pont de Nemours & Co.: (R), 16,500.

W. Samuel Carpenter III, director, E. I. du Pont de Nemours & Co.: (R) 10,000.

Lammot duPont Copeland, director, E. I. du Pont de Nemours & Co.: (R) 29,500.

Henry Crown, director, General Dynamics Corp.: (D) 750; (R) 51,819.

Nathan Cummings, director, General Dynamics Corp.: (R) 44,856.

Harry B. Cunningham, director, Bendix Corp.: (R) 10,805.

Paul L. Davies Sr., director, International Business Machines Corp.: (R) 14,500.

Frederick B. Dent, director, General Electric Co.: (R) 10,500.

C. Douglas Dillon, director, American Telephone & Telegraph Co.: (D) 3,500; (R) 62,000.

Benson Ford, director, Ford Motor Co.: (D) 560; (R) 28,250.

Henry Ford II, director, Ford Motor Co.: (D) 6,060; (R) 54,726.

William Clay Ford, director, Ford Motor Co.: (D) 30,-000; (R) 27,000.

Herbert J. Frensley, president and director, Brown and Root Inc.: (D) 8,900; (R) 4,759.

Harold S. Geneen, chairman of the board, president, and director, International Telephone and Telegraph Corp.: (D) 1,000; (R) 11,500.

Crawford H. Greenwalt, director, Boeing Co., and director, E. I. du Pont de Nemours & Co.: (R) 13,000.

Robert V. Hansberger, director, General Dynamics Corp.: (R) 21,000.

William R. Hewlett, director, Chrysler Corp.: (R) 26,500.

Amory Houghton Jr., director, International Business Machines Corp.: (R) 28,500.

Howard Hughes, president, Hughes Aircraft Co.: (D) 4,000; (R) 247,500.

Thomas V. Jones, chairman, president and director, Northrop Corp.: (R) 133,000.

Earle M. Jorgenson, director, Northrop Corp.: (R) 36,500.

Gustave L. Levy, director, LTV Corp., and **Janet Levy:** (D) 3,000; (R) 115,442.

John A. McCone, director, International Telephone and Telegraph Corp.: (R) 12,000; (NP) 2,000.

James S. McDonnell, chairman and director, McDonnell Douglas Corp.: (R) 37,530.

Augustine R. Marusi, director, NL Industries; (D) 500; (R) 12,500.

J. Irwin Miller, director, American Telephone & Telegraph Co.: (D) 92,864; (R) 43,100.

Roger S. Milliken, director, Westinghouse Electric Corp.: (R) 104,000.

C. S. Harding Mott, director, Bendix Corp.: (D) 1,000; (R) 9,500.

Donald W. Nyrop, director, Honeywell Inc.: (R) 13,-000.

W. R. Persons, director, General Dynamics Corp.: (R) 17,181.

Henry Salvatori, director, Litton Industries Inc.: (R) 150,173; (M) 3,500.

John M. Schiff, director, Westinghouse Electric Corp., and **Edith Schiff:** (R) 41,700; (M) 1,500.

Martin B. Seretean, director, RCA Corp.: (D), 2,627; (R) 114,845.

Hugh R. Sharp Jr.,, director, E. I. du Pont de Nemours & Co.: (R) 25,075.

O. Edwin Singer, director, Gulf Energy and Environmental Systems: (D) 10,000; (R) 5,000.

Howard A. Stamper, director, RCA Corp.: (R) 52,-307.

Vernon Stouffer, director, Litton Industries Inc.: (R) 25,000.

Lewis L. Strauss, director, RCA Corp.: (R) 11,000.

William Paul Thayer, director, LTV Corp.: (D) 9,000; (R) 6,700.

Joseph A. Thomas, director, Litton Industries Inc.: (R) 10,000.

Charles B. Thornton, director, Litton Industries Inc.: ($) 52,636.

Thomas J. Watson, chairman of the executive committee, International Business Machines Corp.: (D) 4,500; (R) 33,000.

George H. Weyerhaeuser, director, Boeing Co.: (R) 25,000; (M) 180.

STATUS OF WATERGATE COURT ACTIONS SEPT. 30, 1974

Fifty-one individuals and 14 corporations had been charged with violations of federal law in connection with various facets of the Watergate scandal by Sept. 30, 1974. The figures below add up to more than 51 because several defendants had been implicated in more than one case. This was the status of the court actions:

• Thirty-three persons had been sentenced or fined and 15 either had served or were serving prison terms. Five were free, pending appeal, and seven were awaiting sentencing. One had been granted immunity to testify. Charges against three had been dropped. One had fled the country to avoid prosecution.

• Thirteen corporations had been fined. One corporation had been acquitted.

• Six men were awaiting trial for their alleged roles in the Watergate coverup: John D. Ehrlichman, H.R. Haldeman, Robert C. Mardian, John N. Mitchell, Kenneth W. Parkinson and Gordon C. Strachan.

Watergate Break-in

Five men, wearing surgical gloves and carrying electronic surveillance equipment, were arrested about 2:30 a.m. June 17, 1972, in the Democratic national headquarters at the Watergate office building in Washington, D.C. Seven men eventually were indicted in connection with the break-in.

Bernard L. Barker, Miami real estate agent, former CIA agent: Sentenced Nov. 9, 1973, to 18 months to six years in prison after pleading guilty to seven counts of burglary, wiretapping and conspiracy. Released Jan. 4, 1974, pending appeal, after serving one year, 19 days.

Virgilio Gonzalez, Miami locksmith, refugee from Cuba: Pleaded guilty Jan. 15, 1973, to six counts of burglary, wiretapping and conspiracy. Sentenced Nov. 9, 1973, to one to four years in prison. Released on parole March 7, 1974.

E. Howard Hunt Jr., former CIA agent and White House consultant: Pleaded guilty Jan. 11, 1973, to six counts of burglary, wiretapping and conspiracy. Sentenced Nov. 9, 1973, to 30 months to eight years in prison and fined $10,000. Released on personal recognizance Jan. 2, 1974, pending appeal, after serving 10 months and five days.

G. Gordon Liddy, former FBI agent, White House aide, general counsel to the Committee for the Re-election of the President, counsel to the Finance Committee to Re-elect the President: Convicted of six counts of burglary, wiretapping and conspiracy. Sentenced March 23, 1973, to six years and eight months to 20 years in prison and fined $40,000.

Eugenio Martinez, Cuban refugee, Miami businessman: Pleaded guilty Jan. 15, 1973, to seven counts of burglary, wiretapping and conspiracy. Sentenced Nov. 9, 1973, to one to four years in prison. Released on parole March 7, 1974.

James W. McCord, former security coordinator for the Committee for the Re-election of the President and for the Republican National Committee: Convicted of eight counts of burglary, wiretapping and conspiracy. Sentenced Nov. 9, 1973, to one to five years in prison. Released on $5,000 bond pending appeal.

Frank A. Sturgis, Miami salesman, former Marine: Pleaded guilty Jan. 15, 1973, to charges of burglary, wiretapping and conspiracy. Sentenced Nov. 9, 1973, to one to four years in prison. Freed by court order Jan. 18, 1974, pending appeal. Parole Board announced March 25 that parole would commence on termination of appeal bond.

Watergate Coverup

An alleged conspiracy among White House and re-election campaign aides to obstruct justice in the investigation of the Watergate burglary. By Sept. 30, 11 persons had been indicted in connection with the coverup.

Charles W. Colson, former special counsel to the President: Pleaded not guilty March 9, 1974, to charges of conspiracy and obstruction of justice. Charges were dropped after he pleaded guilty June 3 to charges of conspiring to violate the civil rights of Dr. Lewis J. Fielding, Daniel Ellsberg's psychiatrist.

John W. Dean III, former counsel to the President: Pleaded guilty Oct. 19, 1973, to charges of conspiring to obstruct justice and to defraud the United States. Sentenced Aug. 2, 1974, to a prison term of one to four years. Began sentence Sept. 3.

John D. Ehrlichman, former presidential adviser on domestic affairs: Pleaded not guilty March 9, 1974, to charges of conspiracy to obstruct justice, obstruction of justice and making false statements to FBI agents and to a grand jury. Trial scheduled for Oct. 1.

H. R. Haldeman, former White House chief of staff: Pleaded not guilty March 9, 1974, to charges of conspiracy, perjury and obstruction of justice. Trial scheduled for Oct. 1.

Frederick C. LaRue, former White House aide and assistant to John N. Mitchell at the Committee for the Re-election of the President: Pleaded guilty June 27, 1973, to charges of conspiracy to obstruct justice. Sentencing deferred.

Jeb Stuart Magruder, former White House aide, former deputy director of the Committee for the Re-election of the President: Pleaded guilty Aug. 16, 1973, to charges of conspiring to obstruct justice and to defraud the United States. Sentenced May 21, 1974, to a prison term of 10 months to four years. Began serving June 4, 1974.

Robert C. Mardian, former chief of the internal security division at the Justice Department, deputy manager of the Committee for the Re-election of the President: Pleaded not guilty March 9, 1974, to a charge of conspiracy to obstruct justice. Trial scheduled for Oct. 1.

John N. Mitchell, former attorney general and director of the Committee for the Re-election of the President: Pleaded not guilty March 9, 1974, to charges of conspiracy to obstruct justice, perjury, making a false statement to a grand jury and to FBI agents and obstruction of justice. Trial scheduled for Oct. 1.

Kenneth W. Parkinson, former attorney for the Committee for the Re-election of the President: Pleaded not guilty March 9, 1974, to charges of conspiracy to obstruct justice and obstruction of justice. Trial set for Oct. 1.

Herbert L. Porter, former aide at the Committee for the Re-election of the President: Pleaded guilty Jan. 28, 1974, to charges of making false statements to FBI agents. Sentenced April 11, 1974, to a five-month to 15-month prison term, of which he would have to serve only 30 days. Released May 23, 1974.

Gordon C. Strachan, former aide to H.R. Haldeman at the White House: Charged with conspiracy to obstruct justice, obstruction of justice and making false statements to a grand jury. Pleaded not guilty March 9, 1974. Trial originally scheduled for Oct. 1. Trial separated Sept. 30 and new date not set.

Illegal Campaign Contributions

Investigation into illegal campaign contributions made by corporations and corporate executives. Twenty-one individuals and fourteen corporations had been indicted by Sept. 30. While most of the indictments were for illegal contributions to President Nixon's 1972 campaign, some were for illegal contributions to Democratic presidential and congressional campaigns.

Individuals

James Allen, vice president of the Northrop Corporation: Pleaded guilty May 1, 1974, to charges of illegally contributing $150,000 in corporate funds to the 1972 Nixon re-election campaign. Fined $1,000.

Richard Allison: see Milk Fund Deal.

Dwayne Andreas, chairman of the board of the First Interoceanic Corporation: Pleaded innocent Oct. 19, 1973, to charges of illegally contributing $100,000 in corporate funds to the 1968 presidential campaign of Sen. Hubert H. Humphrey (D Minn.). Acquitted July 12, 1974.

Orin E. Atkins, chairman of the board of Ashland Petroleum Gabon Inc.: Pleaded no contest Nov. 13, 1973, to charges of illegally contributing $100,000 in corporate funds to the 1972 Nixon campaign. Fined $1,000.

Francis X. Carroll: *see Milk Fund Deal.*

Russell DeYoung, chairman of the board of Goodyear Tire and Rubber Company: Pleaded guilty Oct. 17, 1973, to charges of illegally contributing $40,000 in corporate funds to Nixon's 1972 campaign. Fined $1,000.

Ray Dubrowin, vice president of the Diamond International Corporation: Pleaded guilty March 7, 1974, to charges of illegally contributing $5,000 in corporate funds to Nixon's 1972 campaign and $1,000 in corporate funds to Sen. Edmund S. Muskie's (D Maine) 1972 presidential campaign. Fined $1,000.

Harry Heltzer, chairman of the board of Minnesota Mining and Manufacturing Company: Pleaded guilty Oct. 17, 1973, to charges of illegally contributing $30,000 in corporate funds to Nixon's 1972 campaign. Fined $500.

Jake Jacobsen: *see Milk Fund Deal.*

Thomas V. Jones, chairman of the board of the Northrop Corporation: Pleaded guilty May 1, 1974, to charges of illegally contributing $150,000 in corporate funds to Nixon's 1972 campaign. Fined $5,000.

Herbert W. Kalmbach, personal attorney to President Nixon. Pleaded guilty Feb. 25, 1974, to charges of violating the Federal Corrupt Practices Act and to a charge of promising federal employment as a reward for political activity and for support of a candidate. Sentenced to six to 18 months in prison and fined $10,000. Began sentence July 1.

William W. Keeler, chairman of the board of Phillips Petroleum Company: Pleaded guilty Dec. 4, 1973, to charges of illegally contributing $100,000 in corporate funds to Nixon's 1972 campaign for re-election. Fined $1,000.

Harding L. Lawrence, chairman of the board of Braniff Airways: Pleaded guilty Nov. 12, 1973, to charges of illegally contributing $40,000 in corporate funds to the 1972 Nixon campaign. Fined $1,000.

John L. Loeb, Wall Street investment banker: Pleaded no contest June 7, 1973, to charges of disguising a $48,000 contribution to the 1972 presidential campaign of Sen. Hubert H. Humphrey (D Minn.). Fined $3,000.

John H. Melcher, executive vice president of and general counsel to the American Shipbuilding Company: Pleaded guilty April 11, 1974, to a charge of being an accessory after the fact in the coverup of illegal acts. Fined $2,500.

Harold S. Nelson: see Milk Fund Deal.

H. Everett Olson: see Milk Fund Deal.

David L. Parr: see Milk Fund Deal.

Norman Sherman: see Milk Fund Deal.

George M. Steinbrenner III, chairman of the board of American Shipbuilding Company, principal partner of the New York Yankees: Indicted April 5, 1974, for making illegal contributions to the 1972 campaigns of Nixon and Democratic congressional candidates through an elaborate kickback scheme. The 15-count indictment also charged him with attempting to obstruct two grand jury probes by destroying and falsifying records and by ordering company officers to lie to the FBI and to grand juries. Pleaded not guilty April 19, 1974. Changed plea to guilty Aug. 23, 1974. Fined $10,000 on the charges of illegally contributing to political campaigns. Fined an additional $5,000 on a new charge of being an accessory after the fact to violation of federal campaign laws.

John Valentine: *see Milk Fund Deal.*

Claude C. Wild Jr., former vice president of Gulf Oil Corporation: Pleaded guilty Nov. 13, 1973, to charges of illegally contributing $100,000 in corporate funds to the 1972 Nixon re-election campaign. Fined $1,000.

Corporations

American Airlines: Pleaded guilty Oct. 17, 1973, to charges of making an illegal $55,000 contribution to the 1972 Nixon campaign. Fined $5,000.

American Shipbuilding Company: Indicted April 5, 1974, on one count of conspiracy and one count of illegal campaign contributions. Pleaded guilty Aug. 23, 1974. Fined $20,000 Sept. 3, 1974.

Ashland Petroleum Gabon Ind.: Pleaded guilty Nov. 13, 1973, to charges of making an illegal $100,000 contribution to the 1972 Nixon campaign. Fined $5,000.

Associated Milk Producers, Inc.: *see Milk Fund Deal.*

Braniff Airways: Pleaded guilty Nov. 12, 1973, to charges of making an illegal $40,000 contribution to the 1972 Nixon campaign. Fined $5,000.

Carnation Company: *see Milk Fund Deal.*

Diamond International Corporation: Pleaded guilty March 7, 1974, to charges of making a $5,000 illegal contribution to the 1972 Nixon campaign and a $1,000 illlegal contribution to the 1972 presidential campaign of Sen. Edmund S. Muskie (D Maine). Fined $5,000.

First Interoceanic Corporation: Pleaded innocent to a four-count violation in connection with a $100,000 contribution made in 1968 to the presidential campaign of Hubert H. Humphrey (D). Acquitted July 12, 1974.

Goodyear Tire and Rubber Company: Pleaded guilty Oct. 17, 1973, to charges of making an illegal $40,000 contribution to the 1972 Nixon campaign. Fined $5,000.

Gulf Oil Corporation: Pleaded guilty Nov. 13, 1973, to charges of illegally contributing $100,000 to the 1972 Nixon campaign, $15,000 to Rep. Wilbur D. Mills' (D Ark.) 1972 presidential campaign and $10,000 to Sen. Henry M. Jackson's (D Wash.) campaign. Fined $5,000.

Lehigh Valley Cooperative Farmers: *see Milk Fund Deal.*

Minnesota Mining and Manufacturing Company: Pleaded guilty Oct. 17, 1973, to charges of making an illegal $30,000 contribution to the 1972 Nixon campaign. Fined $3,000.

Northrop Corporation: Pleaded guilty May 1, 1974, to charges of making an illegal $150,000 contribution to the 1972 Nixon campaign. Fined $5,000.

Phillips Petroleum Company: Pleaded guilty Dec. 4, 1973, to charges of making a $100,000 illegal contribution to the 1972 Nixon campaign. Fined $5,000.

ITT Case

An investigation into the possible connection between an antitrust settlement considered favorable to International Telephone and Telegraph Corporation (ITT) and an ITT pledge to contribute as much as $400,000 to help finance the 1972 Republican National Convention. Two persons had been indicted in connection with the investigation.

Ed Reinecke, lieutenant governor of California: Indicted April 3, 1974, on three counts of perjury before the Senate Judiciary Committee, which was investigating a possible connection between an ITT pledge to the 1972 Republican campaign and an antitrust settlement. Pleaded not guilty April 10. Trial began July 15. Found guilty July 27 on one count of perjury. To be sentenced.

Richard G. Kleindienst, former attorney general: Pleaded guilty May 16, 1974, to one count of refusing to testify, a misdemeanor. Sentenced June 7, to one month of unsupervised probation. Suspended sentence of one month in jail and $100 fine.

'Dirty Tricks'

A group of men performed acts of political sabotage and espionage, designed to create confusion and dissension among 1972 Democratic presidential contenders. The chief prankster reportedly was paid by Nixon's personal attorney and received directions from the President's appointments secretary.

Dwight L. Chapin, former presidential appointments secretary: Indicted Nov. 29, 1973, on four counts of making false statements before a grand jury. Pleaded innocent Dec. 7, 1973. Convicted April 5, 1974, on two counts. Sentenced May 15 to 10 to 30 months in prison. Free pending appeal.

Donald H. Segretti, California lawyer, former Treasury Department attorney: Pleaded guilty Oct. 1, 1973, to one count of conspiracy and to three counts of distributing illegal campaign literature. Sentenced Nov. 5, 1973, to six months in prison. Served from Nov. 12, 1973, to March 25, 1974, with time off for good behavior.

George A. Hearing, Tampa accountant: Pleaded guilty May 11, 1973, to two counts of fabricating and distributing illegal campaign literature. Sentenced June 15, 1973, to one year in prison. Released March 22, 1974.

White House 'Plumbers'

A secret White House investigative team set up at Nixon's direction in 1971 to plug security leaks. Seven of the plumbers were indicted for their roles in the 1971 break-in at the office of Dr. Lewis J. Fielding, a psychiatrist who had treated Pentagon Papers defendant Daniel Ellsberg.

Bernard L. Barker (see above): Indicted March 7, 1974, on one count of conspiracy to violate Fielding's rights. Pleaded not guilty March 14. Found guilty July 12. Placed on three years probation July 31.

Charles W. Colson (see above): Indicted March 7, 1974, on one count of conspiracy to violate Fielding's rights. Pleaded innocent March 9. Pleaded guilty June 3, 1974, to another charge, obstruction of justice, and all other charges were dropped. Sentenced June 21 to one to three years in prison and fined $5,000. Began prison term July 8.

Felipe DeDiego of Miami: Indicted March 7, 1974, on one count of conspiracy to violate Fielding's rights. Pleaded innocent March 14. Charge dismissed May 21. Action under appeal.

John D. Ehrlichman (see above): Indicted March 7, 1974, on one count of conspiracy to violate Fielding's rights, one count of making false statements to the FBI and three counts of making false statements to a grand jury. Pleaded innocent March 9. Found guilty July 12 of one count of conspiracy to violate Fielding's rights, one count of making a false statement to the FBI and two counts of making false statements to a grand jury. Acquitted on one count of making a false statement to a grand jury. Sentenced July 31 to twenty months to five years on each count, to run concurrently. Must also stand trial on one perjury charge in a California state court. Free pending appeal.

Egil Krogh Jr., former aide to Ehrlichman: Pleaded guilty Nov. 30, 1973, to one count of violating the rights of Dr. Fielding. Sentenced Jan. 24, 1974, to a prison term of two to six years, suspended except for six months. Released June 21.

G. Gordon Liddy (see above): Indicted March 7, 1974, on one count of conspiracy to violate Fielding's rights and on two counts of refusing to testify before a House committee. Pleaded innocent March 14 to all counts. Convicted May 10 on the two counts of refusing to testify and given two concurrent six-month suspended sentences. Found guilty July 12 on one count of conspiracy to violate Fielding's rights. Sentenced July 31 to one to three years in prison to be served concurrently with Watergate break-in sentence.

Eugenio Martinez (see above): Indicted March 7, 1974, on one count of violating Fielding's rights. Pleaded innocent March 14. Found guilty July 12. Placed on three years probation on July 31.

Vesco Case

Indictments of two former Nixon cabinet members on charges of obstruction of justice and perjury. They allegedly attempted to block a government investigation of the activities of financier Robert L. Vesco in exchange for a $200,000 contribution to the Nixon campaign. The two men were found not guilty. Vesco, who also was indicted, was a fugitive in Costa Rica. A fourth man was granted immunity to testify at the trial.

John N. Mitchell (see above): Pleaded innocent May 21, 1973, to one count of conspiracy to obstruct justice, three counts of endeavoring to obstruct justice and five counts of perjury before a grand jury. Acquitted April 28, 1974.

Harry L. Sears, New Jersey lawyer, director of the Nixon re-election campaign in New Jersey: Pleaded innocent May 21, 1973, to one count of conspiracy to obstruct justice and three counts of endeavoring to obstruct justice. Granted total immunity to testify at the trial.

Maurice H. Stans, former secretary of commerce, chairman from Aug. 23, 1972, to Jan. 17, 1973, of the Republican National Finance Committee, chairman of the Finance Committee to Re-elect the President: Pleaded innocent May 21, 1973, to one count of conspiracy to obstruct justice, three counts of endeavoring to obstruct justice and six counts of perjury before a grand jury. Acquitted April 28, 1974.

Robert L. Vesco, financier: Indicted May 10, 1973, on one count of conspiracy to obstruct justice and three counts of endeavoring to obstruct justice. Fugitive in Costa Rica.

Milk Fund Deal

An investigation into a possible connection between federal milk support payments and illegal contributions by officials of dairy cooperatives.

Corporations

Associated Milk Producers Inc.: Pleaded guilty Aug. 2, 1974, to one count of conspiracy and five counts of illegally contributing over $300,000 in 1968, 1970 and 1972 federal elections. Fined $35,000.

Carnation Company: Pleaded guilty Dec. 19, 1973, to charges of making $7,900 in illegal campaign contributions to the 1972 Nixon campaign. Fined $5,000.

Lehigh Valley Cooperative Farmers: Pleaded guilty May 6, 1974, to charges of making an illegal $50,000 contribution to the 1972 Nixon campaign. Fined $3,000.

Individuals

Richard Allison, former president of Lehigh Valley Cooperative Farmers: Pleaded guilty May 6, 1974, to an unwillful violation of the law forbidding corporate contributions to political campaigns; $50,000 in corporate funds were contributed illegally to the 1972 Nixon campaign. Sentenced to one month unsupervised probation and given a suspended $1,000 fine.

Francis X. Carroll, former lobbyist for Lehigh Valley Cooperative Farmers: Pleaded guilty May 28, 1974, to charges of aiding and abetting an individual to make a $50,000 corporate contribution to Nixon's 1972 campaign. Received a $1,000 suspended fine.

John B. Connally, treasury secretary (1971-72), pleaded not guilty Aug. 9 to charges of bribery, conspiracy and perjury; allegedly accepted $10,000 in bribes from Texas lawyer Jake Jacobsen.

Jake Jacobsen, Texas lawyer, former attorney for the Associated Milk Producers Inc.: Indicted Feb. 21, 1974, for perjury before a grand jury investigating illegal campaign contributions. Charges were dropped May 3 on a technicality. Pleaded guilty Aug. 7 to a single charge of paying former treasury secretary John B. Connally $10,000 in bribes. Sentencing deferred.

Harold S. Nelson, former general manager of Associated Milk Producers Inc.: Pleaded guilty July 31, 1974, to one count of conspiracy; admitted authorizing a $10,000 payment to John B. Connally and over $300,000 in illegal corporate contributions to 1968, 1970 and 1972 political campaigns. Sentencing deferred pending pre-sentence report.

H. Everett Olson, chairman of the board of the Carnation Company: Pleaded guilty Dec. 19, 1973, to charges of illegally contributing $8,900 in corporate funds to Nixon's 1972 campaign. Fined $1,000.

David L. Parr, former special counsel of Associated Milk Producers Inc.: Pleaded guilty July 23 to conspiracy charges. Sentencing deferred pending pre-sentence report.

Norman Sherman, former press secretary for Sen. Hubert H. Humphrey (D Minn.) and partner in Valentine-Sherman and Associates, a computer mail firm: Pleaded guilty Aug. 12, 1974, to one count of aiding and abetting use of illegal contributions of $82,-000 from the Associated Milk Producers Inc. to purchase computer mail lists for use in Humphrey's 1972 presidential campaign and in a number of other Democratic campaigns.

John Valentine, partner in Valentine-Sherman and Associates; Pleaded guilty Aug. 12, 1974, to one count of aiding and abetting use of illegal contributions from the Associated Milk Producers Inc. to purchase computer mail lists for use in Humphrey's 1972 presidential campaign and in a number of other Democratic campaigns.

PROVISIONS OF 1972 CAMPAIGN FINANCE LAW

As enacted into law Feb. 7, 1972 (S 382—PL 92-225):

Title I—Campaign Communications

• Limited the amount that could be spent by federal candidates for advertising time in communications media to 10 cents per eligible voter, or $50,000, whichever was greater. The limitation would apply to all candidates for president and vice president, senator and representative, and would be determined annually for the geographical area of each election by the Bureau of the Census.

• Included in the definition of "communications media" were radio and television broadcasting stations, newspapers, magazines, billboards and automatic telephone equipment. Of the total amount permitted to be spent in a campaign, up to 60 per cent could be used for broadcast advertising time.

• Prohibited radio and television stations from charging political candidates more than the lowest unit cost for the same advertising time available to commercial advertisers. Lowest unit rate charges would apply only during the 45 days preceding a primary election and the 60 days preceding a general election.

• Required non-broadcast media to charge candidates no more than the comparable amounts charged to commercial advertisers for the same class and amount of advertising space. The requirement would apply only during the 45 days preceding the date of a primary election and 60 days before the date of a general election.

• Specified that candidates for president could spend during the period prior to the nomination convention no more in primary and non-primary states than the amount allowed under the 10-cent-per-voter communications spending limitation.

• Provided that broadcast and non-broadcast spending limitations were to be increased in proportion to annual increases in the Consumer Price Index over the base year 1970.

• Provided that amounts spent by an agent of a candidate on behalf of his candidacy would be charged against the over-all expenditure allocation. Fees paid to the agent for services performed also would be charged against the over-all limitation.

• Stipulated that no broadcast station could make any charge for political advertising time on a station unless written consent to contract for such time had been given by the candidate, and unless the candidate certified that such charges would not exceed his spending limit.

Title II—Criminal Code Amendments

• Defined "election" to mean any general, special, primary or runoff election, nominating convention or caucus, delegate selection primary, presidential preference primary or constitutional convention.

• Broadened the definitions of "contribution" and "expenditure" as they pertained to political campaigns, but exempted a loan of money by a national or state bank made in accordance with applicable banking laws.

• Prohibited promises of employment or other political rewards or benefits by any candidate in exchange for political support, and prohibited contracts between candidates and any federal department or agency.

• Placed a ceiling on contributions by any candidate or his immediate family to his own campaign of $50,-000 for president or vice president, $35,000 for senator, and $25,000 for representative.

• Provided that the definitions "contribution" and "expenditure" did not include communications, non-partisan registration and get-out-the-vote campaigns by a corporation aimed at its stockholders or by a labor organization aimed at its members.

• Provided that the definitions "contribution" and "expenditure" did not include the establishment, administration and solicitation of voluntary contributions to a separate segregated fund to be utilized for political purposes by a corporation or labor organization.

Title III—Disclosure of Federal Campaign Funds

• Required all political committees that anticipated receipts in excess of $1,000 during the calendar year to file a statement of organization with the appropriate federal supervisory officer, which was to include the names of all principal officers, the scope of the committee, the names of all candidates the committee supported and other information as required by law.

• Required all political committees to have a chairman and a treasurer, and prohibited any expenditure by the committee without the authorization of the chairman or treasurer.

- Stipulated that the appropriate federal supervisory officer to oversee election campaign practices, reporting and disclosure was the clerk of the House for House candidates, the secretary of the Senate for Senate candidates and the comptroller general of the General Accounting Office (GAO) for presidential candidates.
- Required each political committee to report any individual expenditure of more than $100 and any expenditures of more than $100 in the aggregate during the calendar year.
- Required disclosure of all contributions to any committee or candidate, in excess of $100, including a detailed report with the name and address of the contributor and the date the contribution was made.
- Required any committee that accepted contributions or made expenditures on behalf of any candidate without the authorization of such candidate to include a notice on the front page of all literature published by the committee stating that the committee was not authorized by the candidate and that the candidate was not responsible for the activities of the committee.
- Required the federal supervisory officers to prepare an annual report for each campaign committee registered and to make such reports available for sale to the public.
- Required candidates and committees to file reports of contributions and expenditures on the 10th day of March, June and September of every year, on the 15th and fifth days preceding the date on which an election was held and on the 31st day of January. Any contribution of $5,000 or more was to be reported within 48 hours after its receipt.
- Required reporting of the names, addresses and occupations of any lender and endorser of any loan in excess of $100 as well as the date and amount of such loans.
- Required reporting of the total proceeds from the sales of tickets to all fund-raising events, mass collections made at such events and sales of political campaign materials.
- Required any person who made any contribution in excess of $100, other than through a political committee or directly to the candidate, to report such contribution to the appropriate supervisory officer.
- Required a full and complete financial statement of the costs of holding a presidential nominating convention within 60 days after the end of the convention.
- Prohibited any contribution to a candidate or committee by one person in the name of another person.
- Authorized the office of the comptroller general of the GAO to serve as a national clearinghouse for information on the administration of election practices.
- Required political parties in states where a presidential nominating convention was held to file detailed reports on the financing of the convention with the office of the comptroller general.
- Required that copies of reports filed by candidates with the appropriate supervisory officer also be filed with the secretaries of state for the states in which the elections were held.

Title IV—General Provisions

- Repealed the Federal Corrupt Practices Act of 1925 (2 U.S. Code 241-256).
- Required the Civil Aeronautics Board, the Federal Communications Commission and the Interstate Commerce Commission to promulgate regulations with respect to the extension of credit without collateral by any person, business or industry regulated by the federal government to any person on behalf of any candidate for federal office.
- Prohibited funds appropriated for the Office of Economic Opportunity from being used for any political activity.

1974 NIXON MESSAGE ON CAMPAIGN FINANCING

Following is the text, as made available by the White House, of President Nixon's March 8 message to Congress proposing changes in financing and conducting campaigns for the presidency and for members of Congress. Nixon also proposed that a federal libel law be considered to give political candidates and public officials greater protection from attacks in the press and by opponents.

TO THE CONGRESS OF THE UNITED STATES:

I. Introduction

The American people wield a mighty instrument of free choice as they enter the voting booth. Indispensable to the health and integrity of that process is the accountability of candidates for public office.

Campaign abuses recently publicized and of years gone by, samplings of Congressional and public opinion, expert observation, the experiences of all of us in elective office—all proclaim that the electoral process needs reform and that the accountability of candidates must be more uniformly enforced. I commend the Congress for its own recognition of this need as evidenced by recent Senate passage of two important reform measures, by the introduction of scores of reform bills, and by detailed analyses of this entire area by many Members of Congress in both Houses.

The Executive and the Congress have, therefore, a common goal: reform that works, reform that deals with the very real concerns we have in a way which improves the electoral system instead of simply coating it with the appearance of change.

I feel strongly that the reform we seek must be realistic. For example, I continue my interest in the possibilities of a six-year, one-term Presidency and four-year terms for Members of the House of Representatives. Yet, the advantages of these proposals are not so compelling as to merit driving now for a constitutional amendment. I do, however, urge further consideration of these subjects both by the Congress and the public.

Another such proposal, appealing but in my view impracticable, is the so-called Post Card Registration plan. Its goals are laudatory, but not its practical results.

Testimony before the House Election Subcommittee has already indicated that the proposal's stated objective would not be reached and the target groups not registered. In addition to being an unwarranted Federal intrusion in an area reserved by the Constitution to the States, post card registration would be an administrative nightmare and would cause chaos in existing registration systems. Of even greater importance is the open invitation to election fraud that would be inherent in so haphazard a system. I would add that periodic in-person registration by a citizen involves a personal and political commitment that I would regret very much to see us lose.

All of our solutions in the area of campaign reform must be grounded on the solid experience of nearly 200 years, not merely on the spirited rhetoric which so frequently pervades this arena.

II. Legislative Proposals

On May 16, 1973, I urged the Congress to establish a non-partisan commission on Federal election reform. This blue-ribbon commission would have been composed of political party leaders, Members of Congress and distinguished laymen. Only one House of Congress, the Senate, has focused on it. This lack of action has come at the very time that many Members of Congress and private leaders have been speaking out about the need for vigorous action against campaign abuses.

If it had been created in a timely manner, this commission would have been charged to file a public report no later than December 1st of last year. By now we would have had an authoritative, bipartisan report recommending carefully weighed reforms for Federal campaigns, and perhaps by now we could have been well on the way toward new statutes applicable to the upcoming elections this November.

It is because of this delay that I have directed the Department of Justice to work with my staff in preparing a comprehensive set of reforms for consideration of the Congress in this session. I am hopeful that these proposals, together with other approaches being advanced in Congress, will lead to vigorous debate and solid, effective reform.

Of course, we should not be concerned with Presidential campaigns alone. A massive volume of campaign contributions goes into Senate and Congressional campaigns as well. The problem faces us all, and because we are all concerned, I am anxious for the Congress and the Executive to work together in a spirit of full cooperation. For real progress to occur, we must all consider the paramount interests of the electoral system rather than parochial interests of any party or candidate.

The proposals I urge the Congress to consider as it continues to evolve its own approach fall into four major areas: campaign finances, campaign practices, campaign duration, and encouragement of candidate participation.

A. Campaign Finance

In recent years, political campaigns in America have become increasingly expensive. Because the need for more and more money has become acute in many Federal elections, I regard campaign financing as the most important area for reform, and the area in which reform is most urgently required.

After extensive study of a wide range of suggestions, including the many proposals developed by Congressional sources, I conclude that the single most important action to reform campaign financing should be broader public disclosure. Complete financial disclosure will provide the citizens of our country with the necessary information to assess the philosophy, personal associations, and political and economic allegiances of the candidates.

A number of statutes already exist which require some disclosure, but we can and should expand and improve the process.

Specifically, I endorse the proposal that each candidate in every Federal election be required to designate one single political committee as his authorized campaign organization, which in turn would have to designate one single depository for all campaign funds. With this single committee and single depository, accountability becomes virtually assured, and the unhealthy proliferation of political committees to pyramid and conceal campaign donations would be stopped at last.

I also strongly support the proposed requirement that every donation to these committees be specifically tied to the original individual donor, excepting only donations by a national political party organization. Other organizations could act as agents of individual contributors, but the donor himself would be required to designate the ultimate recipient of his campaign donation. This requirement would do more than facilitate disclosure; it would have the highly positive side benefit of reducing the influence of special interest groups by discontinuing their direct and often very substantial contributions to candidates. Donations to political party organizations, rather than to individual candidates, would not be interfered with and would continue to be identified as to the original donor, as existing law requires.

Even though disclosure is, I believe, the single most important prescription to deal with financing reform, I believe also that donation limits are needed on the amounts that an individual contributor could give to any Federal election campaign. I suggest that a candidate's authorized campaign committee be prohibited from accepting more than $3,000 from an individual donor in any Senate or House election, and not more than $15,000 in any Presidential election. These ceilings would apply in each campaign—primaries, runoffs, and general elections—and would include any contributions earmarked for a candidate through a national political committee. Regardless of the number of Presidential primaries, no candidate for President could receive more than $15,000 from any individual for all of the primaries combined, or more than this amount from any individual in the general campaign.

In recent years there has been a proliferation of "in kind" contributions in the form of paid campaign workers, printing supplies, the use of private aircraft, and other such non-monetary campaign assistance. Because there is as much room for abuse with "in kind" contributions as with financial ones, I believe we should prohibit all "in kind" donations by any organization other than a major political party.

Any "in kind" contribution by an individual would, of course, continue to be permissible, but would have to be disclosed as to both donor and recipient, with an open report of its reasonable value. These personal "in kind" donations would come within the same ceiling limitations as monetary contributions and would apply towards the ceiling amounts for Senate, House and Presidential elections.

I also urge:

• That all donations of more than $50 be made by check or other negotiable instruments, so that large flows of cash can be at least inhibited;

• That all campaign-related expenditures of over $50 be drawn only from the central campaign treasury;

• That all loans to political committees be banned, so that we can end the practice of disguising donations as loans;

• That the donation of physical assets such as appreciated stocks be prohibited;

• And that campaign contributions from foreign accounts and foreign citizens be prohibited.

These proposals, when added to the present disclosure law that took effect in 1972, should assure American voters of the information they need to decide for themselves whether or not a candidate is financing his or her campaign honestly and in an acceptable manner.

The proposals I have offered advance the common goal of restraining campaign expenditures, but they do so without imposing arbitrary limits. It is important to note, as well, that existing law already limits the amount which candidates for Federal office may spend for campaign advertising in the communications media, the most costly part of modern campaigning.

Additional spending limits, desirable as they are at first thought, raise significant constitutional questions. Moreover, they would be unworkable because many citizens furnish direct support to a multitude of groups which in turn support candidates only because of selective positions on narrow issues. They can also be unfair because expenditure limitations can be set too low to provide a challenger with any hope of contrasting his views with those of the better known, federally subsidized incumbent. Finally, a limit appropriate to a geographically small, congested Congressional district could be utterly inadequate for a large one. There are many other district-by-district variations that rigid nationwide spending limits could not fairly accommodate.

I conclude that full disclosure of campaign contributions and expenditures, subject to existing limitations, is the best and fairest approach, one that lets the voters decide for themselves whether or not too much money is being collected and spent. There should not be a limit on the widest possible dissemination of ideas and positions on issues, but I fear that would be precisely the effect of additional spending limitations however carefully dsigned.

Much of the debate over campaign reform has centered around the issue of drawing down on the public treasury to pay for all or part of political campaigns. I strongly oppose direct Federal campaign financing, and I doubt very much that most citizens would favor diverting hundreds of millions of tax dollars away from pressing national needs in order to underwrite politicians' campaigns.

Neither is it right to make millions of Americans pay the cost of the political activities of individuals and parties with which they might totally disagree. This even goes beyond taxation without representation. Thomas Jefferson in the Statute of Religious Freedom said that "To compel a man to furnish contributions of money for the propagation of opinions which he disbelieves and abhors, is sinful and tyrannical."

Moreover, if we outlaw private contributions, we will close the only avenue to active participation in politics for many citizens who may be unable to participate in any other way. Such legislation would diminish, not increase, citizen participation and would sap the vitality of both national parties by placing them on the Federal dole.

In addition, almost any "public financing" measure would give incumbents an unfair advantage. Frequently, a challenger must spend more than the incumbent in order to make his qualifications known and to counterbalance the incumbent's in-office financial advantages. But if the taxpayers are to put up the money, ceilings on such spending would have to be imposed which unavoidably would penalize the lesser-known challengers.

Through the existing tax check-off for Presidential elections and political tax credit or deduction, in 1972 the Federal Treasury was subject to the expenditure of up to $100 million for taxpayer support of political campaign activities. These programs, however, do not sever the crucial tie between the individual citizen and the party or candidate of his choice, and do not carry as great a threat of Federal domination of political campaigns.

I believe our Nation has already seen too many examples of how the use of tax dollars can lead to Federal control. By setting reasonable limits on campaign contributions, and by requiring broader public disclosure, we can guarantee that the American voters are fully aware of who is making the contributions; and the Nation can then leave it to the people themselves to judge the wisdom and propriety of these donations.

Another problem in this area warrants the early attention of Congress. The Internal Revenue Service has recently held that income earned from funds of political parties is taxable under the present Internal Revenue Code. This ruling has caused widespread confusion and uncertainty on the part of political campaign committees. I believe this situation was never intended by Congress and urge enactment of legislation removing any tax or potential tax on any income earned from political party funds.

While strong financing and disclosure laws are necessary, these alone will not ensure the reform we need. For most of the 20th century our campaign laws have not been enforced. Enforcement of the Federal Corrupt Practices Act, a measure riddled with loopholes, has been all but impossible, and enforcement of the Federal Election Campaign Act is difficult because of the proliferation of committees and the lack of central reporting.

Therefore, I endorse the proposal developed in the Congress to establish a Federal Elections Commission to supervise the Federal Election Campaign Act and other election measures.

This independent commission would be bipartisan and would monitor our campaign finance and disclosure laws. It would bring under the umbrella of one agency the current oversight functions of the Comptroller General, the Clerk of the House of Representatives, und the Secretary of the Senate. Membership on the commission should include representatives of the major political parties.

In its supervisory capacity, the commission would serve as a much needed central repository for election records and would have powers to subpoena documents and witnesses to fulfill its duties. It would also be able to refer campaign violations to the Justice Department for appropriate action. The work of the commission would in no way impinge upon Congressional rights and responsibilities, but would expedite the disposition of violations and provide a coordinated supervisory role in overseeing the various election laws.

B. Campaign Practices

Many people have made the point that additional Federal laws are needed to deter or punish criminal, tortious or otherwise improper activities in Federal election campaigns. Existing laws deal with vote bribery, vote fraud, spurious campaign literature and other breaches of campaign ethics, but as in the area of campaign finance, these laws are unclear and have been unevenly and sometimes unfairly enforced through selective prosecution.

I have reviewed several recommendations in this area and conclude it is time for Federal statutes to spell out specifically the prohibition of certain campaign and election day practices. I propose that we prohibit three types of campaign practices:

• Activities which unreasonably disrupt the opposing candidate's campaign, such as the dissemination of false instructions to campaign workers and related disruptive activities, or which constitute a fraud upon the voters, such as rigging opinion polls, placing misleading, advertisements in the media, misrepresenting a Congressman's voting record, or organizing slander campaigns.

• Activities which involve the use of force, such as the organized use of demonstrators to impede or deny entry at a campaign rally, or individual criminal actions which take on a special significance when they are done intentionally to disrupt the Federal election process.

• Those election day practices, such as stuffing ballot boxes, rigging voting machines, forging or altering ballots, or failing to count certain votes, all of which directly affect the electoral process in a most pernicious manner.

I realize that attempting to outlaw certain improper campaign activities requires particular attention to the First Amendment guarantees of free speech and assembly. With this in mind, I have asked the Department of Justice to draft a criminal statute designed to prohibit wrongful practices and to make them Federal offenses if the conduct is engaged in with the specific intent of interfering with the Federal election procedure. I invite especially thorough debate by the Congress in this difficult area.

C. Campaign Duration

In the campaigns of 1972, there were no less than 23 separate State primaries for the Presidential contestants. The extent and duration of these proliferating primary contests have not only extended the length of campaigning but have also materially added to its expense.

I believe deeply in the statewide Presidential primary system. It affords the public a true measure of candidates who have to take their cause to different parts of the country and face the voters with their positions on crucial issues. Because I believe in the primaries but wish to bring some sense of order to the system we now have, I agree with the proposal not to hold any State Presidential primaries or nominating conventions before May 1st of an election year, and I urge that this be done.

Even though moving primary dates later in the election year is the only specific legislative action I offer to shorten campaigns, other helpful measures can be taken without Federal legislation. One way to cut down on the cost and duration of Presidential campaigns is to delay the national nominating conventions until the month of September. I urge the leaders of both national political parties to plan now for the scheduling of their 1976 conventions at this later time.

I know that delaying the nominating conventions may conflict with certain State requirements that a nominee's electors must be selected earlier than September. Therefore, I encourage the States having such requirements to change their laws to conform with this potential action by the national parties. I am reluctant to ask for Federal legislation in this area because it would intrude unduly into the right of each State to determine its election laws, but I am hopeful that the States will cooperate in this important effort. To this end, I am instructing the Department of Justice to give the States such assistance as they may desire in developing legislation to make this possible.

D. Encouraging Candidate Participation

One of the major items on the agenda of campaign reform is the need to encourage qualified people to run for office and maintain a strong two-party system. We should never limit the voter's choice or discourage capable men and women from seeking to represent their fellow citizens.

I urge the Congress to examine its own benefits of incumbency which have mounted over the years. It would be inappropriate for the Executive to propose specific remedies in this Congressional area, but I suggest there is reason for concern over the marked advantages—federally funded—that Congressional incumbents now enjoy over their challengers. Such things as free mailing privileges, use of "public service" broadcast time, and the extensive staff and financial fringe benefits of office have made it progressively more difficult for competent challengers to have a fair chance in Congressional races. I readily concede that the Presidential incumbency advantage is also substantial but there is some protection here in the constitutional limit on length of Presidential service. I urge the Congress to review this problem and to develop reforms that will assure a better balance in Congressional races.

I also propose repeal of the "equal time" provision of the Communications Act of 1934 for all Federal elections. The repeal of this provision would reduce campaign expenditures by allowing the electronic media the flexibility to provide free campaign coverage to the major political candidates, and in doing so would assist our citizens in reaching sound judgments on election day.

Finally, I have asked the Department of Justice to explore the possibility of legislation to reaffirm certain private rights of public figures so that people interested in running for public office can have greater assurance of recourse against slanderous attacks on them or their families. Landmark Supreme Court decisions have severely restricted a public figure's ability to gain redress against such grievances, but I would hope that specifically defined limits can be legislated by the Congress to prevent unscrupulous attacks on public figures. These reforms are not intended to restrict vigorous debate, but to enhance it, to help give it dignity and integrity, and to improve the prospects for good and decent people who today flinch from political participation because of their fear of slanderous attacks.

III. Conclusion

The reforms I have urged here, and that many in the Congress are seeking as well, are designed to open up our electoral process and to correct some of its most egregious abuses.

I am doubtful that any legislation can provide the panacea that some seek to guarantee absolute integrity in the electoral process. If our campaigns, like the communication of ideas in every area of our public life, are to remain free and spirited, they will frequently be caustic and hard-hitting, and some excuses and abuses will inevitably occur.

The central purpose of the reforms I suggest is to get the really important political information out to the people, to let them know as much as possible about their candidates, and to eliminate abuses which cross the boundaries of fair play.

America has had a remarkable history and tradition of campaign electioneering. Given full access to the actions and thoughts of political aspirants, the American people have shown great wisdom at the ballot box over two centuries of self-government. The reforms I propose today are intended to strengthen the will of the people by making our election process more open.

RICHARD NIXON

BIBLIOGRAPHY OF MATERIALS ON CAMPAIGN FINANCE

Books and Reports

Adamany, David, *Campaign Financing in America*, North Scituate, Massachusetts, Duxbury Press, 1972.

Alexander, Herbert E., *Financing the 1968 Election*, Lexington, Massachusetts, D.C. Heath Company, 1971.

Alexander, Herbert E., *Money in Politics*, Washington, D.C. Public Affairs Press, 1972.

Association of the Bar of the City of New York, Special Committee on Congressional Ethics, *Congress and the Public Trust: Report*, "Campaign Financing," pp. 118-153. New York, Atheneum Press, 1970.

Center for Public Financing of Elections, "Campaign Finance Surveys of 1974: Federal Candidates and Their Supporting Political Committees," 201 Massachusetts Avenue, N.E. Washington, D.C. 20002, 1974.

Citizens' Research Foundation, "Contributions of National Level Political Committees to Incumbents and Candidates for Public Office 1971 and January-February 1972." 245 Nassau Street, Princeton, New Jersey 08540, 1973.

Citizens' Research Foundation, "Political Contributions of $500 or More in 1971 and January-February 1972." 245 Nassau Street, Princeton, New Jersey 08540, 1973.

Citizens' Research Foundation, "Political Contributions of $500 or More Voluntarily Disclosed by 1972 Presidential Candidates," 245 Nassau Street, Princeton, New Jersey 08540, 1973.

Committee for Economic Development, "Financing a Better Election System," 477 Madison Avenue, New York, 10022, 1968.

Common Cause, "Analysis of Registered Political Committees' Cash on Hand as of February 28, 1974," 2030 M Street, N.W. Washington, D.C. 20036, 1974.

Common Cause, "1972 Congressional Finances," 10 vols. 2030 M Street, N.W., Washington, D.C. 20036, 1974.

Common Cause, "1972 Federal Campaign Finances: Interest Groups and Political Parties," 2 vols. 2030 M Street, N.W., Washington, D.C. 20036, 1974.

Congressional Quarterly Almanac 1973, "Senate Twice Votes Campaign Financing Reform," p. 741, 1414 22nd Street, N.W., Washington, D.C. 20037.

Domhoff, G. William, *Fat Cats and the Democrats: The Role of the Big Rich in the Party of the Common Man*. Princeton, New Jersey, Prentice-Hall, 1972.

Dunn, Delmer D. *Financing Presidential Campaigns*. Washington, D.C., Brookings Institution, 1972.

Gilson, Lawrence, *Money and Secrecy: A Citizen's Guide to Reforming State and Federal Practices*. New York, Praeger, 1972.

Heard, Alexander, *The Costs of Democracy*. Chapel Hill, University of North Carolina Press, 1960.

McCarthy, Richard D., *Elections for Sale*, Boston, Massachusetts, Houghton-Mifflin, 1972.

Nichols, David, *Financing Elections: The Politics of an American Ruling Class*, New York, New Viewpoints, 1974.

Peabody, Robert L., *To Enact a Law: Congress and Campaign Financing*, New York, Praeger, 1972.

Penniman, Howard, *Campaign Finances: Two Views of the Political and Constitutional Implications*, American Enterprise Institute for Public Policy Research, 1150 17th Street, N.W., Washington, D.C. 20036, 1973.

Thayer, George, *Who Shakes the Money Tree? American Campaign Financing Practices from 1789 to the Present*, New York, Simon & Schuster, 1973.

Twentieth Century Fund Commission on Campaign Costs in Electronic Era, *Voter's Time*, 41 East 70th Street, New York 10021, 1969.

Twentieth Century Fund, Task Force on Financing Congressional Campaigns, *Electing Congress: The Financial Dilemma*, 41 East 70th Street, New York, 10021, 1970.

Winter, Ralph K., *Campaign Financing and Political Freedom*, American Enterprise Institute for Public Policy Research, 1150 17th Street, N.W., Washington, D.C. 20036, 1974.

Articles

Adamany, David, "Money for Politics," *National Civic Review*, April 1970, p. 191.

Adamany, David, "Public Financing: A Cure for the Curse of Slush Funds," *Progressive*, October 1973, p. 38.

Alexander, Herbert E., "The Federal Election Campaign Act of 1972: Is It Working?" *Politiea*, Summer, 1972, p. 21.

Berry, Jeffrey M., "Congress and Public Policy: A Study of the Federal Election Campaign Act of 1971," *Harvard Journal on Legislation*, February 1973, p. 331.

"Campaign Funds: New Rules for Candidates, Backers," *U.S. News & World Report*, April 3, 1972, p. 81.

"Campaign Money: Prospect for Reform," *Time*, April 22, 1973, p. 28.

"Campaign Reform: Taking the Worry Out of Reelection," *Washington Monthly*, September 1973, p. 13.

Cockrell, Joel M., "Campaign Finance Reform: Pollution Control for the Smoke-filled Rooms?" *Case Western Law Review*, Spring 1972, p. 631.

"Congress Wrestles with Campaign Financing," *Business Week*, September 15, 1973, p. 70.

Dollar Politics

In December 1971 Congressional Quarterly published its first book dealing with campaign spending. That volume, *Dollar Politics: The Issue of Campaign Spending*, focused on the techniques of fund raising and campaign spending and on the political background that led to the legislation enacted in 1971-72. The book included a legislative chronology of all congressional action on campaign finance legislation for the years 1945-70, statistical studies of defense contractors' contributions to the 1968 presidential campaign, broadcast spending in the 1970 congressional elections, and statistics on all contributions and expenditures in all 1970 congressional campaigns reported under the provisions of the 1925 Corrupt Practices Act.

Cranston, Alan, "Campaign Funds: How to Cure the Corruption," *Nation*, September 17, 1973, p. 242.

Dawson, Paul A., "Broadcast Expenditures and Electoral Outcomes in the 1970 Congressional Elections," *Public Opinion Quarterly*, Fall 1971, p. 308.

Dean, E. Joseph, "Undisclosed Earmarking: Violation of the Federal Election Campaign Act of 1971," *Harvard Journal on Legislation*, February 1973, p. 175.

"The Federal Election Campaign Act of 1971: Reform of the Political Process?" *Georgetown Law Journal*, May 1972, p. 1309.

"Fund-raising for Political Campaigns: Why the High Costs? Who Will Pick up the Bill?" *Vital Issues*, January 1968, p. 1.

Greene, Wade, "Who Should Pay for Political Campaigns?" *Columbia Journalism Review*, January/February 1974, p. 24.

"How to Cure the Corruption," *Nation*, September 17, 1973, p. 242.

"Public Financing of Campaigns is 'Nonsense,'" *Human Events*, January 10, 1974, p. 19.

"The Question of Federal Financing of National Election Campaign; Pro & Con," *Congressional Digest*, February 1974.

"Senator Buckley on Campaign Reform," *Human Events*, March 30, 1974, p. 8.

"Should Tax Dollars Pay for Politics? What Party Leaders Say," *U.S. News & World Report*, August 20, 1973, p. 31.

Sterling, Carleton W., "Control of Campaign Spending: the Reformers Paradox," *American Bar Association Journal*, October 1973, p. 1148.

"Tax Supported Campaigns," *New Republic*, December 22, 1973, p. 5.

Documents

U.S. Congress, Office of the Clerk of the House, *The Annual Statistical Report of the Contributions and Expenditures Made During the 1972 Election Campaign for U.S. House of Representatives*, U.S. Government Printing Office, Washington, D.C. 20402, 1974.

U.S. Congress, Office of the Secretary of the Senate, *Report on Audits, Field Investigations, Complaints and Referrals in Connection with the Election of the U.S. Senate, 1972. U.S. Government Printing Office*, Washington, D.C. 20402, 1974.

U.S. Congress, House Committee on House Administration, *Federal Election Campaign Act of 1971, Conference Report, December 14, 1971*, U.S. Government Printing Office, Washington, D.C. 20402, 1971.

U.S. Congress, House Committee on House Administration, *Federal Election Reform, Hearings October 2, 1973*, U.S. Government Printing Office, Washington, D.C. 20402, 1973.

U.S. Congress, House Committee on House Administration, *Federal Election Reform, Report October 13, 1971*, U.S. Government Printing Office, Washington, D.C. 20402, 1971.

U.S. Congress, House Committee on the Judiciary, *Statement of Information, Political Contributions by Milk Producers Cooperatives: The 1971 Milk Price Support Decision, Book IV*, U.S. Government Printing Office, Washington, D.C. 20402, 1974.

U.S. Congress, House Committee on the Judiciary, *Statement of Information Submitted on Behalf of President Nixon, Political Contributions by Milk Producers Cooperatives: The 1971 Milk Price Support Decision, Book III*, U.S. Government Printing Office, Washington, D.C. 20402, 1974.

U.S. Congress, House Committee on Ways and Means, *Proposals for the Reform of the Electoral Process, Message from the President, March 11, 1974*, U.S Government Printing Office, Washington, D.C. 20402, 1974.

U.S. Congress, House Special Committee to Investigate Campaign Expenditures, 1972, *Reports January 11, February 12, and June 15, 1973*, U.S. Government Printing Office, Washington, D.C. 20402, 1973.

U.S. Congress, Senate Committee on Rules and Administration, *Federal Election Campaign Act of 1973, Report*, U.S. Government Printing Office, Washington, D.C. 20402, 1973.

U.S. Congress, Senate Committee on Rules and Administration, *Federal Election Reform, Hearings April 11, 12, June 6, 7, 1973*, U.S. Government Printing Office, Washington, D.C. 20402, 1973.

U.S. Congress, Senate Committee on Rules and Administration, *Public Financing of Federal Election, Hearings September 18-21, 1973*, U.S. Government Printing Office, Washington, D.C. 20402, 1973.

U.S. Congress, Senate Select Committee on Presidential Campaign Activities, *Draft of Final Report, Part 2: Campaign Financing*, U.S. Government Printing Office, Washington, D.C. 20402, 1974.

U.S. Congress, Senate Select Committee on Presidential Campaign Activities, *Watergate and Related Activities, Phase III: Campaign Financing, Book 13*, U.S. Government Printing Office, Washington, D.C. 20402, 1974.

U.S. Department of the Treasury, Internal Revenue Service, *Voluntary Tax Methods to Help Finance Political Campaigns, Publication #585*, U.S. Government Printing Office, Washington, D.C. 20402, 1974.

U.S. General Accounting Office, Office of Federal Elections, *Alphabetical Listing of 1972 Presidential Campaign Receipts, 2 vols*, U.S. Government Printing Office, Washington, D.C. 20402, 1973.

U.S. General Accounting Office, Office of Federal Elections, *Report of 1972 Presidential Campaign Receipts and Expenditures*, Washington, D.C. 20548, 1974.

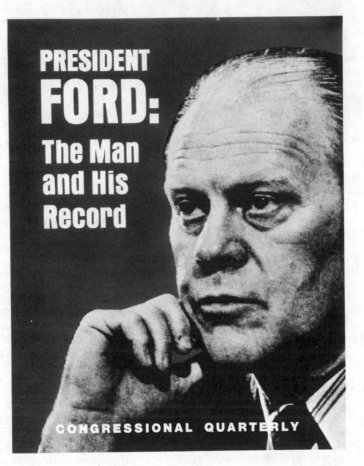